POSTMODERN MANAGEMENT

The Emerging Partnership
Between Employees and Stockholders

William McDonald Wallace

QUORUM BOOKS
Westport, Connecticut • London

2024

Library of Congress Cataloging-in-Publication Data

Wallace, William McDonald.
Postmodern management : the emerging partnership between employees
and stockholders / William McDonald Wallace.
    p.   cm.
Includes bibliographical references and index.
ISBN 1–56720–181–4 (alk. paper)
1. Industrial management. 2. Cooperativeness. 3. Bureaucracy.
4. Industrial management—Employee participation. 5. Stockholders.
I. Title.
HD31.W253   1998
658—dc21   97–41004

British Library Cataloguing in Publication Data is available.

Library of Congress Catalog Card Number: 97–41004
ISBN: 1–56720–181–4

First published in 1998

Quorum Books, 88 Post Road West, Westport, CT 06881
An imprint of Greenwood Publishing Group, Inc.

Printed in the United States of America

The paper used in this book complies with the
Permanent Paper Standard issued by the National
Information Standards Organization (Z39.48–1984).

10   9   8   7   6   5   4   3   2   1

Contents

Preface

During the late 1950s, while I was a graduate student in the University of Washington's Graduate School of Business, I dreaded the quarterly ordeal of registration, when I was often reduced to a state of helpless rage. The administrative staff followed the absolute letter of every rule, even when it made no practical administrative difference but could cause great inconvenience. Rules were rules they would say. I was not alone; nearly all the graduate students detested the "staff bureaucracy" and its officious attitude.

In our classes on management and organization, however, we learned that bureaucracy was the only practical way to organize large-scale operations, and with over twenty thousand students the university was pretty large. Max Weber, a German sociologist from the early twentieth century whose authority and status in those days was immense, was frequently quoted to this effect. His writings on bureaucracy were required reading. Indeed, Weber seemed to take on the aura of a channel of revealed truth, so little did anyone question his conclusions. I glumly concluded he was probably right. In any event, I had been so impressed by another of Weber's works, *The Protestant Ethic and the Spirit of Capitalism,* that I assumed he could do no wrong. In fact, that work became the starting point for my doctoral dissertation about Japan. If, as Weber argued, John Calvin's work ethic had been a major driver of early capitalism in Northwestern Europe and North America, the Japanese must surely have an analogue to it. My interest in Japan had been sparked by several previous trips to Japan. The first two were in the summer of 1948, when, having just finished my freshman year at the College (now University) of Puget Sound, I applied for and got a job as a crew member on an army transport ship. I made two trips between Seattle and Yokohama carrying over soldiers in the occupation force and their dependents. The place was absolutely smashed flat. The debris had been cleaned up by then, but acre after acre of the area between Yokohama and Tokyo was simply vacant rubble. I recall thinking to myself that Japan's economy could never come back.

In the summer of 1950, the Korean War broke out and, after graduating from college, I was called up as a reserve second lieutenant in November 1952. In late June 1953, the army flew some of us as replacement officers to Japan and we spent two weeks in Tokyo before being assigned to Korea. I could not believe the change. Two R&Rs (rest and recreation), in November 1953 and June 1954, further reinforced my first impression. Damage was still evident, to be sure, but the reconstruction was awesome. I began to question much of the propaganda I had heard during the war about the "slave-like" status of Japanese workers. The ones I watched working so hard were clearly not driven by slave drivers. I began to suspect that Japan would rise again and before very long.

I was rotated home in November 1954, worked for about a year and a half, and decided to get an MBA. Just before getting that degree I was invited to enter the doctoral program in Business and Economics with an instructorship. I quickly accepted. I had not thought much about Japan after coming home, but then I had to select a topic for my dissertation, and, as I said, Japan came to mind as an extension of Weber's thesis on the work ethic. I had first thought of surveying all major cultures, but was quickly persuaded to narrow my focus. In my view, Japan was clearly the best non-Western example of dynamic economic growth and, with that, my topic was accepted. My broad conclusion was that what the Protestant ethic had been to Europe, the code of *Bushido* had been to Japan. Both of these ethics fostered hard work and dedication to one's goals, though the goals themselves were initially quite different. And while the West thought in terms of an individual's salvation, the Japanese were dedicated to their group, initially the clan. After the *Meiji* Restoration, the business firm replaced the clan, yet the ethic remained broadly intact.

More to the point of this book, a big question arose in my mind almost at once about Weber's thesis on bureaucracy. The first major piece of evidence I came across was a short book on the Japanese factory and its social system by James Abegglen, then a professor, now one of the top people in the Boston Consulting Group. It was clearly like nothing Weber described. As he described them, Japanese factories worked more like a family or college fraternity. Weber had insisted that bureaucracy should be run as an impersonal machine. The less emotion and sentiment the better, he said. The Japanese, however, ran on emotion and sentiment and aimed for a high *esprit de corps*. This was not only a "work ethic," it was a team's work ethic, not a notable feature of Weber's Calvinism.

Japan had not at that time, between 1959 and 1960, really showed what a powerhouse it was soon to become. It was easy to say that Japan, not unlike Germany, was making a remarkable postwar recovery, and, thank you very much, in good part because of American help and, in Japan's special case, because of "MacArthur's Reforms." I felt that Japan's more organic social order would get more out of people than our mechanistic approach, but it was not then clear it got so much more out of people that Japan could successfully begin to challenge General Motors right in America a decade later.

Weber had not said that bureaucracy was the best system for large-scale operations only in European culture. He made this claim across cultures and over time. Still, my doubt was deflected for a time by another revealed academic truth, namely, behaviorism. Japan's organizations were different because its culture was different. In those days, an aspiring student did not question behaviorism in cultural analysis. (One could be a member of the rival Freudian camp for personal psychology.) Indeed, I titled my dissertation to account for behaviorism: "Cultural Values and Economic Development; A Case Study of Japan." In 1960, after completing everything but my dissertation, I went to work for Boeing as a market analyst. When I finished my thesis and got my degree, however, I took a job in England as a management consultant and from there moved to Brazil.

I had suppressed my doubts about bureaucracy until then. But overseas I began running into a new problem. By the mid-1970s I had lived and worked in a wide range of different cultures with different values. Never mind; bureaucratic behavior remained remarkably similar. Weber could not have been crossculturally correct about the efficiency of bureaucracy, but surely he was correct if one focused on the inefficiencies of bureaucracy. It was then the faint origins of the idea for this book began to form. I pursued a number of blind alleys and had a few false starts, but in the late 1970s the focus began to become clear. Bureaucracy did not work well anywhere and survived only because it had no organic competition with comparable technology. Many books and articles began to appear on Japanese business, including some of mine. But in 1978 I returned to Boeing and a new element began to surface. A shift in world view was becoming evident. I had long ago learned that it was more or less pointless to extol the organic Japanese approach to industrial relations. Any effort to look at the differences vanished under the behaviorist cultural influence. "That is just the way the Japanese are brought up," I heard time and again from people who knew nothing about it and, what is more, had no intention of learning. But such denial would no longer serve once the Japanese began to dig deeply into our markets.

My last few years before retirement from Boeing were crucial to my thinking. After the company decided to adopt a Deming-like continuous quality improvement program imported directly from Japan, I began to witness a cultural transformation like none I had ever seen. At this same time a whole kind of nonmechanistic thinking began to emerge, and many of us at Boeing began to read of the new sciences and of how bureaucratic ways had evolved from the old mechanistic science. It began to occur to me that the United States had taken the Western lead in leaving the modern era behind and creating a whole new world view and behavior to go with it for a postmodern era in the twenty-first century. True, the Europeans, led by the French, were also talking about a postmodern era, but the one they described was influenced by Marx and repeating his mistake. Marx railed against capitalism, but was so hopelessly vague about communism that, once in power, all his hopes were immediately crushed under the same old bureaucracy, one even more despotic than anything found here. The French postmodern movement does much the same thing. It strikes out and curses the evils of the mechanistic, overly "rational" modern era, but it is driven by philosophers with no real responsibility for affairs and it poses no practical alternative of any kind. Unlike the French, Americans are forging new practices and a whole new philosophy, one that incorporates the new science.

ACKNOWLEDGMENTS

My experience of this shift began at Boeing, and there too did my thoughts begin to come together after endless discussions and debates on how best to organize and manage people and on what things like chaos theory implied for our linear and mechanistic world view. Some of these debates were in formal committees, others over lunch or coffee, but they went on from about 1979 to the day I retired in February 1992.

I cannot remember the names of all the people whose thinking went into mine, but five years later here is a list in alphabetical order of two groups of people. The first were those who showed by management style that they were indeed leading the way into a more organic postmodern world. The second group were those with whom I had the deepest discussions. Some people fall into both groups and so I decided not to separate them. My thanks therefore to Fred Bowen, Phil Condit, Tom Craig, Susan Cox, Ewalds d'Silva, George Eaton, Gary Jusela, Jim Hinkhouse, Fred Kelly, Gene Laughlin, Chris Longridge, Mike Little, Jerry Martin, Pete Morton, Jim Moore, Alan Mulally, Jack Pierce, Ed Potts, Fran Thomas, Dean Thornton, and Ray Waldmann.

Outside of Boeing, my dean at St. Martin's College, Jerry Knutson, has given me much encouragement and support. Also, I want to collectively thank many hundreds of students at St. Martin's who have had to suffer through my thinking and theorizing on this issue. Their critical comments on some of my ideas were most helpful. Eric Valentine, my publisher, also provided great help in giving the book its final focus. I am most grateful. A personal friend, Leo Bailey, has also been a big help, especially in "holding my hand" in times of frustration and discouragement.

But if I must single out one individual above all others, it is my wife, Patricia Ann Wallace, to whom I owe the most, both in discussions, proofreading, and affectionate and steadfast support. In many ways this is her book too.

Introduction

Not only is the twentieth century nearing its end, so is the modern era. That era saw the emergence of modern science, modern technology, and during the Industrial Revolution modern bureaucracy as well. With bureaucracy came the rise of modern management. The science part of this package emerged by the seventeenth century, giving rise to a new and mechanistic view of the world, but that view did not reach its pinnacle in management philosophy until the mid-twentieth century. The new science and technology, of course, launched the most dramatic transformation of material standards of living the world had ever experienced, more than in all previous history. But the modern age also had its downside, a spiritual bankruptcy that largely accounts for its passing. This book takes a close look at the consequences of that bankruptcy in business.

These consequences include a shift to a postmodern philosophy and methods now well under way. By the year 2020 and with 20/20 hindsight, I suspect people will wonder why we ever believed in a mechanistic philosophy. At its outset, modern science sparked a dramatic shift in how we saw the universe and our place in it. Humanity was put down hard. The earth and its people were no longer the center of the universe or the purpose for it. After Darwin, humans were no longer God's children, but machines that had evolved as an accident of natural selection acting on random mutations. The universe was simply an impersonal mechanism, a "clockwork" in the early metaphor. The machine, of course, set the modern era apart from the past and quickly became its major symbol. Science and technology, the egg and sperm of the modern era, also created the machines that transformed civilization. A new philosophy also grew out of those machines. It is called *mechanistic determinism, scientific* or *materialistic realism,* or just plain *materialism.* In this impersonal and materialistic view, only matter is real. Modern materialism holds that the human mind, or human consciousness, arises only from matter, and purely as a secondary consequence of complexity, a position called epiphenomenalism. Free will, together with all aspects of human spirituality, are dismissed (by those deeply committed to materialism) as illusions of an otherwise entirely materialistic mind. In practice, of course, not everyone was deeply committed to that modern view. Religions continued, and most people continued to believe, at least nominally, in the existence of God and a spiritual life apart from the material.

MODERN MANAGEMENT

But not business. Both in theory and, for the most part, in practice, business firms were regarded as purely secular, as impersonal and mechanistic institutions. Economics as a social science was, if anything, even more secular and materialistic. If people in business had a spiritual life, perhaps attending church and trying to practice its teachings, they tended to compartmentalize themselves. Church was one thing, business another, more secular and impersonal. Business, government, and academia all began to compartmentalize. In most business firms management departmentalized itself in terms of function. The typical division consisted of production, engineering, finance, and marketing, along with others. This division of labor became part and parcel of the modern era that set great store by specialized function—much as machines were a collection of specialized parts.

But all this has been changing for some time. In one arena after another the modern mechanistic view of the world has begun to break down. Former adherents are now discarding it in droves. This shift actually began decades ago in physics, the birthplace of the modern era. By 1927, a new science, quantum mechanics, had emerged. Ironically, this new science demolished the assumptions that sustained the modern era's mechanistic metaphor. But that knowledge was mainly confined to physics until about 1970, when the shift began to spread to the other scientific disciplines. Even the social sciences began to waver a bit. But the biggest shift has been taking place in business organization and management. Nowhere else has a flight from the modern era been more dramatic. For one thing, in America it had become more entrenched in business than in most other areas of life. And nowhere else did the assumptions of the materialist world view prove quite so bankrupt in actual practice. These assumptions nearly brought down many large and famous American firms, such as Ford, Chrysler, and General Motors. From that crisis in the late 1970s an epiphany began, in Detroit if not Damascus, and one that quickly spread.

The mechanistic model of management always had its critics. For example, the movement called "scientific management" in the late nineteenth century was often criticized. Despite some benefits, labor came to resent being treated as a "cog in a machine." A Charley Chaplin film, *Modern Times*, became a popular symbol of that resentment. (The rise of Marxism was an earlier European backlash to the machine model of industry, but Marxism suffered from being even more materialistic than capitalism, and its recent demise is part of the shift from the modern to the postmodern world.) Despite that setback, the mechanistic mode got a new lease on life around 1960 with the computer. Before 1960, everyone understood that we could not make the vast number of calculations needed to apply the mechanistic model to management. It had thus applied almost exclusively to factory workers and to labor. Managers, professionals, and clerical personnel were rarely treated as machines. With some exceptions, they were more often treated as family, and, not surprisingly, they often responded with fierce reciprocal loyalty to their firms. That soon would change.

The computer revived the mechanistic model under a slightly new label, and it was now hailed as "management science." It launched the most mechanistic approach to management and organization ever tried. The old scientific management paled by comparison. (Note this new version simply reversed the older terms.) Management science at once began to treat white collar workers as cogs in the machine, no longer as "part of the family." Business was to be impersonal, objective, rational, and, above all, quantified. It was a colossal flop because its assumptions were not only wrong but downright dysfunctional.

One false assumption in the mechanistic view is that the world is mathematically linear and hence predictable. Where the world is not linear, quantitative methods such as linear programming will not work. But in truth, the social, economic, and political environment of business, government, and the whole economy is turbulent. Thus, it is also mathematically nonlinear. The difference is straightforward. In a linear world a small change in initial conditions yields the equivalent small change in a future outcome. If you know the initial conditions you can predict the future outcome. But in a turbulent and nonlinear environment small changes in initial conditions can, via positive feedback, cascade into a huge change in the outcome. Even if you know the initial conditions, the outcome is uncertain. The future of any turbulent environment is thus inherently uncertain and unpredictable.

The sudden realization that conditions were turbulent, and thus the future uncertain, came as a shock. That realization played a crucial part of the philosophical epiphany that began in business about 1980. Business had suffered one surprise shock after another after having invested much time and effort in planning based on sophisticated computer models that claimed to be able to predict the future. These models could often predict that tomorrow would be much like today, and when it was they could claim to be right. But these models of modern sophistication almost never called for a major change of direction, except for a few that never took place. The major shocks came in 1974 with the 600 percent oil price hike, in 1979 when oil prices more than doubled again, and in 1986 when, unexpectedly, oil prices suddenly collapsed. Meanwhile, the surge of competition from Japan after 1970 became a sort of escalating shock. The precipitous end of the Cold War between 1989 and 1991 caught the most-informed experts by surprise. More recently the surge in the Internet after 1992 came as a big surprise even to Microsoft, and it had to abruptly shift gears in 1995. The modern econometric methods of forecasting, one part of management science, did not predict any of these surprise events. Still, each of those shocks immediately negated a whole array of costly plans and investments that entailed great dislocations. By the mid-1980s business let go more than half of its economists, the folks who had sold them on the power of computer forecasting.

Surprises and shocks, however, have always been with us. So why, three hundred years into the modern era, did unforeseen events suddenly become a reason to doubt the modern mechanistic world view? The reason is clear enough. Before 1960 the future was thought predictable only in principle. In practice everyone knew that we simply did not have enough computing power to make the needed calculations. Then came the computer, and by about 1960, we began to think we now had that power. Yet, even more important, management acted on that belief by building gigantic planning bureaucracies based on a formula that I call FPCC (forecasting, planning, command, and control). Forecast the future, make plans to meet that future, issue commands to put those plans into effect, and then monitor compliance to those commands with an elaborate management hierarchy armed with an array of controls. This formula works well enough if, for practical purposes, you can make accurate forecasts of the future. That is sometimes possible. But if you cannot make accurate forecasts, and thus cannot "call the turns," FPCC is a program for disaster. It is too rigid, bureaucratically hide-bound, and boss-centered. (Your forecasts tell you how many customers you will have, so why worry about them?) Moreover, FPCC comes with some very costly behavior patterns. It depends on hired labor, fragmented into specialties that focus on their function or job rather than the whole enterprise. Moreover, a policy to depend on hired labor sets up a series of incentives that lead to systematic overstaffing, overlayering, and overregulation. In addition, we typically find endemic job defensiveness, turf battles, and power struggles. Wage rates are not only downwardly rigid, but they tend to ratchet upward. It is almost a euphemism to describe all this as dysfunctional.

For all these reasons, the business bureaucracies that arose after management science cope poorly with the sudden surprises or shifts in direction that are normal to life, business, and economics. For a brief time in the late 1960s, many business executives, most famously Harold Geneen of ITT, thought modern scientific management methods created a "surprise free" business environment. By 1980 that hope was a joke. The new watchword was flexibility, and the modern paradigm had no useful advice to offer on how to achieve it. Business still struggles with that.

POSTMODERN MANAGEMENT

Still, some elements of a more organic postmodern business model are becoming clear. If the old model of business was mechanistic, linear, specialized by function, and managed from the top down by command and control, the postmodern world will be quite different. No longer are lower-level employees seen as automatons. We noted earlier that nonlinear turbulence implies an inherent uncertainty and thus places a big premium on flexibility. Thus, top-down command and control is increasingly giving way to self-managed teams. Instead of working from precise and detailed job descriptions called for by the mechanistic model, more and more employees are being asked to work flexibly and to accept crosstraining across a variety of skills. If specialization was the key to modern career success, an interdisciplinary ability to "multi-task" across functions to demonstrate "band width" is the postmodern ideal. Thus is the modern functional focus quickly giving way to the postmodern holistic focus on the enterprise as a whole, including its goals and mission. This book will focus on how best to create a flexible enterprise.

We can summarize it as follows. The modern world view of business was of mechanistic firms firmly focused on their parts and managed from the top down in a stable and linear business environment. The postmodern business, however, recognizes it must cope with a turbulent and nonlinear business environment. To do that it must become flexible. To achieve flexibility, business firms must transform themselves into more organic, holistic, and participatory enterprises. Unfortunately, most firms have no clear vision of how to accomplish that goal. Many have lost their way. The mission of this book is to provide needed guidance.

The need is clear. Despite some notable successes, the major vehicles of reform, total quality management and reengineering, fail far more often than they succeed. Skepticism about management fads abound. Middle management, for example, often fights the concept of self-managed multifunctional, whole-process teams. The big hang-up is easily described. In the end, the flexible organization requires sustained employee cooperation, which in turn demands trust. But flexibility in a modern bureaucracy also demands layoffs, and layoffs destroy trust. Yet that problem arises only because most firms retain their bureaucratic employment policies. This is to say the typical firm continues to depend on hired labor even as it struggles to get rid of the behavior that policy encourages. That policy acquired a well-established aura of "rationality" because the classical theory of labor, buttressed by later management theory, made it seem that a dependence on hired labor paid specific rates to do specific jobs was the only viable option in large firms. Though hardly any questioned the assumption, it is still false. But as long as it convinces business firms to depend mainly on hired labor, the incentives for bureaucratic behavior will persist. Downsizing will not change those incentives.

THE POSTMODERN CORPORATE PARTNERSHIP

Let us cut to the chase. The solution is partnership between the stockholders and the employees. Partnership imparts the behavioral motives needed to achieve sustained or durable flexibility. It is the only format that does so because it is organic rather than mechanistic. It focuses on the whole, not the parts. All the partners participate in achieving these goals rather than leaving it all to management. All these elements better equip a partnership to cope effectively with a crisis or surprise shocks. Partners are members of the firm, they are not just hired hands.

They have a sense of ownership that a hired hand does not. As Jesus is quoted as saying in John 10:12, "The hired hand . . . does not own the sheep, sees the wolf coming, and leaves the sheep and runs away because the hired hand does not care for the sheep."

A partner's pay, meanwhile, varies with enterprise performance. That fact makes labor costs inherently elastic in a partnership, compared to the downwardly rigid unit wage rates paid to most hired employees in a bureaucracy. A corporate partnership's cost flexibility thus dissolves the bureaucracy's dilemma between trust and flexibility. The variable rates of pay implicit in a partnership avoid the necessity of layoffs. These are necessitated, after all, primarily by the downward rigidity of wage rates, Moreover, a pay system tied to enterprise performance dissolves the incentive to overstaff, overlayer, and overregulate the administrative side. All such behavior will reduce partner income. But downsizing does not remove those dysfunctional incentives. In fact, downsizing a bureaucracy may even stimulate these incentives, much like pruning a tree stimulates more vigorous growth of the branches.

Meanwhile, partnership can set the stage for effective and self-motivated teamwork based on a high esprit de corps. The mechanistic world view, as I mentioned at the outset, does not even allow for the real existence of a spiritual side of life. In business, team spirit is a nonmaterial but very real entity. Esprit de corps is the spiritual side of life in any competitive arena, whether in team sports, the military, or business. The resulting camaraderie is often its own reward. Rivalry adds zest that would otherwise be lacking. The modern world saw competition and cooperation as polar opposites. Capitalism stressed competition, communism in theory stressed cooperation, and both policies missed the postmodern boat. Postmodern business philosophy integrates both competition and cooperation into holistic complements. The Japanese slogan that played a big part in their capturing so many U.S. markets captures the right spirit. That slogan was and is, "Competition between firms, but cooperation within them." Competition enhances social cooperation and team work, provided the team members trust each other. Partnerships create that trust and bureaucracy erodes it. What about employee stock ownership plans (ESOPs)? ESOPs are okay in the abstract, but if the firm continues to depend on hired labor paid fixed rates for doing particular jobs, ESOPs do not accomplish much. An ESOP bureaucracy is no less a bureaucracy.

So far, in groping toward the postmodern business world, top management refers to the concept of partnership over and over. They talk of partnering with customers and suppliers. As for the firm's own employees, top management urges them to "take ownership of their own work processes," and to "focus on the customer." They are urged to work as enthusiastic and cooperative team players, all as if they already had banded together in formal partnership. But that is precisely what is missing, a formal partnership with the stockholders and each other. Rhetoric is no substitute for the real thing. If you want people to act like partners, the solution is simple enough: offer them partnership. That is the message of this book.

PLAN OF THE BOOK

Forming a partnership from scratch is not particularly difficult, but making a successful transition from a bureaucracy can be. This book provides some guidelines for making that transition, but before embarking on that project it helps to first have a clear understanding of just why and how bureaucracy goes wrong. Such understanding helps overcome the false "aura of rationality" so embedded in the bureaucratic policy of depending almost exclusively on hired employees.

Accordingly, Part I looks mainly at Bureaucracy. Chapter 1 takes a look at the earliest origins of bureaucracy. Faced with a new problem of constructing large-scale irrigation networks to make it possible to farm dry areas, early civilizations responded with the first coercive organizations to marshal the necessary labor. That is contrasted with the origins of partnership, which evolved as a way of fostering cooperation and sharing in early hunter–gatherer societies. Chapter 2 moves on to the story of how and why the mechanistic model of business bureaucracy took such firm root in Britain and America and not in Japan. Chapter 3 takes a close look at the basic source of bureaucratic dysfunction. Here we introduce a relatively new concept, *autopoiesis*, a variant on the "law of self-preservation." A factor in life generally, in organizations it drives to preserve identity and status, and we see how bureaucracy fails to work with that drive and is thus defeated by it. Frustrated autopoiesis largely accounts for systemic overstaffing, overregulation, and overlayering. In Chapter 4 we look more closely at how the computer gave rise to FPCC, at Robert McNamara's role in promoting it, and why it failed so badly. Chapter 5 looks at the paternalism in the stable bureaucracy and at how the turbulent beginning in the 1970s made job security impossible to continue given rigid wage rates. In Chapter 6, we zero in more closely on the late industrial bureaucracy's systemic wage-rate ratchet. It began in 1933, and after World War II gave rise to the postwar wage/ price spiral. We turn to a related issue in Chapter 7 and see how and why rigid wage rates converted a 1930 recession into the Great Depression. By way of contrast, we will see that in that same period between 1929 and 1933, economic sectors that had flexible pay managed to maintain output and employment. The major examples are American agriculture and Japanese industry.

In Part II we turn to Partnership. Chapter 8 gives an overview of corporate partnership and why it solves the problem of bureaucracy. We explain why members paid in terms of corporate performance lose all incentives to overstaff, overlayer, and overregulate. In so doing, they lay the groundwork for high esprit de corps and cooperative teamwork. We will see why, given partnership, partners willingly strive to downsize the enterprise if that is really necessary. Here too we will look at the macroeconomic consequences of widespread corporate partnership. In Chapter 9 we deal with the difficult issue of transition from bureaucracy to partnership and show how certain steps taken in advance of suggesting partnership can smooth the transition. In Chapter 10, we explore the implications of widespread partnership for the whole economy and how it would at long last foster full employment without inflation and yet cope with economic turbulence and dynamic change.

The appendix relates some of the strange new realities of life and matter revealed by such new sciences as quantum mechanics and chaos theory. These new findings not only undercut the old mechanistic model of the modern era; they fully validate the shift to partnership. The new science is mainly an adjunct. The change in business is being driven by the failure of the mechanistic model to compete with the organic Japanese system. Thus, with the exception of autopoiesis, I refer only occasionally to these new sciences in the body of the text and confine most of that discussion, for those interested, into the appendix. Still, these new findings provide a certain unity by which the flight from modernity in other fields such as medicine can be understood as part of a broader whole.

PART I

BUREAUCRACY

Chapter 1

Origins of Bureaucracy

PREMODERN BEGINNINGS

Why and how did bureaucracy begin? This is an interesting question, because for about two or three million years our ancestors lived and worked in small organic clans hunting and gathering. The evidence from both recent times and ancient history suggests that hunter–gatherers enjoyed that organic way of life. They left it reluctantly, usually under pressure of circumstance.[1] Primitive peoples in a wide variety of environments hunted and gathered in this cooperative organic social order. Historically, it has been observed nearly everywhere, in the Arctic north, in the steaming tropics, in the mountains, on the plains, and in the forests, savannas, and deserts. The similarity of this organic social order in so many different settings suggests that the psychology associated with its way of life, one featuring muted dominance and friendly cooperation, is rooted in our genes. In any event, our distant ancestors knew little of the authori-

tarian and often coercive management style associated with bureaucracy. So again we ask our question: why bureaucracy?

The answer is that organic partnership, as it applied to primitive
hunting, proved too successful. By about thirty thousand years ago
humans had become the earth's master hunters. The surprising part
is that this success came in the face of comparative physical weak-
ness and an absence of the fighting fangs and claws common in other
species. As individuals, we humans were next to helpless. But we
did stand upright, we had opposable thumbs, and more important,
we had both the capacity and the robust desire to cooperate with
each other in the hunt. Teamwork in the use of crude hand crafted
weapons thus made up for and went well beyond our lack of physical strength. About twenty thousand years ago came the invention
of long-distance weapons. The bow and arrow so improved the productivity of hunting that a population explosion began. Hunting territory soon grew scarce. Since it takes up to twenty square miles to
feed a person living the life of a hunter–gatherer, the whole earth
could support comparatively few of us, perhaps ten million in total.
As hunting grounds became scarce, our ancestors had to depend more
on gathering fruits, roots, herbs, and perhaps grains. Before long,
people in widely scattered locations began learning how to cultivate
crops, especially grains. Then they began to farm such crops, though
full-time farming emerged gradually. In many cases, hunting and
farming coexisted. It usually took several generations to complete a
community's transition to farming. Some American Indian tribes both
hunted and farmed when the Europeans arrived.[2]

Farming, however, was but a transitional step toward the emergence
of the first bureaucracies. The early farming communities retained the
hunter–gatherer social order of mutual cooperation, but farming also
vastly increased the earth's carrying capacity for the human species. It
takes only a couple of acres of good land to feed one person, even
with primitive techniques. The transition from mostly hunting to
mainly farming was well established about ten thousand years ago,
and thus the growth of human population began to accelerate. No
longer nomadic hunters, humans could rear far more children than
before. As nomadic hunter–gatherers, each mother could carry only
one infant at a time. Fathers had to carry weapons and other items of

survival and, of course, remain ready to fend off predators. So it was rare for women to bear more than three children. Mothers often avoided sex while nursing a child and did not wean an infant until it was three or four.[3] In settled farming communities, however, even young children could help with the chores. Larger families thus paid big economic and social dividends. As the population exploded, however, a new crisis soon began to emerge. The farmers began to run out of well-watered farm land because they produced more children than the farms on which they grew up could support. As these surplus children matured, they had to find new land to farm. Before long, they had been forced into much dryer areas. Land was still in plentiful supply, but water for the crops was not.

HYDRAULIC FARMING

This water shortage led not only to the development of bureaucracy but to much else as well, including political government and organized religion. Forced to farm dryer lands, people near large river systems such as the Tigris and Euphrates in Babylon (present-day Iraq) learned how to build irrigation canals. The canals began in small communities and at first depended, as before, on mutual cooperation and the sharing of work. This communal system of canal building, however, began to break down when the need for larger systems arose. For the first time in human history, the need for large-scale construction projects became evident. According to Karl Wittfogel, the most thorough student of that era, the need to build these irrigation canals then led to the first "civilized" human communities, complete with organized government and religion.[4] Both were necessary to justify the coercive organizations these communities had to create in order to build and maintain large-scale irrigation networks. Thus, Wittfogel entitled his book *Oriental Despotism*. The despotism that canal construction brought in tow began about six thousand years ago. In various guises, these "hydraulic societies," as Wittfogel calls them, arose in Babylon, Egypt, India, and China around the same time.

Of course, there was no proletariat available from which to recruit labor. Moreover, humans had no cultural experience of large groups working together across many different local communities to build extensive projects according to some plan. Nor did human culture, up to this point, have any tradition to justify forcing people to work outside their local communities. According to Wittfogel, organized religion came into being to justify forced labor by command of divine authority. Before this time, most work was done without need for formal bosses. Early tribes had no chiefs. Tribal authority usually rested in some version of a "council of elders." To move from this early method of cooperative working to formal structures divided into specific functions and ruled from the top down by command and control was a huge step to take. There had to be some minimal acceptance of it by the people to whom it would apply. Organized religion achieved that acceptance.

People in these early farming communities were already well aware that forces over which they had no power, such as the weather, could spell the difference between a good harvest with plenty for all and a bad harvest followed by hunger. The weather gods had to be placated. Everyone saw the need for that. Shamans emerged, claiming special powers to placate whatever gods they believed in. These shamans began to organize communal ceremonies to celebrate the spring planting or the fall harvest. They in fact became a channel through which these gods "spoke." The priests soon began to issue "god-given" commands to the people. Shamans from adjoining communities began to coordinate their celebrations. Before long, they began (informally at first, later more formally) to become a priesthood that cut across the local communities. The priests might then elect one of their number as a chief priest. The chief soon acquired political powers across these communities. Eventually, the tribal gods somehow informed the priests of the need to build bigger and longer canals to bring water to the whole community. Each local community was asked to supply the necessary labor, and perhaps at first they did so willingly.

Meanwhile, some communities got into territorial disputes with other tribes or had internal disputes within their own tribe. The disputes with other tribes called for warrior bands, often directed by the chief priest. Moreover, the chief priest might be called on to adjudicate disputes between the communities within the tribe. A process of centralizing power began that ended when the chief priest had become a "god king" with dictatorial powers.[5] The volunteer labor drafts needed to build canals became compulsory, a sort of tax. Called *corvee* labor, it worked not unlike the road tax of early Western communities in the United States, where farmers could work on roads instead of paying a tax in cash. Once the organization was formed to build and maintain canals by *corvee* labor, it was a short step indeed for the god king to use involuntary labor to build temples, palaces, pyramids, or other such monuments. The first coercive bureaucracies had come into being through the rise of despotic theocracy, all as an integrated response to a water shortage.

Huge changes followed. First, hydraulic farming was often very productive, and it became possible to store surplus grain. We see the beginning of wealth. Surplus wealth in its turn made civilization possible because it enabled people to specialize outside farming. Merchants and shippers, as well as artisans specializing in various trades, gave rise to commerce between communities. That same surplus of wealth enabled other people to specialize as priests, warriors, and rule makers, and this gave rise to organized religion, large-scale government, and standing armies.

THE RISE OF CASTE SYSTEMS

With such division of labor came big increases in productivity. The artisan who can work full time crafting tools, for example, can produce more and better tools compared to a farmer who makes tools as a sideline. But with the division of labor into occupational specialties we also see the beginnings of a caste system. A caste system uses the division of labor to create a hierarchy of social status. One's status in this hierarchy derives from the ascribed rank or order of importance to society of one's occupational specialty. Within that broader occupation, social status gradations arise from the ascribed importance of the position one holds or the specific job one does.

Who did the ascribing? Priests for the most part, usually by claiming to be speaking on behalf of higher divine authority. Are we surprised that they placed themselves at or near the top? They of course shared the glory with warriors and government officials, but sometimes the dividing line between these groups was fuzzy. Lower in the ranking came those who actually did the work: farmers, artisans, merchants, unskilled laborers, and sometimes an untouchable class to do work the priests regarded as unclean.

The various occupations might hold different ranks depending on the society involved. It might or might not be possible to rise from a lower- to a higher-ranked occupation. The old Hindu caste system in India, for example, locked one into one's occupational caste at birth. Japan, however, allowed for some mobility between castes, especially through marriage or by adoption.[6]

Slavery was a variation on the theme of caste servitude and probably started by making prisoners of war into slaves. Slaves or serfs were common throughout the world until quite recently. Even the ancient Athenians, despite their democracy, used slaves for most work. Rome was also a slave-based empire, and the Christian Bible makes it clear that slaves were common and involuntary servitude was accepted as a normal condition.

Involuntary servitude has, of course, been on the wane for the past two hundred years, in good part because of the Industrial Revolution. For one thing, machines began to replace people for much of the heavy lifting or other drudge work. For example, better sails began to displace galley slaves at about the time of Columbus. Then, three hundred and fifty years later, steam engines on ships began to displace the still large crews needed to mind the sails. People were still needed to shovel coal, but by 1915 fuel oil and the steam turbine displaced coal-fired steam engines along with the "black gangs" that shoveled coal. By 1970, no more than two dozen people could crew a large container ship, one of which could probably carry more grain than the entire merchant marine of the Roman Empire with its thousands of galley slaves.

The Christian religion undercut the traditional divine sanction for caste. The Gospels made it clear that Christ evangelized all segments of society, including slaves. Still, for the next fifteen hundred years, caste, slavery, and serfdom remained common, even in Christian lands. Then, during the Protestant Reformation and the rise of John Calvin's Puritan work ethic, the idea of caste came under a dark theological cloud. All legitimate work was blessed in the eyes of God, according to Calvin.[7] Even Catholicism's Benedictine Order took a motto that roughly translates as "To work is to pray." Nearly any kind of productive work served the purpose in either case. One might have thought that caste came to an end, and on one level it did. People who remained self-employed were relatively free of caste, and for nearly three hundred years after the Protestant Reformation most of the labor force (primarily farmers, but also those in other small enterprises and cottage industries) remained self-employed. But then came the Industrial Revolution in the mid-eighteenth century. As it spread, so did bureaucratic organization. Within one hundred fifty years, bureaucracy accounted for most of the labor force. We had become a nation of hirelings.

"RATIONAL" BUREAUCRATIC CASTE

Yet despite this cultural shift to the work ethic, caste remained a firm part of bureaucracy's social order and still does today. In the early days of the modern era that emerged between 1453 (with the invention of the printing press) and 1687 (with the publication of Isaac Newton's masterwork) very few people worked in bureaucracy, but as modern science and technology gave rise to the Industrial Revolution after about 1750, justification for caste in the newly emerging industrial factories shifted. Divine authority was out. Instead, the rational division of labor (made famous by Adam Smith in his *Wealth of Nations*) became the justification for caste.[8] These new (mostly textile) factories usually featured powered machines driven first by water and then by steam. Not implausibly, the factories using these machines were themselves often seen as analogs of machines. The jobs that people did were equated with the parts of a machine, and were deliberately made as simple, mechanical, and mindless as possible. Reductive methods of analysis might be employed to design the jobs for the best effect. This mechanistic approach to organization did not much apply to management staff until after World War II, when it reached its apex long after the Industrial Revolution began two hundred years earlier. Reductive rationality was called job evaluation or position classification. It tried to rank jobs in supposed order of their importance to the firm, but this is what a caste system is all about. This rank order was needed to establish a valid basis for different pay rates, because the pay rates in bureaucracy are attached to jobs. A job's pay rate, of course, is then a rather precise measure of the job holder's relative social status. Thus, the twentieth-century practice of modern job evaluation is closely analogous to that developed by various priesthoods about six thousand years ago. The source of justification changed, but even here we can see a common thread. In both cases caste was justified by the highest authority, an authority that shifted from religion to science and reason. In both cases we also deal with "revealed truth" of sorts, shifting merely from "divine revelation" to a new revelation by rational analysis.

The Protestant religion and modern science initially disowned the caste system. Under Calvinism, work—including work of common labor traditionally reserved for the lowest castes—had taken on a social dignity unique in the civilized world.[9] This new egalitarian view of work, however, survives well mainly in an organic setting—as was at first the case. At least 80 percent of the workforce was self-employed or worked in small organic family partnerships such as farms, shops, or cottage industries. The great bulk of hired workers were then domestic household servants. These servants were usually put into a job-based pecking order; that is, a bureaucratic caste system where the abstract job defined both the identity and relative status of the person who held the job. That made some sense: Domestic servants were hired to help consume, not produce, wealth.

CREATING A CASTE SYSTEM

Even when productive work of all kinds enjoys a cloak of divine morality, the use of hired labor for permanent staff tends to create a de facto caste system. For example, suppose an entrepreneur opens a small shop making some hot new ski accessories. She does all the work at first and thinks nothing of sweeping out the place, feeling not in the least demeaned by doing "janitor's work." As her business expands, she may decide to hire some help, but even now she may continue to sweep up at the end of the day. Now suppose her new sports line is a big hit. She expands output and decides to hire more help. Greater sales volume forces her to spend more time running the firm and on finance, administration, and marketing. She puts production in the hands of a hired manager who hires additional equipment operators and a janitor to do the sweeping up so that the operators can concentrate on production. Meanwhile, the owner herself has hired other people to do the accounting and purchasing and help with administrative chores. Of all the new hires, let us assume the janitor was the least skilled and thus paid the least. Suddenly, everyone doing a job that is paid more than the janitor will feel demeaned if asked to do the "janitor's work." They feel or sense a loss of "caste" within the social system created by the owner's decision to use the job as the basis for paying hired help at different rates.

People in nearly every culture resent being asked to "work beneath their station." In some cultures such a request is taken as an insult. Middle class people "lose caste" in many parts of the world if they "stoop" to do their own cooking and housework. That is "servant's" work. And these (hired) servants are often ranked in the traditional bureaucratic fashion, with identity and status attached to the job. In Victorian England and America, the job of butler was usually the top for males. For females the top job was housekeeper. Below them in various pecking orders were footmen, maids (upstairs and downstairs), cooks, kitchen helpers, gardeners, chauffeurs, and nannies. In my own experience abroad, I found that servants themselves strictly observe these job boundaries; they do each other's work with great reluctance. Meanwhile, the "masters" often maintain a strict social distance from the "hired help."

THE DIVISION OF LABOR

The division of labor into specialized skills can produce enormous gains in productivity, and on this fact bureaucracy is very clear. The very term *bureaucracy* implies the division of labor. The term itself is an extension of the French word *bureau,* which is usually translated into English as "department." Thus, we organize work into departments like accounting, purchasing, marketing, production, engineering, and human resources. Each of these departments is in turn subdivided further. Humans have practiced division of labor for thousands of years, even back to hunting and gathering, but they have by no means always created a social order around it.

Adam Smith, of course, made the division of labor a high principle of organization in the very first pages of his 1776 landmark book, *The Wealth of Nations.* He opens with a description of a pin factory and clearly shows how the division of labor achieved enormous increases in productivity compared to the older craft system of production. Smith pointed out that if craftsmen made pins by doing all the jobs themselves they could produce perhaps ten a day. But take ten men and give each a special task to do, such as drawing the wire, cutting the wire, putting points on the cut wire, putting on the pin head, packing the pins in paper, and so on, and these ten men could each turn out perhaps a thousand pins a day, ten thousand between them.

Smith's arresting example, made with such striking clarity, helped make *The Wealth of Nations* a bestseller in its own time.[10] It has remained in print and sold well ever since. All this time it has remained the classic example of how the division of labor improves productivity, but the sheer power of Smith's argument obscured a weak but silent assumption, namely that *hired labor* was the only relevant employment relationship. Smith did not even discuss the possibility of working in partnership. He carries on with the presumption of hired labor throughout his book such that one is led to conclude that "labor" necessarily refers to "hired labor." Economic theory has treated it so ever since.

Smith pointed out that free hired labor tends to work more efficiently than do slaves. But he also made it clear that hirelings work under the master–servant relationship. Throughout his book, Smith uses the term "master" to mean manager or owner. He repeatedly used the term "servant" as a synonym for the hired employee. It apparently did not occur to Smith (as one hundred years later it did to the Japanese) that if hirelings are motivated to work more efficiently than slaves, then by the same reasoning partners clearly have more incentive to work efficiently than do hirelings. After all, a hireling has no voice in policy and does not participate in profits as partners do. This point is developed in more depth later on.

THE "RATIONAL" ECONOMIC MAN

I will argue that bureaucracy's job-based caste system is a major source of dysfunctional behavior. This caste system almost self-organizes once a decision is made to depend on hired employees as permanent staff rather than partners. Again, early economic theory nearly always assumed that large firms would use hired labor, not partners.

They seemed to limit partners to small family-like enterprises such as cottage industries, farms, or retail shops. Moreover, the relationship between the hired employee and the firm was assumed to be an impersonal exchange of time for money. The relationship was then dehumanized by assuming that hired labor was just another commodity to be bought and sold impersonally on the market. Such thinking became part of the classical canon of economic theory as the "commodity theory of labor." The commodity theory was part of a broader new theory of human behavior in the marketplace. It was dubbed the theory of the "Economic Man."[11] Economic Man aims to maximize his profits (or other sources of income) to the exclusion of all else. The theory of Economic Man almost explicitly excludes loyalty, esprit de corps, and camaraderie from the marketplace, including the firms who compete in the market. All such sentiments become irrational to Economic Man in his quest for more income (whether from profits, wages, rent, etc.) or, the other side of the coin, paying a lower price. Economic Man is the consummate rational calculator. He devotes his life entirely to his own individual self-interest. He was thus in endless competition with his "fellows," even within a firm. Classical Economic Man never could and never did experience camaraderie with his fellow workers, the very experience upon which depends sustained, effective teamwork.

Noneconomists have, of course, long scoffed at this theory. Even some early economists, such as America's Thorstein Veblen, ridiculed the theory of Economic Man.[12] In fact, most economic texts today hardly mention it except in passing. Today, almost no economist actually promotes the commodity theory of labor or its related concept of Economic Man. Nevertheless, those concepts remain firm foundations of economic theory regarding market behavior. Confronted with that fact, most economists simply brush off this criticism quickly by conceding that neither the commodity theory nor that of Economic Man is realistic and, they add, was never meant to be. These concepts, they say, are merely convenient abstractions focused narrowly on market behavior and used purely as a tool or instrument of prediction. "Judge this theory," they insist, "not by how realistic it is, but by how well it predicts economic behavior in the marketplace." (In formal philosophy this defense of a theory is called *instrumental-*

ism, where a theory or model is used purely for making predictions.) As for predictions, modern economists are quick to point out, no other social science does as well.

In fairness, this instrumental defense has some logic. The theory claims that in the market humans are greedy profit maximizers (Economic Man), and it does yield good predictions of market behavior. For example, all else equal, people around the world prefer to pay a low rather than a high price for a given good or service. Again, all else equal, people nearly everywhere tend to buy more when the price of a good drops and less if its price goes up. Such behavior is what the classical model predicts, and it is usually correct. The Marxists attacked the theory to promote communism, but never really attempted to refute it. Instead, the communists, led by Lenin, tried to get around such greed by command and control. After nearly three-quarters of a century the effort failed. Experience shows that market prices left free to fluctuate will allocate scarce goods and services among rival claimants better than any alternative scheme. The price mechanism is not perfect, of course, but it is still far superior to any yet tried alternative general method of allocating scarce resources.

So what is the problem? Just this: However well the model of Economic Man predicts our behavior as independent buyers and sellers in the marketplace, it fails dismally when it comes to predicting the behavior of people working together. Here, that model makes terrible predictions. The theory does not, for example, predict the rise of trade unions formed to achieve gains through collective action. One could argue that collective bargaining is a variation on the profit maximizing theme by a group instead of a person. Perhaps so, but the theory does not make room for people banding together for collective actions, however greedy. Greed is to be pursued entirely by individuals who act solely on their own behalf. Early on, the trade union movement falsified this individualistic part of classical theory. So, in fact, did Marxism. Meanwhile, time and again unions have gone on strike for "principle" even when they have known the wage gain they are likely to get will not recoup the wages lost in the strike. Under the theory of Economic Man, such behavior is merely dismissed as irrational.

The classical theory of Economic Man also failed to predict or account for the rise of Japan. How, with so few natural resources and so far behind in modern technology, could Japan catch up with the West so quickly, first after 1868 and again after 1945? The competitive advantage Japan holds, most of their business competitors now agree, is superb industrial teamwork based on esprit de corps. Precisely such behavior is excluded by classical and modern economic theory of business-firm behavior, now usually called microeconomics. Here, it should be made clear, this exclusion is not culturally specific: It claims to apply in all cultures. Economists have in recent years tried to use cultural differences to explain away Japan rather than adjust the theory, but the theory's deeply embedded assumptions about individualism are also deeply flawed.

The Japanese, of course, rejected the West's commodity theory of labor as a prime example of occidental inscrutability.[13] The Japanese made the conscious choice to have nothing to do with it. They knew perfectly well that labor was not another commodity such as cotton or coal. The Japanese also knew that good teamwork arises from esprit de corps, which, in turn, involves human emotions, sentiments, and feeling, all of which are thought to be irrational in Western theory. The Japanese for their part thus deliberately devised employment policies that aimed to elicit esprit de corps. They consciously decided *not* to expand their new factories with hired labor after about 1875, but rather to bring people in more or less as family-like members of the firm. They modeled these new factories on an organic family farm or cottage industry. Though they aimed to adopt Western technology, the Japanese knowingly rejected Western industrial-relations practice (and of course theory) in the process of trying to catch up.

Yet Westerners looked at military esprit de corps in a much more realistic light, about the same way as the Japanese did. The Japanese thus copied Western military models of organizaton for using modern technology, again both in theory and in practice. They used Britain's Royal navy as the model for their Imperial navy, and Prussia's army (and its General Staff) as the model for their new Imperial army. But the Japanese rejected as absurd the British model for industrial relations, thinking it not only unreal and illogical, but immoral as well

(Japan's motto during this transition was "Western science and Eastern morals").[14] Yet, at the same time, the Japanese had little concern about adopting the impersonal market model when it came to competition between firms (here the Japanese motto became, "Competition between firms, cooperation within them," and this indeed is the postmodern goal Western firms are striving to achieve). In short, where the classical market model is realistic (competition between independent entities in the marketplace, be they corporate or individual) it gives good predictions. Where it is unrealistic (people working together within the firm), it systematically gives terrible predictions.

The Japanese merely continued to use the ancient organic model in order to achieve their goal of creating industrial enterprises that could achieve the teamwork and cooperation they knew they needed to catch up with the West. They wanted to make the workers members of the enterprise, where both owners and workers found it in their common interest to achieve the same goal. The Japanese wanted nothing to do with the adversarial relationship that Japanese observers witnessed in England in the 1860s. They knew systematic internal rivalry would kill any chance of Japanese firms catching up with Western technology.[15]

Westerners often claim Japan's organic industrial relations are a legacy of Japan's feudal past. But the West, like Japan, also has a feudal past based on a hierarchy of organic loyalties held in place by a set of master–servant relationships. Most people think that in Europe the rise of capitalism buried that feudal past (Marx strongly promoted that view). To the extent this is true, it is also misleading. It is true the modern West shifted from a feudal organic to a modern mechanistic world view, but capitalism kept the master–servant relationship, a bedrock of feudalism, nearly intact. The very word *capitalism* suggests that capital dominates labor after all. The Japanese, on the other hand, quickly abandoned the master–servant relationship in their new factories in favor of something akin to partnership. So while the West did abandon the organic feudal model in favor of its new mechanistic model, that new model retained the feudal master–servant relationship. Japan made the reverse transition. It kept the organic model but shifted its base to partnership and threw out the feudal master–servant relationship.

The West has long cherished the illusion that Japan took a different road in response to the feudal imperatives of their own culture,
and not as a deliberate act of rejection of the Western model of mechanistic rationality. In this way, Western economists isolated the Japanese organic model as a cultural aberration, one they could safely
ignore. Japan's unique culture, they argued, made it reasonable for
them to do what they did as a means of shifting from a feudal to a
modern system of industrial production. But, many went on to argue, once that transition was complete, Japan would be forced to
adopt the Western mechanistic model of rational organization. That
was not to be, and it is in fact turning out to be the other way around.
Once they made the transition, the Japanese discovered they had a
great competitive advantage and they promptly used it to dig deeply
into Western markets. In self-defense, Western managers began moving closer toward Japan's organic model of industrial organization.
Top management also sacked more than 50 percent of their own hired
economists at about the same time. These people had proved that
they could not predict major market shifts and as a group had failed
to warn their American employers about the competitive dangers
posed by Japan's organic approach. Instead, almost the whole profession dismissed Japan's organic approach as a temporary cultural
aberration that soon would pass away.

ENCLOSURE AND THE COMMODITY
THEORY OF LABOR

The truth is that the West's economists were the ones in thrall to a
"cultural aberration." By that I mean the commodity theory of labor
owes its acceptance, in the face of all logic to the contrary, to a unique
historical event. This event took place in Britain, beginning about
1400 or so and ending just after the Industrial Revolution began. I
refer to the Enclosure Movement, in which a large part of Britain's
rural population, mainly tenant farmers, were displaced by sheep.[16]
Large landowners, mostly aristocratic, discovered they could make
more money by raising sheep than they could by retaining tenant
farmers to grow crops. The reason was the rising price of wool. Raising sheep for wool takes little labor compared to growing crops, and

so the bulk of tenant farmers were displaced. Having no other means of support in the countryside, these displaced souls drifted into the towns and cities.

Britain's rural refugees soon degenerated into a social disaster. With no means of support and no organized welfare system, many turned to crime and drink. They put the infamous "London gin mills" in business. Families fell apart, as did the moral code. Mothers left their babies to the parish orphanages as "foundlings" because, married or not, they could not care for them. The need for parish orphanages soon shot up. The infants they got were often malnourished or victims of what we now call fetal alcohol syndrome. The orphanages, themselves grim and sometimes cruel places, dumped their male charges out on the street at about age fifteen. These boys were typically alienated, angry, and rebellious. A few fortunate ones might find masters who would take them on as apprentices or domestic servants, but many of them promptly joined gangs and turned to a life of street crime as depicted by Charles Dickens in *Oliver Twist*.

The British authorities grew frantic as the Enclosure continued to bring in fresh refugees to keep a vicious circle of self-reinforcing positive feedback going. Joblessness, poverty, alcoholism, and crime all led to new foundlings abandoned to the orphanages. Prisons overflowed. Drastic penalties were invoked, including execution for theft. Nothing seemed to work. The problem continued and created eversharper class divisions. The British government finally turned to "transporting" this "criminal riff-raff" abroad. The American Southern colonies became the first dumping ground for many of Enclosure's refugees or their descendants. They became indentured servants, in effect slaves, on the tobacco or cotton plantations. True, some gained freedom after seven years, but with penalties for bad behavior many died as de facto slaves. After the blacks began coming in from Africa, Australia became the favorite dumping ground for the Enclosure's refugees. There they became the first colonists. In America the indentured servants gave rise to that part of the South's culture now called "red necks," initially labeled "white trash," of which there was no really comparable group in the North. Such "white trash" were largely Anglo-Saxon Protestants.

Back in Britain, the refugees of the Enclosure became the world's first industrial proletariat—before industrial jobs actually became available. They constituted the bulk of the labor force for the new (mainly textile) factories that began to arise in the mid-eighteenth century. Long cut off from the land, this first proletariat had become rootless, alienated, malnourished, lacking in much self-discipline, dirty, slovenly, and generally regarded by the middle classes as human scum. In the seventeenth century, many of the boys out of orphanages were turned over, often involuntarily, to the Royal navy or merchant marine. Ship captains soon discovered that the lash was a vital tool for managing these "recruits." They could not otherwise expect their orders to be carried out or, worse, faced mutiny. The British army also drew heavily from this class and found a need for similar harsh discipline. Again to the middle classes this proletariat appeared reprehensible and even frightening. As the Duke of Wellington put it after his great victory over Napoleon at the Battle of Waterloo, "I don't know if my soldiers frightened Napoleon or not, but by God they certainly frighten me."[17]

Thus, it is hardly surprising that, after the Industrial Revolution began to create more jobs than it displaced, factory owners did not rush to embrace this proletariat into an organic family-like partnership. True, the refugees were hardly the architects of their own circumstances, and many people saw that. For example, Sir Thomas More wrote of them, "Your sheep that were wont to be so meek and tame, and so small eaters, now as I hear say, be become so great devourers and so wild, that they eat up and swallow down the very men themselves. They consume, destroy and devour whole fields, houses, and cities."[18]

Queen Elizabeth I was also upset. Early she saw that sturdy rural folk were being converted into poverty-stricken urban "scum." The army was upset because, in the first instance, when the tenant farmers disappeared so did the bulk of the people who had time to train as archers for the vaunted English long bow, Europe's most feared weapon at the time. All this breast beating and remorse, however, did little to change the behavior of the Enclosure's refugees. Crime, for example, continued to escalate. If hired for factory work, they were often lazy and nearly always dirty, the picture of sloth. Unless coerced by strict bosses, they seemed inclined to work as little as possible. Of course, as the level of coercion rose, their motives to work declined unless they were forced to do so.

It is no wonder that middle-class economists demoted such "low class," even "subhuman" people into commodities to be bought and sold impersonally in the market. To employ this lot as anything other than hirelings to be kept firmly in their social place and at arm's length, strictly subordinated under a harsh "Theory X" style of management, would have been far too much to ask of most of the factory owners. Yet for all that, the Enclosure was a unique situation. It created unique social conditions that could only have distorted the way Enlightenment thinkers regarded the industrial labor force in Britain. For the Enclosure, new factories would have had to recruit labor directly off the farm, as was the case in Japan. Had the recruits come directly off the farm, the factory owners might well have brought these workers into some more organic arrangement. The Germans did so. As William Manchester's history of the German industrial empire founded by the Krupp family reveals, the family took a strongly paternalistic view of their labor force right from the outset.[19] The Krupps were contemptuous of the British approach. Nor were Germans strong supporters of British classical economics founded by Adam Smith. And Karl Marx, a German by birth and upbringing, did not look to Germany for his worst horror stories of the exploitation of labor. Nearly all his examples are British.

Still, it was the British who established the management and organization practices as well as the economic theory behind them that shaped the Industrial Revolution that first emerged in Britain. Both the practice of industrial bureaucracy and the theory behind it were deeply influenced by the social consequences of the Enclosure Movement, but the Enclosure was not the only British influence. Britain also played a prominent role in the formulation of modern science, which gave rise to the intellectual spirit of the Enlightenment. The mechanistic model of the universe that grew out of early modern science helped justify industrial bureaucracy and its compartmentalization on the intellectual level, even as it did in medicine and academia. This model continued to play a major role right up to the apex of bureaucratic command and control in the late 1960s.

NOTES

1. Karl Wittfogel, *Oriental Despotism* (New Haven: Yale University Press, 1963).

2. Lewis H. Morgan, *Houses and House Life of American Aborigines* (Chicago: University of Chicago Press, 1965); originally published in 1881.

3. Wittfogel, *Despotism*.

4. Ibid.

5. Ibid.

6. William McDonald Wallace, "Cultural Values and Economic Development, A Case Study of Japan," Ph.D. diss., University of Washington, Seattle, 1963.

7. Max Weber, *The Protestant Ethic and the Spirit of Capitalism*, trans. Talcott Parsons (New York: Charles Scribner's Sons, 1958).

8. Adam Smith, *The Wealth of Nations* (London: Stratten & Cadell, 1776).

9. Weber, *Protestant Ethic*.

10. John Kenneth Galbraith, *Money* (Boston: Houghton Mifflin, 1975).

11. Ibid.

12. Thorstein Veblen, *The Theory of the Leisure Class* (New York: Macmillan, 1899).

13. Wallace, "Cultural Values."

14. Ibid.

15. John Roberts, *Mitsui: A Record of Three Centuries* (New York: Weatherhill, 1976).

16. Robert L. Heilbroner, *The Making of Economic Society*, 8th ed. (Englewood Cliffs, N.J.: Prentice Hall, 1990).

17. William McDonald Wallace, "The Great Depression Reconsidered: Implications for Today," *Contemporary Economic Policy* 8 (2) 1995: 1–15.

18. Heilbroner, *Economic Society*.

19. William Manchester, *The Arms of Krupp* (Boston: Little, Brown, 1968).

Chapter 2

Modern Bureaucracy

Unless a firm first rids itself of the policies that create bureaucracy, dysfunctional behavior will persist. Downsizing cannot correct the problem, because bureaucracy is not a function of size. Bureaucracy arises from employment policies that assume permanent employees should work as hirelings at specific jobs paid at specific rates. ESOPs may or may not help. They will help little if, as workers, the employees remain hirelings who happen to own stock. Hirelings sell their services to a buyer, usually called the employer. The buyer–seller relationship works well if the sellers of labor are independent of the buyers, but much less well when people work as hirelings in a subordinated relationship. The buyer–seller relationship has then been muddled with that of master and servant and is not the best bet for creating wealth.

Before looking at why, let us first consider where the pure buyer–seller relationship works very well, namely in a client–contractor relationship. Here, the contractor is typically paid an agreed sum to do a specific job. The job is usually a project such as fixing the plumbing, repairing the roof, or resurfacing the parking lot. The contractor gets paid for the job and then moves on to other jobs, usually with other clients. Contractors may also do ongoing tasks such as running the firm's cafeteria and providing it with janitorial services or landscape maintenance. These contracts usually run for a definite period of time. The client–contractor relationship can also work well if one firm has a subcontract from the general contractor. This is so common in construction it hardly needs mentioning. However, a manufacturing firm could be the general contractor who designs and assembles the product using parts made by the subcontractors to the contractor's specs. If the parts are common items that can be had off the shelf, they can be purchased from vendors. In fact, many firms trying to slim down to "core competency" have decided to outsource the production of items that other firms make better and cheaper. This move often makes sense, but not as a way of eliminating bureaucracy.

Meanwhile, clients and contractors are both independent. The person or firm hired to do a job manages their own work once they know what the client wants. The contractor is not a servant to the buyer and the buyer does not stand as master over the contractor. It is often an impersonal market exchange. This is also true in a domestic household when a housecleaning service provides the cleaning woman to do the work. The cleaning woman is now a contractor, not a personal servant, even though she may be providing a personal service. To be sure, a few gray areas can appear if the client is big and the contractor is small, but, in general, the client specifies the job to be done and the contractor decides how to do it. The client is not only hiring work, but knowledge and skill. For the client–contractor relationship, some aspects of the commodity theory are reasonable. There is nothing necessarily wrong with an impersonal and market-driven relationship between client and contractor. Paying for the job done is entirely logical. Contracting with specialists is also reasonable. A plumber will probably fix your broken pipes quicker and better than a jack-of-all-trades.

THE DYSFUNCTIONS OF HIRED LABOR

What logic, then, justifies using hirelings as regular staff for ongoing in-house work, work that includes the firm's "core competencies?" Why confuse the buyer–seller with the master–servant relationship? Inertia partly explains it. Most firms have always depended on hired labor. Thus, rather than being thought out, the policy is taken for granted. But that policy also has a mechanistic logic that goes right back to the commodity theory of labor. That theory explicitly calls for the use of hirelings, but that policy poorly serves the employer who adopts it. Why? Because, unlike the use of outside contractors, the buyer–seller relationship for permanent staff sets up a series of dysfunctional incentives with costly consequences. First comes a climate of job defensiveness, one that leads directly to turf battles and power struggles. Second comes a group of three costly interrelated practices: overstaffing, overlayering, and overregulation or red tape. This package of dysfunctions cuts right across cultures and so can be observed in bureaucracies around the world. To be sure, the broader culture usually imparts certain idiosyncrasies and local color. Still, complaints about overstaffed, rule-obsessed bureaucracies with such distended chains of command that no one ever makes a clear decision (except to say no) are common complaints that are voiced around the world and have been for years. In general, the larger the organization the worse this gets. Still, hirelings in small firms often show job-defensive behavior. Again, the problem is not one of size but of relationships. To change the behavior, change the relationships. Keep the relationships you have got, and you will keep getting the behavior you have been getting.

IDENTITY, STATUS, AND THE MOTIVES
OF DYSFUNCTION

The relationship that motivates people to behave defensively about their jobs is the buyer–seller relationship (people hired to do a specific job paid at a specific rate). That policy imparts a job-centered identity to the staff. Implicitly at least, the hireling's employment depends on that job. Cut out the job and you cut out the hireling, who in turn becomes job defensive. All it takes to bring that defensiveness front and center is a perceived threat to the job. The context in which the work takes place also determines the perception of threat. I do not just mean a threat of a layoff. That is perhaps the worst threat, but cutting out layers of management and hence future promotion prospects is also threatening. Having another person or department take over some of your job's duties is another threat. Not only is a person's working identity tied up in the job, so is his or her pay and, hence, status relative to other jobs, because the rate of pay measures status more or less precisely. The agreed equity principle of compensation for hired employees is equal pay for equal jobs, more pay for more important jobs, and less pay for less important jobs. Few critics of bureaucracy would criticize that principle. It appears the soul of rationality, and in a sense it is. But that principle nevertheless creates an instant caste system that inhibits flexible teamwork and thus limits corporate performance.

AUTOPOIESIS AND SENSE OF SELF

Here we need to look at two aspects of human nature. The first concerns a person's sense of self. All humans try to preserve their sense of self in the face of constant change in the environment. Our material bodies, of course, undergo constant change day by day, even minute by minute, as they take in fuel and oxygen and eliminate the waste products of metabolism. All the atoms in our bodies come and go. So do the cells made of those atoms that, in turn, make up our tissues, fluids, organs, glands, and bones. Yet, through all this transformation and turnover of living matter, we maintain this constant, if immaterial, sense of self. We maintain it throughout our development from childhood to adulthood and into old age. Our urge to maintain this constant sense of self is an aspect of the law of self-preservation. But preservation as used here refers not to life as such, but to one's identity within that life. A new term, *autopoiesis*, has recently come into use to label this urge to preserve self-identity in the face of constant change.[1]

Autopoiesis applies to all levels of life and relates to the power of self-organization that biologists increasingly argue partly accounts for the very possibility of life. Only through the powers of self-organization in the service of autopoiesis can your body heal itself from a wound without need for our DNA to encode umpteen million specific healing instructions for every conceivable kind of wound or injury. A general imperative to heal suffices. Self-organization takes over and handles the healing specifics within broad parameters. The same process works on DNA itself. Often harmed by cosmic rays or other factors, DNA is always repairing itself, as Dr. Andrew Weil points out in his 1995 book, *Spontaneous Healing*. A growing number of biologists in fact argue that without self-organization evolution could not happen.[2] Indeed, it does not happen entirely from the natural selection of random mutations. Critics agree that both forces are vital to evolution. They agree that if a random mutation confers a survival advantage in some context, natural selection assures that the trait is passed on to future generations. Some traits, however, are much more complex than that. For example, echo ranging by bats confers a major fitness advantage. But there is a problem here. Before echo ranging could actually happen, separate mutations had to bring forth a connected series of parts in just the right order. The parts first had to come into being and then get assembled in the proper sequence. Not until the sequence was complete could echo ranging actually take place to impart a fitness advantage upon which natural selection could act. Yet the bat had to expend energy on maintaining these temporarily functionless parts until the whole series had come together.

How can we thus explain through natural selection the whole sequence of steps that culminated in echo ranging? Again, each separate mutation provided no extra fitness. Hence, natural selection had no basis for passing it on to later generations of bats. In other words, to make echo ranging functional, not only the mutation for each step was random, but so was its survival. In that case, and on probability calculations, the time required for random chance to produce the right order far exceeds the age of the bat species itself. This issue of randomly selecting the separate parts of some whole in the right order to produce the whole is a variation on the old joke that given an infinite number of monkeys pecking away at an infinite number of typewriters, at some infinite future date one of them would assuredly type *Hamlet*. But, as noted earlier, the bat did not have infinity to work with.

Researchers at the Santa Fe Institute have argued that, in general, if sequential changes in the parts were to happen randomly, it would take an infinite amount of time to get the order of the sequence right.[3] Michael Crichton uses echo ranging by bats in his recent novel *The Lost World*, the sequel to *Jurassic Park*, to illustrate how life required self-organization to work with natural selection to facilitate evolution within the limits of actually available time. And it is more than coincidence that the opening scenes of Crichton's best-selling novel take place within the Santa Fe Institute, the leading think-tank on self-organization. Self-organization, we might note, appears not to work deterministically, but by trial and error toward a broader vision. It is often messy and imprecise, but it seems to work without the need to create detailed plans for a contingent, usually uncertain future.

AUTOPOIESIS AND SELF-ORGANIZATION

Self-organization is not just a biological concept, of course. As an aspect of autopoiesis, it clearly applies to human organizations. As a scientific term and concept, self-organization is relatively new. It cuts across chemistry and physics, as well as biology, to economics and the other social sciences. But if the term itself is new, its effects have been observed under different names for decades. In fact, Adam Smith's classical economics is an excellent example. Smith stressed the importance of self-organized markets guided by the "invisible hand" of competition. What Smith said on this issue in 1776 is still true. Despite one innovation after another; despite constant flux and transformation in the economic environment; and despite the vagaries of fad, fashion, and simple taste, self-organization of markets, however imperfectly, maintains a better balance between supply and demand than any human-directed command economy has ever come close to duplicating. When the communists finally admitted as much, the Cold War ended.

Even when the mechanistic model of organization was thought efficient and taken for granted, most students of social organization took note of the self-organized informational networks that grew up within but apart from the formal bureaucracy. They called such informational networks the "informal organization," which in turn gave birth to the "grapevine" or "rumor mill." Information that was spread by such networks often drove mechanistic managers nuts. Indeed, throughout history, despots have had to devote considerable resources either to quashing or, if they were smart, infiltrating these self-organized social networks because they were often a fertile breeding ground for palace revolts.

Actually, no mechanistic organization can function without these self-organized informal networks. A bureaucracy may not function very well with them, but without those networks a bureaucracy or any organization enmeshed in its own red tape could hardly function at all. As a green second lieutenant during the Korean War, I wondered at first how the army ever got anything done given its mountains of army regulation manuals. The sheer volume of them terrified me. Once on duty, however, the light dawned. Many NCOs had developed great skill at working off the books and under the table to outflank regulations that threatened to bring things to a halt. These NCOs in fact ran the army's day-to-day routines. Their informal networks, often forged in the NCO clubs, cut right across units and their formal chains of command. In my experience, the NCOs left the commissioned officers out of their networks, much to my relief.

Again, autopoiesis relates to self-organization at all levels, even among the cells to heal injury to the body. It drives us as individuals to take action to protect ourselves from some threat to our identity. It drives groups of people within the organization who feel threatened to take steps to damp down the threat and thus preserve the integrity of the group's identity. On a larger level, we often can see an organization trying to preserve its identity in some crisis and watch individuals leap into action to save the day, spontaneously, without prior direction. Whole communities can also spring into self-organized action when disasters such as floods or earthquakes strike. In the spring of 1997, the worst flood in two hundred years hit the rural Grays Harbor coastal community where my wife and I live—twenty inches of rain fell in thirty-six hours. Our little tree farm along the Satsop River quickly became an island surrounded by water. The county officials and Coast Guard all responded quickly enough, but, apart from that, so did hundreds of private citizens. They responded entirely on their own, spontaneously, undirected, and with no prior planning but with a view to preserve the community. Friends put up friends for the night who were kept from getting home by high water. Those with four-wheel drives helped rescue cars stalled in high water trying to get home that night. Other folks used such vehicles to bring in supplies for those who could not get out. After the waters receded, neighbor helped neighbor dig out the mud and debris and then helped clean up. Some churches donated money to flood victims from other churches and so on.

Such self-organized and yet unplanned efforts help communities bounce back from such disasters far more quickly than would otherwise be possible. Clearly the process is similar to the ways that the cells of our bodies cooperate to repair a wound spontaneously, without detailed plans or specific directions but with a clear mission to maintain a healthy self. In the next chapter we shall take a close look at the specific and costly dysfunctions that arise when bureaucracy distorts the natural course of self-organization and autopoiesis. Entangling red tape, bureaucratic bloat, and distended chains of command are the classic results.

IDENTITY AND SOCIAL STATUS

Meanwhile, we humans maintain our sense of self through many social changes. We get married, have children, move from one place to another, change careers, and so on, all the while maintaining our sense of self. But this self needs more than a body, it also needs social identity that lets it relate to other people. Having social identities within social relationships is what makes for a social animal. A constant self can have numerous social identities at the same time, for example, as members of a certain race or ethnic group, as a citizen of a specific country, or as a member of a club, political party, church, interest, or self-help group. We, of course, are concerned with employees who work for an organization.

A general principle is this: Our social reality is a function of our social relationships. A "self" has no social identity apart from its social relationships. Try to identify yourself without invoking your relationship with other people. Now define the "real you" independently of such relationships. In any event, the "real you" changes from one set of relationships to another. You behave one way as a parent to your children and in an often much different way as a child to your parents. So too with a superior–subordinate, doctor–patient, or teacher–student relationship. How you behave in many ways is going to depend on which side of what social relationship you find yourself on. So, who is the "real you?" Again, the "real you" varies depending on the relationships you are talking about and where you fit in to them. But if you do not have a clear social identity based on definite social relationships, you will tend to feel disoriented, perhaps alienated, and probably depressed. Such reactions may not arise from unclear casual relationships from which you can easily walk away, but adverse reactions will certainly surface if your status is unclear or your if identity is in danger in any organization on which you depend for a living.

THE STATUS IMPERATIVE

Social relationships imply status differences. Again, the status of a doctor is different from that of a patient, a teacher from a student, a superior from a subordinate, a parent from a child, and, within a family, that of elder child from younger child. The general rule for healthy social status is twofold. First, we need a clear and stable status to go with our social identity in the short run. Second, in the longer run, our status needs to rise as we gain experience in the organization. For example, students need to rise in status as they learn more. Schools systems worldwide do this systematically. They promote the child from the first to the second and then to the third grade and so on. This steady promotion goes on for twelve grades of grammar and high school, and yet another four for college. Note that this continuous rise in status comes within the continuing social identity of student. Almost every adult in the United States has grown up in this system; one is steadily "promoted" in status by advancing in grade as one acquires more academic experience. True, the school system, perhaps for lack of parental involvement or good teachers, may fail to impart as much knowledge as it should, but such failure does not change the promotion principle.

Promotion as recognition for more experience is natural and healthy. It is completely in tune with our human nature, forged as it was over two or three million years in hunter–gatherer clans. Those clans evolved the formula that more experience equals more status. In principle, however, bureaucracy rejects the formula. It thus creates serious problems for itself. This conflict drives us underground to try to beat the system and get more social status as we invest more effort and acquire more experience in the organization. We react badly if the additional status does not come as naturally as it does in the school system. Frustrated, we take steps to get the additional status. If we succeed, the bureaucracy suffers, mainly by overstaffing, overlayering, and overregulation, an interactive, mutually reinforcing package. But if our efforts fail, the bureaucracy still suffers, as we become depressed, alienated, lethargic, and gradually turn into bureaucratic deadwood. Many of us then become masters of wooden compliance, or worse, of malicious compliance (we may follow our orders to the letter, even knowing they will backfire, to discredit the boss who frustrated us).

Most managers fear this reaction, at least intuitively, so many give in and promote by seniority. But the "hard heads" often strongly believe that promotion should be based strictly on merit. With good reason they fear promotion based on seniority. If people are promoted into higher paying jobs because of seniority rules, as many union contracts specify, some will not be able to handle the better job. If they flop at the outset, however, it becomes a blessing for the firm (you can perhaps fire him or her) but a black eye for the person who did the promoting. More typically, people perform marginally, well enough to avoid the sack but not well enough to make a contribution. Meanwhile, the hard heads are coming to recognize that merit is also a land mine. Good performance on one job may seem to justify promotion, but it by no means guarantees good work in the higher job. In fact, some spectacular failures have occurred here. To illustrate, Anthony Eden performed brilliantly as Britain's Foreign Minister. So Eden succeeded from Churchill as Prime Minister, only to fail miserably—and in foreign affairs—during the Suez crisis of 1956.

Overall, and despite fears about promoting by seniority, most bureaucracies feel compelled to do it to keep internal peace. The typical ploy is to claim to promote on merit but in fact use seniority. This becomes evident when we statistically regress pay against time served and find that the two almost always rise together nicely. The seniority system of job promotion no doubt mismatches people and jobs all the time, but that is probably a lesser evil than the systematic creation of deadwood.

Of course, the best solution is to put the best person in the job, regardless of seniority or his or her past performance in other jobs. At the same time, a poor performance on a low-ranked job does not imply bad performance at a higher level. (As a nineteen-year-old Bill Gates put it, "It will be hard to deal with me unless I'm in charge."[4]) The problem is that we cannot be sure who will do the best job. Paper qualifications and personal interviews, while not worthless indicators, are notoriously unreliable. Often the most relevant information falls through the cracks even if the data presented are correct. But the uncertainty problem has a reasonable solution, namely the same trial and error upon which self-organization relies. If Fred or Laura appears well qualified, try him or her out. If one of them fails, try another job that he or she can handle. Unfortunately, this straightforward solution would traumatize a bureaucracy's social order based on its de facto job–caste system.

Meanwhile, the pay equity principle that applies to jobs ignores an important fact of life: The relative importance of a job can vary widely. It can also change unexpectedly, as a result of surprise events or circumstances. A sales job may be vital when plenty of surplus capacity exists, but falls in importance sharply after a big sales backlog accumulates. Design engineers may be vital when rapid changes in technology force frequent design changes, but that importance drops sharply once technology stabilizes. In any event, when a connected series of jobs all have to be done well before the good or service can be sold, the rank order of importance of any job in that chain is objectively indeterminate. Interdependence among jobs undercuts the effort to determine job rank order, even in a stable environment. The effort itself adds no value to the goods or services being produced. It may even subtract value if, as a result, some employees feel their jobs were shortchanged.

We will see in Part II how partnership between employees and stockholders works with human needs for identity and status to avoid the problems bureaucracy usually encounters by fighting those needs. As we will see, a partnership between capital and labor addresses the identity and status issue naturally, without contortion or concoction. First, however, we need to look at the way bureaucrats who feel impelled to defend their jobs to preserve their identity or status do so. They use common methods around the world. These methods, however, create costly concoctions and contortions in the organization and its work.

NOTES

1. Margaret J. Wheatley, *Leadership and the New Science: Learning about Organization from an Orderly Universe* (San Francisco: Berrett-Koehler, 1992).

2. Michael J. Behe, *Darwin's Black Box: The Biochemical Challenge to Evolution* (New York: The Free Press, 1996). See also Robert Wesson, *Beyond Natural Selection* (Cambridge: MIT Press, 1994).

3. Stuart Kauffman, *At Home in the Universe: The Search for New Laws of Self-Organization and Complexity* (New York: Oxford University Press, 1995).

4. "The Private World of Bill Gates," *Time*, 13 January 1997, p. 48.

Chapter 3

The Autopoiesis of Job Defense

Our social relationships create our social identities. Our identity, however, comes with a specific status relative to others. Autopoiesis impels us to preserve the integrity of that identity and its present social status, but as we gain in experience we expect our social status to rise above those with less experience. If the organization ignores that need, autopoiesis comes to the surface. It urges us to take steps on our own behalf. We might quit, of course. Or we might band together with others who also feel frustrated, say by a lack of promotion opportunities. One way to unblock that frustration is to create "make-work," add people to do that work, add new levels of management to supervise, and *voilà*, our promotion ladder has more rungs.

If that tactic does not work, we may turn to personal infighting. We might undercut our rivals to make them look bad. Hopefully we and not they get the coveted promotion. Failing that, we may retaliate against the system in some way. We might try practicing covert sabotage, or more subtly and more likely, try practicing malicious compliance. But if none of this gets us promoted and quitting is impractical, then what? If we do not go into depression, we may just mentally tune out of the job. We comply woodenly with whatever we may be asked to do to keep the money coming in, but we do as little as possible to keep the job. We can then look elsewhere in our lives to achieve a sense of self-respect and acquire higher status, perhaps in a church, a club, or a hobby group.

For the organization, all these employee reactions are dysfunctional. Managers usually know that. To avert such reactions to status blockage, managers may try to preempt them by making seniority a major consideration when promoting people. That is not always bad; experienced people get promoted, after all. Nevertheless, seniority often results in a mismatch of people with jobs, and once that mismatch takes place, it can be tough to change it.

RED TAPE

Meanwhile, these independent employee actions or reactions take place within the "informal organization," something that inevitably self-organizes around the formal bureaucratic organization created to do the work. In a bureaucracy, this self-organized informal organization will begin to invent make-work that adds little or no value. Yet more often that not such make-work soon becomes incorporated into the official routine. For example, reports are written that no one really reads or cares about. Studies are made that have little to do with the work at hand and no particular bearing on the future. Procedures are written, often in the name of safety, that often do little to improve safety and much to slow down operations. These procedures then require others to monitor them for compliance. The rule books, procedures manuals, and policy handbooks get fatter and fatter, more and more difficult to follow, and often include mutually contradictory instructions. Regulations can bring order out of chaos, of course, but once they pass the point of diminishing returns they become dysfunctional. The metaphor "red tape" captures well the reason for the dysfunction. Operations can become so entangled in specific rules that everything slows down. Little gets done, as citizens trying, say, to get a building permit approved have learned the hard way. But the same is true within a business. I once observed a practical example of this in the United Kingdom in the early 1960s as a consultant in a large steel works. In those days, British trade unions had total control of the shop floor.[1] If the unions wanted something that the management resisted, the unions had a simple tactic that nearly always worked. They threatened to "work to rule." The unions had honed this weapon of malicious compliance to a very sharp edge. The members would follow each and every management safety and union contract work rule to the letter. It was not that this tactic slowed things up. If rigorously applied, work to rule brought things to a dead stop without the workers actually going on strike. Management almost invariably caved in if faced with that threat. Any company that attempts to operate on the basis of a complex set of regulations and procedures becomes vulnerable to some variation on this tactic.

In practice, the more complex the regulations become, the more the formal organization requires the help of an informal organization to bail it out. To get things done, employees may form tacit cabals to bypass rules that pointlessly interfere with the operations. This can be dangerous for the employee, of course. If something bad happened when a rule was being bypassed, the risk is to the employee. Overwhelmingly, management is likely to assume that the violation caused the problem and then go punish the "wrongdoer" accordingly. If he or she responds with the defense, "Hey, don't pick on me, everyone does it," it will be sanctimoniously rejected. Management will respond with, "Rules are rules, and rules exist for a good reason—as you have just proved. Other people may well disobey rules, but that fact does not justify you doing so. You're fired."

After a Los Angeles earthquake, according to one of the physicians present, the hospitals were suddenly inundated with many injured citizens requiring emergency treatment. The chief physician took it upon himself to suspend the administrative rules for admittance. That allowed the medical staff to begin at once to treat the injured. The staff's productivity skyrocketed by a factor of nearly 500 percent in terms of patients treated per hour compared to periods when they followed those rules. The problem with trying to run a business strictly by the book, using regulations to specify every action taken, comes down to this: Any set of regulations comprehensive enough to cover all contingencies will be too complex to be understood. Any set of regulations short enough to be understood will be too short to cover all contingencies.[2] It is this dilemma that makes a purely mechanistic, rule-driven organization hopelessly inefficient, even impossible. Judgment and intuition will always be needed to decide when the letter of a law or regulation interferes with its spirit, or, put another way, when applying the rule defeats its own purpose.

This is an issue that complicates social life in general. When should we follow the rule and when should we disregard it, perhaps in unusual situations, to preserve its purpose? Philosophers and theologians have long debated this issue. One school holds that we should follow the rules to the letter. That is, generically speaking, the legal fundamentalist's position. In this view, the law, especially if attributed to God as its source, is absolute. It applies at all times and in all situations. Virtue lies in submitting to these rules. Sin is disobedience, period, end of discussion. At the extreme fringe, within religion and outside it, fundamentalists reject the notion that the letter and spirit of the rules conflict. The spirit is the letter and the letter is the spirit. Rules are rules, and not mere guidelines. Letting violations pass, in this view, is an open invitation to anarchy. Grant people the right to decide for themselves when to obey and when to ignore a rule and you have granted each person a de facto license to make their own rules as they see fit. Many people will violate any rule that they find is inconvenient or that stands in the way of their instant gratification of fleshly pleasure, in this fundamentalist view. Their argument has a certain validity, but it also takes a rather jaundiced view of human nature.

A more liberal argument is that a rule has no meaning in the abstract. Rules have specific goals, be it order, safety, health, efficiency, or whatever. Otherwise, why bother with a rule? Thus it can apply only in specific concrete situations. Yet the specifics can vary so much and so widely that no "one rule size fits all" can work. If tailored to fit every situation, it would be too complicated to follow or understand. If rules are not taken in good faith as guidelines, and if it is not recognized that the spirit and letter sometimes can part company, then one is in trouble. Each situation must have its own rule, and new situations are always coming up. Thus, the fundamentalist view opens society, the church, the organization, or whatever to a need for an ever-expanding proliferation of rules to cover every new contingency and thus becomes hopelessly ensnared in red tape. Before long, one cannot even turn around without unwittingly violating the letter of some rule or another. The rules, in effect, have long passed the point of diminishing returns. Instead of rules preserving order through the rule of law, the red tape actually creates disorder. Under the table, so to speak, we have reverted to the arbitrary rule of men. For example, when two rules conflict without a clear order of precedence (as when federal law trumps state law), some person has to decide which one has precedence. Such decisions can be made arbitrarily, and can vary from one "judge" to another. Such efforts to disentangle red tape can hardly be described as the rule of law. Still, a strong commitment to the rule of law tends to create a fundamentalist bias, one of following the letter even when it conflicts with the spirit. This bias often applies to police. Traffic police, for example, often ignore technical violations that did no harm and put nobody at risk, but if their superiors measure their "productivity" on patrol by the numbers of citations they issue, harmless technical violators can suddenly find themselves hammered.

Bureaucrats also tend to be fundamentalists, biased to enforce the letter of any law that is visibly violated, even if for good reason. Broadly, bureaucrats have the same motives that drive the police, a priesthood, lawyers, or government regulators. "Enforcing the law" is their job and that job activates an autopoietic response to preserve that job's identity in a self-consistent way. But just as important to those whose jobs and job identities arise from laws, rules, or regulations is the fact that they can enhance their job and career by extending these laws and rules into new territory. Subconsciously, autopoiesis will bias them to do just that. Defense lawyers will lobby for ever more complex rules of due process. Priests tend to interpret scripture to prohibit new categories of behavior. Bureaucratic regulators will lobby for ever more complex, extensive, and confining regulations to apply to the public (and to themselves, for that matter). A business bureaucrat does the same thing with internal policy and procedure.

The ultimate if largely implicit goal is to relieve those being regulated of all independent initiative. We can turn to Plato to see how far some would carry this.

The greatest principle of all is that nobody, whether male or female, should be without a leader. Nor should the mind of anybody be habituated to letting him do anything at all on his own initiative, neither out of zeal, or even playfully. But in war and in the midst of peace—to his leader he shall direct his eye and follow him faithfully. And even in the smallest matter he should stand under leadership. For example, he should get up, move, or wash or take his meals only if told to do so. In a word he should teach his soul, by long habit, never to act independently and be utterly incapable of it.[3]

Any large organization would quickly seize up if employees actually followed Plato's advice. Still, his remarks underscore the desire some folks have to control and micromanage other people's lives down to the last detail. Plato was perhaps the first person of note to confess this need, and in so doing he perhaps inadvertently profiled the expected behavior from employees who worked "as cogs in the machine" during the early days of scientific management. Such cogs are to do nothing on their own, of course, even as your car's spark plug is not to spark until "told" to do so.

Plato wanted leaders to micromanage people's lives directly, but laws or regulations can be used for much the same purpose. The rise of Christianity offers an illustration. By the time of Christ's mission, that branch of the Jewish priesthood known as the Pharisees had formulated hundreds of detailed rules covering nearly every aspect of Jewish life.[4] The Jewish religion was in fact built around God's Law, first brought down from Mt. Sinai by Moses as the Ten Commandments and with later additions. The Jews saw themselves as the people chosen by God, the creator not just of the Jews but of all humans, to live according to these laws. A thousand years later, more or less, Christ argued, in effect, that the Pharisees had carried all this past the point of diminishing returns. He began breaking some of the laws, by consorting with gentiles, for example, or healing on the Sabbath. By doing so Christ incurred the wrath of the Pharisees. He responded to their criticism of his healing by arguing the Sabbath was created for man, not man for the Sabbath, and continued to heal. He used the par-able of the good Samaritan to show how the specifics of the Pharisees' rules actually undercut God's broader message. Among other things, these rules prohibited touching the dead. If violated even inadvertently, one had to drop everything and head back to the Temple in Jerusalem to undergo a ritual cleansing. Such a rule would clearly inhibit helping a sick person found along the road. He might be dead. The good Samaritan, however, ignored the risk, picked up the sick person, and brought him to an inn to help him recover. Thus, the Samaritan put the spirit of God's broader goals ("love thy neighbor as thyself") ahead of the Pharisees "red tape" that clearly interfered with a community's ability to provide mutual support.

Christ also downplayed Jewish dietary rules. These he apparently felt were of little significance in God's eyes. That issue, together with the requirement for circumcision, began to split the gentile Christians off from the Jews during the mission of St. Paul. Paul felt it was self-defeating to insist that adult gentiles submit to Jewish circumcision or diet as a condition for accepting Christ. That cavalier attitude was too much for the Jews, even outside Palestine, where Paul concentrated his missionary efforts. Jews outside Palestine had long allowed gentiles attracted to monotheism into their synagogues, but kept them at distance. Paul's preaching on behalf of Christ seemed to appeal to gentiles. The numbers so attracted began to grow. A former Pharisee himself, Paul had come around to Christ's view of the law. It provided useful guidelines but should not be obeyed in a way to defeat the underlying purpose of God's Law. The Jews, after all, supposedly were to bring God's Law to all nations. So why restrict association with gentiles? Why try to impose so many rules upon them? Still, a big question remains. How can we tell when to obey and when to ignore a rule? Paul seemed to suggest that faith was the answer. In fact, Paul points out, faith was what sustained the Jews from the time of Abraham to that of Moses and the beginning of written scripture and law, a period of several hundred years.[5]

Most Jews, including some of the original twelve apostles, did not go along with Paul. They had some angry debates on this issue, apparently with Peter and James resisting Paul. Finally, the debate of "faith versus the law" ended as the gentiles began to form their own churches. They broke away from the Jews, and Christianity became a gentile religion. For the next three hundred years the new Christian faith grew rapidly, largely through self-organization, despite Roman persecution. Then, about A.D. 330 the Roman emperor Constantine decided to convert to Christianity. He made Christianity the official religion of the whole Roman Empire, and it has remained Europe's dominant religion ever since.

Then came a great irony. As Christianity became the official religion, the same motives that drove the Pharisees to elaborate and extend Mosaic law began to take hold among the Christian clergy. The church began to develop an elaborate church law alongside scripture, just as the Jews had done earlier. And once again, about a thousand years later, some of the clergy got restive, much as Christ had done. Led by Martin Luther just after 1500, a new revolt against these elaborate and often corrupted church rules broke out. Luther insisted that Christ's message has been lost sight of. The Protestant Reformation swept away church rules. With the help of the printing press, invented about fifty years earlier, the Bible had already become a big best-seller by Luther's day because, by previous standards of hand copying, it was now dirt cheap. The Protestants were inclined to encourage each person to read scripture for themselves. For its part, the Catholic Church and priests had not stressed Bible reading by the laity. They had kept it more or less to themselves, which made it much easier to control its interpretation. In fact, very early in Christian history, two influential bishops, Irenaeus and Tertullian, discouraged lay reading of the newly compiled Bible. It had become evident to these bishops that the diverse writings found in the Bible lent themselves to a wide variety of interpretations (does one take an "eye for an eye" or "turn the other cheek?"). They quickly concluded it was the job of the Church working through the priesthood to interpret the Bible and pass it on to their own congregations as lessons during Sunday services. After Christianity became Rome's official religion, the views of Irenaeus and Tertullian became more or less official policy.[6] Thereafter, the now-official church, led by the pope, began to add new rules over the next few hundred years. Those laws, of course, helped the pope become much more powerful and influential than any king in feudally fragmented Europe during its Dark Ages.

After the Reformation, the Protestants quickly began to interpret scripture in different ways, just as Irenaeus foresaw. And as he had feared, new sects grew up around the different views of just what scripture said or meant. Except perhaps for the Quakers and a few other small sects, the Protestant priesthoods themselves began seeing their main job as the "proper interpretation" of scripture. They then began to reject dissenters. Before long, the fundamentalists emerged, trying to end all this confusion by insisting on a "literal" interpretation of the Bible—God said it, I read it, that settles it.

Making and interpreting rules and laws has always been bread and butter to the clergy. That is one of the priesthood's main jobs in the Judeo–Christian–Islamic tradition if the job becomes a church-supported career. If it is, the temptation to keep extending the rules is overwhelming. Doing so both enhances the status of the job and tends to increase the need for priests. Once the priests push the rules too far, a backlash may occur. A new prophet comes along with a new message of renewal and a "back to basics" approach. But after the prophets have passed away, the next generations of priests sooner or later begin once again to complicate the rules by extending them further and further.

Bureaucrats tend to behave in exactly the same way and for the same reasons. My extended discussion of priestly behavior mainly aims to point out the generality of this process and the long history behind it—the Catholic Church, after all, is the oldest organization in the West. Again, bureaucrats in any bureaucracy have more or less the same incentives that have applied to priests. Besides, business too has its prophets of reform. They emerge periodically and begin to attack the red tape and its rigidity. They may urge reforms such as reengineering, TQM, a learning organization, or whatever. Such reforms may well help—for a time. But, for either a priesthood or a management, if your job accords you your primary social identity and is also a career upon which you depend for a living, the urge to extend the rules through which you exert the authority of your office quickly reappears. As soon as the reformers have left the scene, as they always must, autopoiesis will again work on your identity. If your identity is that of manager, and that job is to exert some control, control is what you will try to exert. That is as true of the affairs of a business as of a church. In a bureaucracy, that control is usually expressed through rules and regulations. That being the case, the temptation to judge subordinates in terms of their compliance to your rules is all but irresistible. When things seem to be going badly, the temptation to regain control by imposing new rules and regulations can become all but overwhelming. As a reformist manager you may be happy to go along with empowerment and self-managed teams, if in fact those teams deliver the goods. Things will seem to be going well. You then gladly accept the somewhat wishy-washy role of "coach" or "facilitator" as opposed to "boss." You can still bask in a sort of enlightened and liberal aura of "reformer."

But suppose trouble develops. Perhaps one of those self-managed teams really screws up—even self-managed teams are human. "How could those idiots have done that," you ask yourself. You can handle one or two screwups if they are not too serious. Still, screwups by subordinates that happen on your watch make you look bad. You begin to rethink those reforms. Who did Deming think he was, anyway? Look at what happened to Baring Brothers Bank when they turned loose that idiot, Nick Leeson, to do his own thing in the Far East financial markets. He lost so much money speculating in yen that he brought down the whole bank before the top command even knew what was happening. You begin to conclude that what this outfit needs is a little more top-down command and control. With each screwup you are tempted to formulate a new rule or procedure that, had it been followed, would have prevented error. Or at least you convince yourself of that. A fundamentalist position (assuming the letter is the spirit) begins to assert itself. The rules soon proliferate but none dare call it red tape. Whether or not the reforms come apart on your bureaucratic watch, they will come apart sooner or later. The old red tape, the old tendency to add administrative staff and more layers of management at any excuse, will return, in one way or another, at one time or another.[7]

But such recidivism is not driven by status blockage alone. Self-consistency in terms of one's identity is what autopoiesis is all about. Indeed, we often accept an excuse for some action that caused harm when the person can say, "I [or he or she] was only doing my job

according to the rules." If one's job is to make laws, write regulations, or lay down rules, autopoiesis will drive you to do just that. It
will also inhibit you from dwelling on the law of diminishing returns. You will not much worry about reaching the point where useful regulation ends and dysfunctional red tape begins. Even if you
accept the principle of diminishing returns as a valid abstraction, your
subconscious biases to defend the integrity of your identity will still
urge you to believe that those diminishing returns are a comfortable
distance down the road.

This "just doing my job" aspect of autopoiesis was well illustrated
in a recent *Time* article, "Knowing When to Stop."[8] The subtitle read,
"Doctors go to heroic lengths to keep terminally ill patients alive—
often against their wishes." Citing a research study published in the
Journal of the American Medical Association, the *Time* article went on to
explain why doctors behaved that way. The researchers began by
conceding that many terminally ill patients were kept alive by heroic
measures long after all hope of recovery had vanished, prolonging
the agony of the patient, often at great cost to the survivors. For example, they noted that 40 percent of the patients sampled had been
kept alive in intensive care entirely through breathing machines and
that half of these patients had reported severe pain. The researchers
hypothesized that this situation arose primarily because of poor com-
munication between patients and their families on one hand, and the
doctors and other hospital staff on the other.

A controlled study was done in which half of more than four thousand patients were given traditional hospital care. No effort was made
to communicate patient wishes. The other half, or two thousand patients, were given the special attention the researchers hypothesized
would avoid needless pain and expense. Care was taken to make
sure the doctors and hospital staff knew of the patients' and their
families' wishes not to receive heroic care. The researchers expected
to see big differences in results between the two groups, but when
they analyzed the data they were shocked. To quote the researchers,
"We were stunned to find [the extra effort] didn't make a bit of difference. The tools the experts thought would work didn't." One re-
searcher suggested, in effect, an autopoietic reason. "Physicians are

taught to save lives, and that death is failure," she said. So regardless of what the patient wanted, and regardless of the pain gratuitously inflicted, and despite knowing full well that death was imminent anyway, doctors and nurses did everything they could to prolong life to the bitter end. That was their job, and that was also autopoiesis in action to maintain the integrity of job-based identities. True, not all doctors do that, and Dr. Kevorkian quickly springs to mind. People in all kinds of jobs sometimes create other identities for themselves. If these other identities become primary, from the standpoint of autopoiesis, the primary trumps the secondary if the two conflict. Perhaps the prophets of reform emerge from such people.

CHAIN OF COMMAND VERSUS
THE PROMOTION LADDER

Let us now focus more closely on the conflict between the need for good communications and the imperatives of social status. A good chain of command has as few links as possible. Short chains preserve the integrity of communications up and down. Long chains with many links are well known to distort communications; the more links the worse the distortion. In practice, each link in the chain edits or filters out the information it gets before passing it on. In long chains with many sources of information, this editing, filtering, and the related "gatekeeping" function can hardly be avoided, and in long chains the editing by one link is edited yet again by other links going up or down the chain. Important information gets left out, its meaning is changed, or both. Sometimes this is accidental, but it is often deliberate. For example, lower levels tend to filter out bad news on the way up, hoping to avoid the well-known fate of messengers thereof. Another notorious form of editing concerns the NIH ("not invented here") factor. In bureaucracy, as a rule, the employees are forced to compete with each other for the boss's favor. If someone has a good idea that wins acceptance, they get the credit. They are suddenly rivals and one up on you for pay raises or promotion. Internal competition thus imparts a motive for you to put down anyone you see as an actual or potential rival, and that will obviously include their ideas. The point here is that wisdom supposedly attaches to office, and the higher its level, the more wisdom and knowledge one holding the higher position supposedly possesses. The top job is even held to impart infallibility in some cases, and decisions coming from it can never be criticized. While this god-like wisdom ethic prevailed among the "pilots in command" of Pan American Airlines during the early years of the jets, the airline lost ten 707s, the worst safety record of any airline flying that jet. Sensing the problem, in 1974 Pan Am switched to a cockpit team system among the crew, and the airline never lost another 707.[9] Pan Am thus provided early proof that teams work better than dictatorships.

Now assume a lower-level employee comes up with a great idea on how to simplify and improve some work process. Worse yet, suppose her idea, once stated, seems obvious. I ask myself, "Why didn't I think of that?" Perhaps I subconsciously feel threatened. This lower-ranked person may be promoted around and ahead of me (this happens all the time). Subconsciously my frightened "child within" urges me to react (a bureaucrat's "child within" has good reason to take fright). I can deal with this potential threat in at least three ways. First, I can just ignore her proposal and pretend I did not receive it or that her memo got misplaced. This tactic amounts to a pocket veto. Second, I can tell my innovative subordinate that I am very busy. I will try to get to her idea as soon as I can but, honestly, it will take a while. I thus buy time to think up reasons why it should be vetoed. Third, I can simply veto it outright with or without a stated reason, perhaps with an aura of imperial disdain. Whichever, such filtering quashes innovation in a bureaucracy, and the bigger it is, the less it can innovate. That is true even without an NIH factor. Let me illustrate by assuming a very low NIH factor. Therefore assume that every boss on every level of approval accepts and passes on with undiminished enthusiasm fully 50 percent of all new ideas put to him or her (a 10 percent rate would be more realistic). Now assume six levels of approval before final approval. Of one hundred new ideas you submit you could expect your boss to approve fifty of them and your boss's boss twenty-five. About twelve would survive to level three, while six would make it to level four. Three of your ideas still survive to reach level five, and one or two might make it to level six. If it takes, say, a month to develop an idea to the point of submission, you must spend perhaps one hundred developmental months to get one idea accepted. With that batting average, most people give up. In practice, people who come up a new idea a month and who also have the drive to develop it to the point of submission month in and month out are very rare. But assume that you recruited for such people and they had thirty-year careers or 360 months. Of the 360 developed new ideas submitted for approval over their career at the assumed approval rate, perhaps five or six might get accepted during a whole career. At the same time, there may be more than six levels of approval. Given ten such levels, the odds drop to nearly zero. You may get no approvals over your whole thirty-year career.

The great bulk of groundbreaking innovations come not from within large and well-endowed bureaucracies, but from outside them. They come from innovators working in their fabled garages, usually with limited resources. Many of them are refugees from bureaucracy's NIH factor. Those really driven to innovate either avoid or soon leave multilayered hierarchies. They start their own firms in the fashion of Bill Gates and Paul Allen.[10] The market can also take a frightful toll on these innovations if they are put to the test. But a market rejection reflects a failure in practice, not a failure to get the innovation approved. With few exceptions—the first transistor out of Bell Labs, the first PC out of IBM—the great majority of innovations that have a high impact come from the margins of the mainstream or even completely outside it. When the KGB, as a result of its spying on us, came to realize this fact, they encouraged Gorbachev's reforms. They saw that the Soviet system forever precluded much real innovation. In many cases, more than thirty approval levels were needed and again, given a 50 percent approval rate, of one billion new ideas none would likely survive. Meanwhile, those with a talent for innovation had no private sector to which they could retire to try it on their own. As a matter of ideology, the USSR had effectively banished market competition and therefore any hope, as the KGB saw it, of reaching some sort of technological par with capitalism.[11]

In practice, many of the intermediate links between the value-adding work and the decision-making levels are redundant. They create jobs and facilitate promotion to be sure, but add no value for the customer and may even from subtract it. The subconscious "inner child" of most middle managers thus has much to be fearful about. Many jobs and even whole units reporting to mid-level managers are highly vulnerable, as a decade of downsizing proves. In an era of reengineering, most middle managers have become openly expendable. Hundreds of thousands of them have been laid off in the campaign to de-layer management hierarchies. Some people argue that multilayered hierarchies with their redundant levels are a thing of the past, but in bureaucracy the pressure to add rungs to the promotion ladder will continue. If pay and status are tied to the job, and if the jobs along the chain of command make up the main promotion ladder, the pressure to add redundant levels or links will continue unabated. We have already seen evidence of this after recent pruning attempts. As with plant life, pruning tends to invigorate bureaucratic growth a short time later. After the downsizing, if sales pick up at all, the old pressures to add levels, and the old reasons for doing so, remain fully in force, as pointed out earlier.

TIME-TESTED STRATEGIES

From about 1960 until about 1980, it was often easy to get new layers of management added on. A new excuse for doing so came to hand. One only had to lobby for more staff and a shorter span of control—and thus more levels—in the name of improving either forecasting, planning, control, or all three. The reason was that the mainframe computer began coming into its own, and with it came a new, if brief, era that featured a computer-enhanced mechanistic model of bureaucracy.

This new model was built around a strategy that I call FPCC—forecasting, planning, command, and control. How it worked, the mechanistic logic behind it, and why it failed so badly are the main focuses of the next chapter. Here we need only note that it proved a bonanza for unblocking status frustration inherent in a bureaucratic pyramid with a short chain of command. The glory of FPCC was that one could enhance one's career prospects, as well as those of subordinates, without any need to bring such self-serving issues up. The ethic that came with FPCC would have balked at those reasons anyway, because FPCC was not "people centered"—aggressively not—partly as a reaction to the human relations school that management science and FPCC had just displaced. The human relations people, according the new apostles of FPCC, were just so many wishy-washy do-gooders, full of talky talk. Management science expressed as FPCC (the acronym is mine, but it captures the typical sequence) disdained human relations "squishiness." FPCC insisted on objective logic and reason and demanded precise quantitative measures. If you could not express it in numbers, forget it.

So how did the computer become a vehicle of adding levels and jobs when the fear had been that it would wipe out administrative jobs by the thousands? Let me recount an example from my own early experience at Boeing. I worked in the market research and planning group located in the sales department. Our job was to make market forecasts of airline traffic, and based on those forecasts, we made a forecast of Boeing's market share or a sales forecast for Boeing jets. From the sales forecast, and with the help of other planning groups, we compiled a business plan including a production schedule. This sequence was no boondoggle. It had to be done because it took many months between the time an order was booked until the airplane was delivered, and a big part of the airplane consisted of purchased parts, for example, engines, the electronics, and even large parts of the fuselage. (Boeing designed and built its own wings, considered then as now to be the crucial core competency.) But it was also crucial to keep cycle time as low as possible, because if you could not deliver when the airline wanted the new airplane, it might go to a competitor. There were three in the United States, namely, Douglas, Lockheed, and General Dynamics. Several other firms in Europe produced jets, such as Caravel, BAC-111, and Trident. Boeing thus had to estimate sales and set production schedules in advance of booking actual orders, or those orders might not materialize. Still, at the time we knew our forecasts, and hence all the plans that we later based upon them were, at the bottom, best guesses. No one pretended we were dealing in science. Then came the IBM 360, the real beginning of the computer age. Now, suddenly, the constraints of costly computation seemed to disappear, and Laplace finally came into his own.[12]

Before long it became known to us that a group led by Dr. Lawrence Klein of Wharton's Graduate School of Business had developed a macroforecasting model of the U.S. economy. It contained hundreds of separate equations and could spew out forecasts on nearly any significant sector of our economy by quarter, by year, and for five years ahead. While our traffic forecasts required other data on price and quality, the economy provided the income to buy. Meanwhile, the unit was under some pressure to "become more scientific." Wharton's computer model, a product of the best brains in the Ivy League, was heaven sent. Not only did it provide us with a facade of science, it helped us to justify more real "boss" managers, more levels, and thus a longer promotion ladder. Though that was not what Klein thought he was selling, it was one of things we were buying, for we had earlier learned a harsh truth. In those days, and in common with most firms, an "individual contributor" (a manager with no subordinate staff) could go only so high in salary—and not very high at that. True, we all had "management status," but such status was largely a facade. We got that status for the benefit of Boeing's airline customers, with whom we had frequent contact.

Being an individual contributor was fine when coming into the group and for a while thereafter. But then autopoiesis would cause people to get restless. Moreover, the personnel department did not really care how good a job you did; they could authorize no raises beyond the top allowed for the individual contributors. They were not being mean minded, they were just following the rules. In my case, I had made a well-received traffic forecast that had restored some confidence in the future at a time when traffic growth had stalled out and pessimism was spreading. If I showed my more optimistic forecast to one customer or supplier group, I must have showed it to a hundred or so over the next two years because events suggested it was proving correct.[13] I made the pitch so often I could have done it in my sleep. My boss truly wanted to get me a fat raise, but personnel told him that I had already topped out. I had to have people reporting to me before they could even consider it. Being a creative chap, my boss said he could arrange that. He reorganized his unit, gave me a new title, and reassigned some of the people reporting directly to him to report directly to me. Informally, I was expected to continue doing my job and they theirs, but that device got me about a 20 percent raise so I was delighted. Besides, in the executive dining room I could now utter those magic words that confirmed me as a real manager. If some technical issue came up, I could now say, "Okay Tom, I'll have *my guys* get with your guys to look into that." But those very words also made the people who had been demoted a level unhappy. They conceded that I deserved a raise but not at their expense.

Now came the Wharton model. Suddenly we had an excellent excuse to create more supervisory management jobs to deal with it. It also gave us an excuse to launch other new projects that could use even more people, computing things that could not be computed before. So we lobbied the vice president of sales to subscribe to Wharton. Since Klein's model supposedly took the guesswork out of our forecasts, we got quick approval. It helped that business was booming, and the model forecast the boom would continue. Now other deserving but frustrated folks could be "saved," as I had been earlier, by getting their own subordinates.

At first, the adding of new layers was seen largely as a device to get around personnel's promotion limits. The new layers were not taken that seriously. My "guys" could still go to my boss without asking my permission. But after the IBM 360 became common, new managers began taking these new layers very seriously. They began to insist that their "guys," and by now a few "gals," follow a strict chain of command. Everyone began to keep their studies a secret from others, especially the computer printouts. Everyone began to use the computer for even heavier number crunching. Such crunching, it was hoped, would reveal new, possibly surprising, quantitative relationships. If it was tightly controlled, we could use such new information to leverage our group's status. Demand for computers thus soared. Before long, Boeing had acquired the largest inventory of mainframes of any private company on earth, according to Boeing's then CEO, T. Wilson.

In theory, all those new computers should have allowed us to do ten times the analytical work with perhaps 10 percent of the people. After all, the computers did drudge calculations previously done by those loud, slow, electromechanical monsters that made a horrible racket in nearly every Boeing office, and did it a million times faster. Instead, Boeing's headcount went ballistic, hand in hand with computer usage. In a couple of years the marketing end of the sales department shot up from about forty-five people to more than four hundred. The number of levels rose even faster. Before the bottom fell out in 1969, the marketing department had forged more links in its internal chain of command than possessed by an eighteen-thousand-man World War II army division over forty times larger. Boeing had ballooned into a monstrously bloated bureaucracy.

Then airline traffic growth suddenly ceased, just as our forecasts called for 12 percent annual traffic increases more or less forever. So much for the computer removing uncertainty about the future. From more than one-hundred thousand employees in the Seattle area in 1968, Boeing collapsed to about thirty-eight thousand by early 1971 as tens of thousands of people were laid off. A famous billboard sign soon appeared in North Seattle: "Will the last person to leave town, please turn out the lights."

One of my own better forecasts was to see this drop coming. Proactively, I shifted jobs a few months in advance and went back overseas as a consultant early in 1968. I was at once confronted with even more grotesque examples of bloated overstaffing, overlayering, and overregulation. I had seen that earlier in Brazil. Now I was soon to see it again in Uruguay, followed by Thailand, Indonesia, and Malaysia, and later yet in South Vietnam, Nigeria, Jordan, and Honduras. I had always thought that culture dictated a nation's style of organization, but no longer. The evidence seemed clear. Bureaucracy itself, working through the incentives established by its own policies, accounted for the overstaffing, overlayering, and overregulation. How else could one explain so similar a pattern of organizational behavior in so wide a variety of cultures?

In Chapter 4, we will look more closely at the FPCC model, the positivist philosophy behind it, and why that model failed so badly and so often in practice. Indeed, the failure of that model played the major role in causing business to lose faith in the impersonal and mechanistic approach that had sustained it throughout the modern era.

NOTES

1. E. Owen Smith, *Productivity Bargaining: A Case Study in the Steel Industry* (London: Pan Books, 1971). This book describes our consulting project at the Steel Company of Wales in Port Talbot in the mid-1960s.

2. To my students I immodestly refer to this dilemma as "Wallace's Law."

3. Karl Popper, *The Open Society and Its Enemies*, vol. 1 (London: Routledge & Kegan Paul, 1945), 3.

4. A good overview is given by Dr. Elizabeth McNamer in her lecture on Paul in an audio series on Western civilization published by The Teaching Company, Springfield, Va. For a biography of Paul, see A. N. Wilson, *Paul: The Mind of an Apostle* (New York: W. W. Norton, 1997).

5. See Paul's Letter to the Galatians 3:6–12.

6. Elaine Pagels, *The Origin of Satan* (New York: Vintage Books, 1995). See also her *Gnostic Gospels* (New York: Vintage Books, 1989).

7. John Micklethwait and Adrian Wooldridge, *The Witch Doctors: Making Sense of Management Gurus* (New York: Times Business Books, 1996).

8. "Knowing When to Stop," *Time*, 4 December 1995.

9. Robert Gandt, Chapter 11 of *Sky Gods: The Fall of Pan Am* (New York: William Morrow & Co., 1995).

10. Bill Gates, *The Road Ahead* (New York: Viking, 1995).

11. This view was expressed at a March 1991 international conference of Wharton Econometrics in Philadelphia by the East European Group's presenters.

12. Pierre Laplace (1749–1827) was a French mathematician and astronomer who claimed that Newton's laws enabled perfect prediction given enough computing power.

13. William McDonald Wallace and T. F. Comick, *A Forecast of United States Domestic Airline Traffic, 1961–1975: TSR-747* (Renton, Wash.: The Boeing Co., 1961).

Chapter 4

Management Science
and FPCC

THE SLOAN MODEL

The classical bureaucratic structure of a departmentally divided hierarchy proved unwieldy with the rise of very large firms in the later stages of the Industrial Revolution. Standard Oil of New Jersey (Exxon), du Pont, Sears, and General Motors all reached this conclusion early in the twentieth century. The man who, more than anyone else, solved this structural problem was Alfred P. Sloan, General Motors's most famous CEO.[1]

Peter Drucker described Sloan's reform as "federal decentralization."[2] What Sloan did was delegate operating authority to the operating divisions. Finance aside, each division controlled all the functions within it. GM's semiautonomous new divisions were built around its automobiles (Chevrolet, Pontiac, Oldsmobile, Buick, and Cadillac) as well as around other products, such as locomotives and aircraft engines. Corporate headquarters retained "federal" control over financial affairs because Sloan insisted on comprehensive and centralized financial controls at the top. He feared that a costly mistake in one division could jeopardize the whole firm. Sloan's solution of federal decentralization brought what had been an unwieldy sprawl quickly under control. GM's share of the market rose from 18 percent when Sloan took over in 1923 to over 40 percent by the time he retired. GM's market share topped out at about 45 percent by 1970. Moreover, GM was the only automobile firm to remain profitable throughout the Depression, if just barely in 1933. Thus Sloan seemed to have found the ideal format for a bureaucracy in the modern industrial world. It could handle large-scale manufacturing operations efficiently and for many different products. From the late 1930s to the early 1970s, GM was the largest and the most prestigious private manufacturing enterprise on earth.

Sloan's reforms became the model for many other firms, but, decentralization notwithstanding, Sloan's bureaucracy remained authoritarian, top down, and mechanistic. As John Micklethwait and Adrian Wooldridge put it, "Sloan's great achievement was to do for management what Henry Ford had done for labor—turn it into a reliable, efficient, and machinelike process. Indeed, Sloan's system was thought to be an effective antidote to temperamental pioneers like Ford."[3] Sloan believed in multilayered hierarchies and in giving managers a relatively narrow span of control. He wanted his top managers to focus on strategic planning, the "big picture." The job of lower-level managers was to carry out those plans. Planning and doing were kept separate. The seniors planned and the juniors did, or at least issued the direct orders to do. A fashionable definition of management was "getting things done through other people."

THE BOSS IS THE CUSTOMER

After World War II, Peter Drucker wrote a book about GM which he called *The Concept of the Corporation*. It was his first best-seller. Before long, Sloan's model became a sort of national standard or, in today's terms, a "benchmark" for large manufacturers. But Sloan's model was not customer focused. As Jack Welch, CEO of General Electric, apparently said, Sloan's model "turned management's face toward the CEO and its ass towards the customer."[4] Welch's pithy remark points to a problem endemic to any organization that depends upon hirelings: If you work for hire, the firm's customer is not really your customer. Your boss is your customer. The firm's customer does not hire or fire you, the boss does. We define customers as those who can decide to buy, refuse to buy, or cease buying. In effect, any resource that hires itself out sells its services. Whoever has the power to purchase your services is therefore your customer. You do very well to keep that fact firmly in mind if you want to remain a hireling. Bosses, of course, like the idea of being the customer because, as they say, "The customer is always right." That attitude, while a useful part of the buyer–seller relationship in general, is dysfunctional for the enterprise for two reasons when it applies within. First, it distracts employees from focusing on the firm's real customers, those who provide the revenue. Second, it encourages a strongly departmental point of view, as we have already said. Turf battles and internal power struggles often follow.

McNAMARA'S VARIANT: FORECASTING, PLANNING, COMMAND, AND CONTROL

Some of the criticism against Sloan's original model, however, has been overdrawn. True, it did view wage labor as "cogs in a machine," but it never treated management and professional staff that way. A manager's life in Sloan's GM was very secure, even in the Depression. At the same time, Sloan's model began life in 1923, when few people believed we could make accurate forecasts of business conditions. The Depression itself came as a shock, but GM handled it well. Sloan took the practical uncertainty of the future into account. He thus allowed for considerable flexibility in planning despite his highly structured management hierarchy. Not only did Sloan's GM weather the Depression well, it quickly and efficiently converted to defense production following the attack on Pearl Harbor. After the war, and with GM as its class industrial act, the United States quickly found itself the world's overwhelmingly dominant industrial power. In 1950, with but 6 percent of the world population, the United States produced nearly 50 percent of the world's gross national product.

Much of the recent criticism directed at Sloan's model should really target Robert S. McNamara. He, far more than Sloan, viewed

managers as cogs in his machine. Moreover, McNamara turned
Sloan's approach into a rigid and inflexible planning monstrosity built
on some heroically false assumptions. He did this not at GM, but at
Ford Motor Co. Mr. McNamara in fact came to Ford as one of a team
of "whiz kids" right after the war ended. Under Tex Thornton, the
team had sold itself to Ford on the strength of the great job this same
team had done for the Army Air Corps in World War II by applying
the quantitative methods of management science. Ford, indeed, was
in a desperate state. Old Henry, a cantankerous autocrat then well
into his dotage, had nearly destroyed the company. It was losing
money at an enormous rate. At the urging of the U.S. Navy, young
Henry and his grandmother successfully conspired to ease old Henry
out before he finally destroyed his own creation. Grandson Henry
was only twenty-eight, but he was smart enough to know that he
could not turn things around by himself, so he hired some top executives away from GM and put them in charge. They were shocked.
They found absolute chaos, no financial controls, and no real accounting system. Nobody at Ford had a clue about the cost of anything.

Tex Thorton's team was given the job of putting in an accounting
system and financial controls. Young Robert McNamara was to become the most famous of its rising stars, in part because he was perhaps the most enthusiastic advocate of management science. As
McNamara rose in Ford, he fashioned what I call the FPCC model.
Beyond any question, the "whiz kids" helped turn Ford Motor Co.
around. They brought order out of chaos. Ford stopped losing money
and became profitable. Using Sloan's structure as the foundation, they
began to demand an ever more rigorous financial analysis of all investments and to impose ever more comprehensive financial and
other controls.[5]

By 1960, McNamara had become President of Ford, and in that
same year John Kennedy won a close election to become President of
the country. One of the President-elect's first appointments was to
name Robert McNamara as his Secretary of Defense. Even Republi-
cans applauded the choice. With enormous prestige, McNamara's
reputation as the very apotheosis of a "modern manager" was richly
deserved. That, however, was also the problem, as the Pentagon was

about to learn. Upon taking office, McNamara imposed his FPCC model on the Pentagon and would later use it to "manage" the Vietnam War. No doubt his systems improved some things. Scientific management is not bad per se. It has its place, and it can be useful, but, overall, the philosophy that McNamara brought to these methods proved to be a disaster for both the military and the nation. His philosophy included an obsession with top-down control. His decisions were often based on specious measures, and he refused to give serious weight to such nonmaterial but still real entities as military esprit de corps. As one senior officer put it, "His eyes would glaze over whenever I began discussing such issues as morale. McNamara insisted that if you made rational decisions based on objective measures, good decisions followed. That, he said, took care of morale."

Let me illustrate this last point with an example from management science in action during World War II, where it all started in the RAF.[6] Early in the war, the maintenance on fighters such as the Spitfire was performed in the squadrons. Each fighter pilot had his own crew chief, who in turn supervised the mechanics who maintained, refueled, and rearmed the airplanes. After the Battle of Britain and as the bomber command expanded, the need for mechanics also increased. Someone did a study and decided that less manpower would be needed if fighter plane maintenance was handled in centralized maintenance facilities. The results of the study seemed conclusive, and so the RAF began a transition to centralized maintenance. Toward the end of the transition, Hitler launched his V-1s (the buzz bombs) toward England. The first (largely unguided) missiles, the V-1 could be intercepted by the faster fighters, but overall the fighters' record was none too good. Most V-1s were shot down by radar-guided antiaircraft artillery. Still, headquarters noted that one fighter squadron had far more "kills" than any other. There seemed nothing exceptional about the pilots or their planes. Then they discovered that this squadron managed to get its planes up and down, that is, do more sorties, than any other fighter squadron. They did not do that much better per sortie, but they could do more sorties. Why? Because it was the last fighter squadron in England that still maintained its own airplanes with its own crews. It seems that strong bonds usually developed between fighter pilots, crew chiefs, and the mechanics. The crews vied with each other to get their "guy" back in the air first. They took pride in their jobs and felt personally engaged in the combat mission. The maintenance study was likely correct as far it went, but it did not go far enough. It did not take morale and esprit de corps into account, and overlooked how good team spirit fostered good teamwork between pilots and the maintenance crews, while that in turn much improved a fighter squadron's combat utilization rate. Management science overlooked such nonmaterial relationships time and again. That was not so much from bad faith but because they lacked convenient measures of the nonmaterial but still vital elements of the equation. For that reason, most practitioners of operations research and other quantitative techniques, in common with McNamara, simply ignored such issues (What is esprit de corps? What is it made of? How do you measure it?). Moreover, when one starts probing such intangible entities with a reductionist approach, the entity tends to do a disappearing act. It is perceived as a whole or not at all.

During the Vietnam War, the Pentagon, under McNamara's direction, made three big mistakes—aside from the political mistake of getting involved in the first place. I, for one, sympathize with the argument that the United States should have washed its hands of that civil war once South Vietnam made it clear that it could not or would not fight effectively without our help. Even McNamara came to see that, and has written his personal *mea culpa* in his recent memoirs. The politics, however, is a different issue. The mistakes I refer to were made in prosecuting the war itself. The first mistake was to micromanage the war from ten thousand miles away. The second was to rely on reported "body count" as valid information for making decisions. People in combat are notorious for overestimating the damage they do to their opponents. During the Korean War, the Air Force reported destruction of more trucks than China produced. In Vietnam, army patrols had to "report" body count numbers of Viet Cong killed from artillery barrages or air strikes they often could not even see. It was clear that their superiors wanted big numbers, and so the troops happily reported big numbers even when they did not have a clue. As these estimates came in from the patrols, everyone knew they were often phony. Still, these numbers were passed up the line and consolidated with "estimates" from other patrols. These consolidations were added up for the whole theater of operations and passed on to the Pentagon. McNamara now had a "big picture" based on body count. He concluded that the Viet Cong's losses had been so great that they were on the verge of collapse, and he publicly stated that the war would soon be over.

A few days later, the Viet Cong launched the Tet Offensive, their biggest offensive by far of the whole war. Tet came as a terrible shock, completely by surprise. It was a political disaster. Temporarily left to themselves, the army and marines actually inflicted a terrible defeat on the Viet Cong, but the political damage had been done. McNamara's whole approach had been thoroughly discredited. As a result, President Johnson saw fit not to stand for reelection later that same year (1968), and he then kicked McNamara "upstairs" to become president of the World Bank. Having learned little or nothing from his experience in Vietnam, McNamara put his mechanistic-methods magic to work at the World Bank, much to the agony of the bank's employees. The results were similar but less well publicized. Under McNamara, the World Bank financed hundreds of specious investment programs justified by numbers little better and often worse than Vietnam body counts. Enormous waste ensued.

Philosophically, McNamara was a logical positivist. This philosophy assumes that one can make statements both true and provable within a given system. Its apostles believe you can deal in certainty. In practice such certainty usually requires you to measure whatever you are dealing with objectively and precisely. If you cannot, nothing valid can be said about it, and so you have no business talking about it. Ludwig Wittgenstein ended his most famous work on logical positivism with words to that effect.[7] Wittgenstein later backed away from that stern position, which was to be disproven in the early 1930s by Kurt Gödel. He proved mathematically that one could never prove all true statements within any system of arithmetic. Some of the proof must come from outside. An oft-quoted example has Plato saying, "Aristotle is a liar," with Aristotle responding, "Plato speaks the truth." There is no way to resolve the self-referenced contradiction embedded in these two sentences. However, Gödel's disproof remained mainly in the province of pure mathematicians until the 1970s.[8] Meanwhile, the positivists went merrily on their way long after Gödel's work. They kept on, like the cartoon cat who keeps running past the edge of the cliff before realizing he is in thin air, looks down, and promptly crashes to earth.

Philosophy aside, in the real world of business, management must daily deal with intangibles, real but nonmaterial entities. For business, as with the military, these intangibles include such things as morale and esprit de corps. In finance, "goodwill" is another old and well established example. One can estimate a value for goodwill and even carry it on the books. Still, goodwill lacks any objective material substance such as land, capital equipment, inventory, work-in-process, or even cash in the bank. That is rapidly becoming true for knowledge as well, according to many observers, such as Thomas Stewart, who insists that the financial value of knowledge has already surpassed the value of physical assets.[9] For example, in 1997, perhaps 3 percent of Microsoft's book value could be explained by its physical assets. Taking into account the $9 billion or so the firm has in the bank, such assets explain less than 20 percent of its market value. The rest, according to Stewart and others, represents intangibles such as knowledge and expertise.

Again, McNamara strongly believed that what you cannot measure has no meaning. Halberstam gives an amusing illustration of such thinking in his history of Ford. Ford engineers, concerned with rusting car bodies after a winter of driving on salted icy roads, developed a far better way of bonding paint to the car body in 1958. They developed an "electropainting" technique, where the car's body was used as one electrical pole and the paint as the other. It worked brilliantly. The paint bonded firmly into every nook and cranny. The engineers quickly patented the process. They calculated what new facilities Ford would need to apply the process to the Ford product line. After the friendly folks in finance studied this proposal, they vetoed it. "Oh sure," they agreed, "It's a nice process, but it costs too much. You claim you'll make it up selling more cars because of quality? Prove it. You can't? Forget about it then." But the bean counters did agree, since the company had already "wasted" research funds on it, to license the new electropainting process to their competitors. Not until the Japanese rubbed Detroit's nose in the quality issue twenty years later did Ford finally install their own process on all their own cars.[10]

Aside from his skepticism about the reality of intangibles, McNamara seemed to accept Pierre Laplace's assumption of a purely linear—hence predictable—universe.[11] If it were entirely linear, then our future state of affairs would in fact be embedded in current conditions. Given enough computational power and the proper methods of extrapolation, we could indeed make accurate forecasts. In such a linear world we could indeed "master the future." This view is called mechanistic determinism by most philosophers, scientific materialism by others. Up until about 1960, however, even a dedicated determinist knew we lacked the computing power to make accurate forecasts. But then came the electronic computer, and hopes blossomed. By the time the IBM 360 emerged in 1964, many people thought we had enough computing power. Putting econometrics together with management science, the positivists insisted that, despite Doris Day's hit tune "Que Sera Sera," "the future would be ours to see" after all. McNamara strongly promoted this view. He argued that through a combination of corporate and government planning based on computer-driven forecasts, the nation could avoid disasters such as the Great Depression. (In 1960, the Depression was still a fresh memory in the minds of everyone over thirty.)

I myself was a forecaster in those days. I would perhaps have balked at taking a hard-line position on positivism and mechanistic determinism, but the mechanistic assumptions implicitly behind those schools of thought were "in the air." I took it for granted that there was a specific future out there, one that included a specific volume of airline traffic, then the focus of my forecasting interests. My job was to devise a clever algorithm that would reveal this future. I did not, as I do now, see the future as contingent on all the choices made between now and then. If pressed, I would likely have agreed with Laplace that free will or choice was an illusion. Our choices, I might have argued, were simply driven by whatever had happened to us in the past. Still, I spent very little time with such thoughts and grand abstractions. As a forecaster I simply assumed the future was "out there"—until I came across Chaos Theory and Edward Lorenz's "butterfly effect" and, from the first "postmodern" science of quantum mechanics, Werner Heisenberg's Uncertainty Principle.[12] Together they convinced me, as a matter of principle, that our future is for the most part truly uncertain (see Appendix).

Meanwhile, a host of firms sprang into being to take advantage of the vision of accurate forecasts. Data Resources, Inc., Wharton Econometrics, and others that fell by the wayside were launched. Alan Greenspan tried his hand at this game, as did UCLA's Business School. At one time or another while I was at Boeing, we subscribed to them all. Each one developed a sophisticated econometric macromodel. Drawing on input data put out by the commerce department and elsewhere as measures of existing conditions, they would run their equations and the model would then crank out forecasts by the quarter, the year, five years, and sometimes even twenty years. Other firms, such as Mathematica of Princeton, New Jersey arose to create other kinds of models that we could use for operations planning. They found eager corporate clients. Soon, many CEOs of large business firms, nearly all of them once bitter critics of central government planning, "saw the light." When they thought they could exert more control over their own firms through central planning, they became instant enthusiasts.

It was now "scientific" and so many CEOs authorized comprehensive strategic planning departments to centralize the business planning function. New investments, large or small, could be analyzed with a quantitative sophistication never before imagined possible. Every proposed new investment could be analyzed to make sure it would achieve a targeted ROI (return on investment). As a result, the operating divisions found themselves with much less authority than they had under Sloan's model. An era of micromanagement from the top down had begun, and why not? If you know what the future will bring, and only you (sitting comfortably at the top) have access to this newly computerized crystal ball, why would you not take control? It is the only rational thing to do (we know what is going on because we have the 360s and they do not). Top-level planners could now access the big picture in a way those below could not. Therefore, the job of people on the lower levels was crystal clear: Follow orders, comply with the plans given them, and follow the called for schedules. What more was there to discuss? We certainly do not need to know what they think. Their view has a narrow focus and is functionally parochial, so they best keep still.

In business schools of the late 1950s, the apostles of this emerging management science (MS) would take the intellectual high ground from the suddenly outmoded "human relations" (HR) professors who had previously held it. The MS types dismissed the HR professors—whose program could be summed up in one dismissive sentence, "Don't fire Mary"—out of hand. In any event, the HR professors flew on intuition, according to the MS profs, who were convinced the day of the intuitive manager had come and gone. Rational quantitative decision making was the new order. These evangelizing professors of quantification rarely would identify themselves as logical positivists, but that was indeed their philosophy. If you could not talk about your issue in rational, objective, and, above all, quantitative terms, you were out to lunch. You did not belong in modern management; no sense in fighting it. Before the computer arrived, linear programming, queuing theory, or multiregression analysis might take dozens of mathematicians weeks to solve. The computer could do it in hours or even minutes. Managers who failed to use this new technology to make decisions were doomed to fail. Managers who adopted management science, the MS profs argued, would make so much better decisions that they would drive the intuitive managers from the market.

I was in graduate school at the University of Washington when this transition took place, and the messianic fervor of the quantifiers was awesome. Taylor's scientific management had come too soon, they conceded, and was also too crude. But now, armed with the computer, management science would be much different. The young professors promoting the new order felt themselves to be the heralds of a newly revealed positivist Truth. We graduate students began

debating whether the computer would displace white collar workers in the millions or merely the hundreds of thousands. We had little
idea of how the internal dynamics of bureaucracy would quash that
prospect before it got started. No new technology in history, not even
the typewriter, created such an explosion of administrative jobs as
did computers. Within a decade, many large corporations, under the
impetus of computerized management science, would transform
themselves into overstuffed bureaucracies full of planners. Moreover,
their planning would become so rigid and sterile that instead of driving others out of the market with their "rational decisions" and their
vaunted powers of central planning, they themselves would perish
or come close to it. Much as was true of the late USSR, these firms
had been ossified by rigid plans and then strangled in the planners
red tape, lacking in any financial flexibility because of costly and cost-
rigid bloat.

A thin little book, *Parkinson's Law*, written largely tongue in cheek
by British professor C. Northcote Parkinson, came out about this same
time. It should have alerted us to what actually did happen. Parkinson
argued that in a bureaucracy administrative work expands, regardless of the value-adding work, at about 5 percent per year. Using
British examples, he showed how the number of civilian bureaucrats
in the Admiralty skyrocketed from two thousand in 1914 when the
British fleet possessed sixty-two battleships to nearly thirty-four thousand by 1954 when the Royal Navy possessed no battleships at all
and had fewer ships in other categories as well. That was not all. By
1954, the bulk of the British Empire had also vanished. Still, the number of bureaucrats in the Colonial Office rose by 500 percent over the
high point of the Empire in 1935. In that year there were a trim three
hundred seventy-two people in the Colonial Office. By 1954, the number had soared to one thousand six hundred sixty-one. Professor
Parkinson noted that the uniformed services followed a different
trend. As the number of ships in the Royal Navy fell, so too did the
number of officers and enlisted men.[13] That difference has important
implications that Parkinson noted but failed to explore. We shall plug
that gap, but defer our discussion of it until we reach Part II.

Similar trends appeared in America. During the mid-1970s the
number of students in Seattle's school districts fell about 25 percent.

The number of teachers also dropped, by about 12 percent. The number of administrators, however, rose by 25 percent.[14] Everywhere in education similar relationships seem to appear. The number of administrators outpaces the growth of students and teachers, often by wide margins, as does the red tape they make. Ironically, and just after his book, many American firms seemed to have enacted Parkinson's Law for themselves as FPCC took hold. My experience at Boeing was repeated over and over elsewhere. As one Boeing vice president in engineering, the late Bill Hamilton, said to me in 1967, "Well, we just have to accept that Parkinson's Law is simply a fact of life in the modern corporation and get on with it." Get on with it we did. A year later the company nearly fell off the cliff, but from that trauma, the worst in Boeing history, the seeds of a new and postmodern era were sown. They finally began to bear fruit in the mid-1980s, as Boeing put itself through an enormous cultural and management transformation.

My own experience in that transformation, after a ten-year absence between 1968 and 1978, stirred a recognition in me that the modern era and its presumptions was passing, not just in scientific theory, but in the business world as well. The collapse of FPCC in business and the disintegration of the Soviet Union were simultaneous events and both related to the passing of the modern era. In 1992, the Czech poet and president Vaclav Havel declared that the fall of the Soviet Union forever would discredit its "cult of objectivity" and bring about the "end of the modern era." The modern era, Havel went on to say, was "dominated by the culminating belief, expressed in different forms that the world—and Being as such—is a wholly knowable system governed by a finite number of universal laws that [humans] can grasp and rationally direct for [their] own benefit."[15]

NOTES

1. A. D. Chandler, Jr., *Strategy and Structure* (Cambridge: MIT Press, 1962). See also Alfred P. Sloan, *My Years with General Motors* (New York: McFadden, 1965).

2. Peter F. Drucker, *The Concept of the Corporation* (New York: Mentor, 1983).

3. John Micklethwait and Adrian Wooldridge, *The Witch Doctors* (New York: Times Business Books, 1996).

4. Ibid.

5. David Halberstam, *The Reckoning* (New York: Avon, 1986).

6. Max Hasting, *Bomber Command: The Myth and Realities, 1939–1945* (New York: Dow Press, 1979).

7. Ludwig Wittgenstein, *The Tractatus* (London: Kegan-Paul, 1922).

8. D. R. Hofstadter, *Gödel, Escher, Bach: An Eternal Golden Braid* (New York: Vintage, 1979).

9. Thomas A. Stewart, *Intellectual Capital: The New Wealth of Organizations* (New York: Doubleday, 1997).

10. Halberstam, *The Reckoning*.

11. George Gilder, "The Materialist Superstition," *The Intercollegiatge Review* 1 (2): 1996.

12. James Gleick, *Chaos: The Making of a New Science* (New York: Viking, 1987). A good discussion of Heisenberg is found in Margaret J. Wheatley, *Leadership and the New Science: Learning about Organization from an Orderly Universe* (San Francisco: Barrett-Koehler, 1992).

13. C. Northcote Parkinson, *Parkinson's Law* (Boston: Houghton Mifflin, 1957).

14. William McDonald Wallace, "Speaking Out," *Seattle Times*, 23 August 1976.

15. Havel, quoted in John Horgan, *The End of Science: Facing the Limits of Knowledge in the Twilight of the Scientific Age* (Reading, Mass.: Addison-Wesley, 1996), 23.

Chapter 5

Our Most Important Resource

Time and again top managers repeat the slogan, "People are our most important resource." Most of them sincerely mean it. Still, many employees are cynical. That slogan is hypocritical unless embedded in policy. In fact, it cannot be embedded in a policy that depends on using hirelings. The slogan is often used as a rhetorical device to calm fear and instill trust among the hirelings, but trust quickly turns to rust when, caught between the rock of declining revenues and the hard place of hired labor's rigid unit costs, top management has little choice but to shove their "most important resource" out the door and onto the street.

Given hired labor and a big drop in sales revenue, that shove is inevitable. Otherwise the whole firm risks bankruptcy. To paraphrase "Chain Saw" Al Dunlop, who laid off tens of thousands of workers in the mid-1990s, "I hate to lay off all these people, it's hard for me, and I know it's tragic for them. But better I lay off some now rather than see everyone out of work later when the firm goes bankrupt."[1]

As Micklethwait and Wooldridge recently put it, "Even the most paternalistic companies, which ran themselves rather like welfare states, have been forced to join the bloodletting, ruthlessly sacrificing managers as well as workers."[2] In much of the postwar period, when revenues were growing or at least holding stable in real terms, bureaucracies often provided excellent job security. Up through the 1970s, firms such as IBM, AT&T, Procter and Gamble, Eastman Kodak, Weyerhaeuser, and most of the oil companies offered de facto lifetime employment. That security applied mainly to salaried staff, but in some cases to hourly workers as well. In such cases, most employees trusted the company and were very loyal. Their security really depended on strong growth which masked the underlying cost rigidity of hired labor. True, some of these firms, such as GM, protected white-collar staff even during the Great Depression. But in those days overhead office workers were perhaps one in ten. The great bulk of labor costs were accounted for by direct blue-collar hourly workers. When sales plunged between 1930 and 1933, those workers were dumped by the millions and industrial unemployment hit 40 percent.

After World War II, better technology slowly reduced the need for blue-collar manual workers. At the same time, the need for white-collar workers, managers, and technical and professional staff shot up. As we noted earlier, systemic bureaucratic make-work accounts for much of that rise. By about 1955, white-collar workers equaled the number of blue-collar workers. Thus, the office staff, or "knowledge workers" as Peter Drucker began calling them, soon became the dominant payroll cost even in manufacturing firms. Indirect costs thus began to surpass direct costs. No firm could maintain employment security for cost-rigid-hired knowledge workers without rising sales. They had become too numerous. If sales took a sustained drop, white collar paternalism vanished. It ended at once in cyclical sectors such as commercial and defense aerospace. "Management by bellows and meat ax," to use another of Drucker's pithy expressions, became the norm.

Elsewhere, if growth remained robust, as at IBM, AT&T, Delta Airlines, Eastman Kodak, and the oil companies, paternalism remained in force. Combined with a steady rise in pay as they gained seniority,

Drucker's knowledge workers typically developed a sense of trust and loyalty during the "sizzling sixties." Then came the "shocking seventies." Two OPEC oil price hikes shook the world economy. Japan emerged as a global force to create a genuine crisis in the United States on top of OPEC. In the mid-1980s, oil prices collapsed, again by surprise, catching many firms in a trap. Many in the oil business had borrowed to take advantage of rising oil prices. They and the banks who had lent them money suddenly found themselves bankrupt. Many Texas Savings and Loan banks were caught in this trap. Just then the personal computer entered the market. As more powerful PCs were developed, a shift from mainframes to them began. New powerful PCs helped create whole new opportunities for those willing and able to reengineer whole operating systems. At the end of the 1980s, the Soviet Union began to implode, again by surprise. The Cold War was over. The evil empire had perished, so the military was ordered to begin a major downsizing, forcing mergers and cutbacks among the defense contractors. Defense was accustomed to these ups and downs, but this down was different; it looked permanent. And the other sectors had much less experience in coping with sharp downturns.

These shifts and shocks shook up markets around the world. The paternalistic bureaucracy was especially vulnerable. The logic of hired labor's rigid unit-labor cost now had to be confronted. Especially for firms using FPCC, the problem was exacerbated by bureaucratic bloat. Massive layoffs followed in once "safe" firms, such as IBM. No one seemed safe any more. Even as these layoffs took place, new firms were creating new jobs as quickly or faster. And those jobs were not just in fast-food outlets. High-tech firms such as Intel, Hewlett-Packard, Microsoft, and scores of others created thousands of new well-paid jobs. Almost one-fourth of Microsoft's employees, for example, became stock-option millionaires. Bill Gates became the richest man in the world and his cofounder, Paul Allen, was not far behind. But for the most part, these new high-tech jobs went to the young (in 1995 the average age at Microsoft was 32). The big layoffs, however, hit mostly older employees in their forties, fifties, and sixties. They were reengineered, de-layered, downsized, or consolidated out of their jobs by the likes of "Chain Saw" Al.

IT'S OUR CALL

But it is naïve to assume that the logic of rigid rates paid to hire-lings induces them to accept layoffs as a simple fact of life that they must learn to accept. For one thing, hirelings typically have no real choices. In the corporate sector, we work as hirelings or not at all. That is not true for those of us who have money we want to put to work. We have two main options in the corporate sector. We can put our money to work for hire as our first option. Second, we can choose equity, a partnership of sorts. In other words, as investors of capital, we can hire out our money by holding debt and getting paid a fixed rate. Or we can hold stock, becoming partners with other stockhold-ers, and earn a variable rate of return. It's our call. We know the tradeoffs. If we want a certain fixed rate of return, we hold bonds. If we want capital appreciation as well as an income, we hold stock. We know the risks of both options. In hard times, stock prices may drop. Dividends may also fall. If we do not like that risk, we can get bonds and accept the other set of risks. With bonds, inflation may erode the value of our fixed interest income. Moreover, if the firm uses our money wisely and makes a huge return from it, we will get no more than the agreed rate of interest. But if the firm uses our money unwisely, we still get our fixed rate. If we think the firm is on to something big, then we forget bonds and buy stock. Again, it's our call. So are the consequences of that call, for better or worse. If stock prices drop or dividends fall we may not like it, but then we made the choice to buy that stock. If, on the other hand, inflation picks up to erode the value of our interest income, we may not like it, but again, it was our choice. Every choice we make entails risks, even the choice to do nothing.

IT'S THEIR CALL

When we want to put our skills and knowledge to work in the corporate sector, we do not have the same choices. We are not asked whether we would prefer to work for hire or in partnership. We work as hirelings, period, and that is their call. Forcing that choice upon us may or may not correspond to our own special needs. Sometimes, of course, it clearly does. Often it does not. But more to the point, that forced choice often works to the disadvantage of the corporation itself. It traps the firm in a bureaucratic format that imparts to its hirelings a host of dysfunctional motives that can hurt the firm. These motives, if not always obvious, are always latent.

In fact, the corporation wants it both ways. It expects its hirelings to accept the risks of working for hire—for example, being laid off, not having a voice in policy, and not participating in upside gains or windfall profits—as if the buyer–seller relationship had been selected by the hirelings rather than imposed on them. At the same time, corporations would like the hirelings to work hard and selflessly to make and indeed improve the profits in which they will not share. The hired hands are also expected to accept new technology gladly, without resistance, even if it may cut out their jobs and put them on the street. In short, the corporation expects the hirelings to work and behave as if they were partners but to forego the advantages of partnership. That is why Chain Saw Al's argument, even if narrowly correct, is broadly hypocritical. He has no compunction about imposing the downside risks on hirelings of firms that deny them the option of partnership.

Of course, that denial of options is not uniquely Al's sin. He could argue that the single option is simply the way we do business in America. Everyone knows that. He might then go on to claim that hirelings do in fact have other options. They can always work for themselves (and about 10% or so do) or form partnerships with each other. Again, if narrowly put, that is true. In the real workplace, however, the other options are academic for about 80 percent of us at any one time. They are impractical for a whole host of valid reasons, including lack of capital to survive the start-up phase, lack of a skill marketable in a small enterprise, and so on. Physicians, who once were nearly all self-employed or worked in small partnerships, are today increasingly being forced to work for hire in an HMO or large clinic, because medical insurance often forces patients into HMOs or large clinics. The red tape of both private insurance and Medicare have combined with the cost of medical malpractice insurance to make medical self-employment increasingly impractical. In a related way, the cost of medical insurance, once hardly an issue, makes self-employment by anyone less attractive. So does the fact that FICA taxes take 15 percent off the top, driving many self-employed young people or older retired people to work off the books and thus avoid all payroll taxes.

IT'S STILL THEIR CALL, BUT IT'S CHANGING

We have already seen how the motives imparted by the buyer–seller relationship between a firm and its permanent employees can hurt the firm. It imposes an adversarial relationship between stockholders and employees; that is, between people who invest money and people who invest skill and knowledge. Why on earth should they be adversaries? There is no good reason, and the policy imposing it is entirely gratuitous. It came about as the result of historical accident and a now discredited mechanistic world view. Clearly, the natural relationship between knowledge and money seeking a common goal is one of partnership. There are reasonable exceptions, to be sure, for temporary occasional work, the contracting out of ancillary operations such as janitorial work, and so forth. Moreover, a hired employment relationship may well suit both parties at the entry level of nonskilled work such as students working in fast-food outlets. Contingency work could suit perhaps 20 to 30 percent of the labor force. That leaves 70 to 80 percent, of which perhaps 10 percent are already working as partners or are self-employed. We are left with perhaps 60 percent of the workforce employed as hirelings, which makes no real sense for either employer or employee.

MANAGEMENT GURUS AND THEIR FADS:
THE EARLY YEARS

During and after the upheavals that followed the collapse of FPCC, many management theorists began proposing new solutions. Management theorists had been around for a long time. The first one we know about lived over three thousand years ago during the Jewish Exodus from Egypt. Moses' father-in-law, Jethro, was concerned that

Moses could not handle everything himself. So Jethro advised Moses to create a hierarchy of managers.[3] Through them Moses could provide overall direction, leaving the details to his underlings. Still, Jethro offered only structural advice. The first comprehensive management theory was written by the Greek philosopher Plato about two thousand three hundred years ago in *The Republic*, perhaps the most famous work of Western philosophy. In it, Plato argued that a ruling elite should monopolize power and authority. They are often called the "philosopher kings." To this day, Plato remains the spiritual godfather of all intellectuals who thirst for power and feel such power is theirs by natural right. Frustrated by being denied that role, they direct their resentment toward the bourgeoisie, according to the late American philosopher Allan Bloom.[4] Those greedy, money-grubbing barbarians usurped the intellectuals' natural rights in the Industrial Revolution. The intelligentsia sees its natural role as civilization's secular priesthood, empowered to call the shots much as they did as in ancient Babylon or Israel.

Plato is thought to have been horrified by the specter of "mobocracy" or a tyranny of the mob. But his star pupil Aristotle argued that Plato's plan would merely replace mobocracy with "snobocracy." Either one degenerates into tyranny. Aristotle, as the apostle of the "Golden Mean," argued for control from the center, that is, by the middle classes, today's bourgeoisie. Aristotle's views evidently prevailed, yet Plato's views remain prominent among the intelligentsia—and they are legion—who feel shortchanged. Karl Marx found a ready audience among them with his antibourgeois, anticapitalist tracts such as the *Communist Manifesto*. The whole Marxist movement was made up of frustrated middle class intellectuals who thirsted for power but had none. Marx had a clever strategy for masking that lust for power, and frustrated intelligentsia have followed it ever since. Instead of whining about how the bourgeois barbarians had shortchanged them, these wannabe philosopher kings sublimate their lust by taking up a plausible cause, especially one that fingers those terrible bourgeoisie as the villains. For Marx, the victims of those villains were the working class. In fact, workers had much to complain about. They were probably worse off in Marx's day than were the feudal serfs, their direct ancestors. Primitive Native Americans were clearly better off as hunter–gatherers. Some of the black slaves on American cotton plantations probably lived a healthier and less traumatic life than did the bottom half of the British industrial proletariat, circa 1830, if Friedrich Engels' description of Manchester is correct. Their traumatic life, of course, made them an ideal vehicle through which to promote the intelligentsia's lust for power in the modern industrial world. If this view seems cynical, consider what happened to the workers once the Marxists managed to take control of the Russian Revolution in 1917. Under Lenin, the Marxists pushed the workers to the sidelines promptly and forcibly. Lenin quickly centralized all political power in the party and in the Kremlin. All thought of worker-run Soviets vanished. These workers had been had. They served mainly as the vehicle in which far-left intellectuals rode into power. Once they got it, they kept it, all of it. The workers became industrial serfs.

After World War II, the appeal of Marxism faded, partly because of the Cold War, but more likely because of the rising living standards of capitalist workers. The average worker in the United States or Europe began to live far better than workers under communism. By 1970, industrial workers in the West often owned their own new middle-class homes, practically always owned a car or even two, and had started voting Republican in large numbers. The industrial worker had eagerly become coopted by the hated bourgeoisie. Workers could no longer be of use as a plausible vehicle for the intelligentsia's power trips.

In 1970 a new vehicle surfaced. This one could not betray the intellectual's hidden agenda by voting Republican. With increasing speed, academic intellectuals lowered their figurative red flags of Marxism. They now picked up the new and bright green flag of environmentalism. Before very long ex-Marxists had practically taken over leadership of the environmental movement. They could still finger as villains the selfish, money-grubbing, and still-hated bourgeoisie. The earth's environment was being sacrificed, trashed in fact, on the alter of capitalism's profits. What was especially nice was that this new cause not only enabled them to continue their war against the capitalists, but the aging Marxists among the greens could also vent a growing resentment against blue-collar workers. They had become prosperous under capitalism against all Marxist theory. That galled: This theory was supposed to be scientific. As the hard hats began to vote Republican in 1968, Marxists began to conclude that, deep down, "The masses are asses." By taking up the green flag, they could use environmentalism to stick it to these hard hat apostates. Besides, white wine and brie cheese intellectuals could never really stand those gross red necked, beer swilling hard hats, who are, after all, every bit as greedy as the capitalists. So without a tinge of guilt, the ex-Marxists gladly urged new environmental controls, wrapped in yards of red tape that would squeeze out blue collar jobs by the hundreds of thousands, in the woods, in construction, and in the factories. These Marxists turned environmentalists were happy to see such jobs disappear in the name of protecting Mother Earth.

They were beginning to assume their "natural" (secular) priestly function, in part by taking up thousands of those new regulatory jobs in government created in response to environmentalist pressure. And, of course, Western environmentalists did not bat an eye when, after the Cold War ended, the late Soviet Union turned out to have trashed its environment on a scale that surpassed by far the worst capitalist excesses. Autopoiesis, perhaps, forced them to ignore such data so that they could continue to revel in their politically correct identity as antibourgeois bigots. Thus, they continued to blame all environmental problems on bourgeois greed for profits. In short, ever since Plato, the main management theory put forth by the intelligentsia is simply this: Put us in charge, and, as we are the best and the brightest, give us all the power. But like Marx, they have nothing very specific to say about how they will use their power once they get it, except, perhaps, like Joe Stalin, to keep copies of Machiavelli beside their beds.

That brings us to the first management theorist of the modern era, Niccolo Machiavelli (1469–1527). His book, *The Prince*, broke brand-new ground. While Plato or Marx might stake a claim for power based on high purpose, Machiavelli did not. He wrote a purely amoral and pragmatic "how to" manual for those who had power and wanted to hold on to it. He outlined the methods necessary to keep power. His advice mixed perfectly good common sense with dirty tricks and a willingness to lie, cheat, or steal to keep power. For example, he was not above selecting some trusted lieutenant to act as a hatchet man and go into an area to ruthlessly suppress the opposition. Our Prince would go in after the heads had rolled, profess to be horrified by his lieutenant's excesses, and then pacify the locals by ordering his lieutenant beheaded. Machiavelli renounced counterproductive cruelty, however. Have your subjects love you if possible, he said, but do not count on their love to keep you in office. If times get tough, the love leaves by the next stage. To weather such storms you must assure them that, however much they love you, they should also fear you. The Prince must cultivate fear, but not hate. Machiavelli was adamant that the Prince should avoid hate. Never, Machiavelli insisted, should the Prince seize a man's property or his women, as such acts almost guaranteed hate. Hate, unfortunately, can overcome fear and thus be fatal to the Prince.

Aside from the early economists such as Adam Smith (on the right) and Marx (on the left), no one wrote much about management philosophy during the early Industrial Revolution. For one thing, that was before the owner–managers felt impelled to turn control over to hired managers. The owners began doing that in the last half of the nineteenth century, beginning with the railroads. The era of modern Big Business was underway. After the railroads came steel, oil, and meat packing and other processed foods made possible by canning. With the opening of the American West, large firms began to manufacture large combines to harvest the grain. Then, early in the twentieth century, came electrical power followed by electrical appliances and the auto industry. By 1929, industry employed the biggest segment of the labor force, and hired managers had become an important component of it. These managers needed updated theories to work from.

We have already mentioned F. W. Taylor, who with others, such as Frank and Lillian Gilbreath, created the first genuine management "fad" called "scientific management." With great sincerity they believed the mechanistic approach to performing work would benefit everyone. And no doubt it helped bring order out of chaos in some places. Ford's assembly line was also much influenced by "Taylorism." That method made cars cheap enough for workers to buy and their wages high enough to buy them, thus beginning the era of working class affluence. Other management theorists followed who took somewhat different tacks. These include Mary Parker Follet, Chester Barnard, Henri Fayol, and others, but none of them really quarreled with the modern era's mechanistic world view. Moreover, all of them more or less took for granted the idea that capital should dominate labor. Some, such as Mary Parker Follet of the United Kingdom and Elton Mayo of the United States took a more humanistic view of labor. Mayo based his theories about human relations on the research conducted in the Western Electric Company's telephone assembly plant in Hawthorne, Illinois, in the late 1920s. Mayo and his group discovered by direct observation that workers who were infused with esprit de corps could raise production well above the norm, even under bad working conditions. They also learned the many ways in which workers who felt that management was trying to exploit them could hold productivity down through coordinated peer-group pressure. Workers frequently frustrated the time and motion studies dear to the heart of the scientific management movement by building enough unneeded physical movements into their work that some would survive. Workers thus gained free time and lower production norms. Woe betide the worker who dared exceed such norms. These "rate busters" were often cold shouldered. If that was not enough of a wake-up call, a crack on the head usually did the job.

Mayo and his associates went on to create the human relations movement, initially at Harvard's Business School, from where it spread rapidly to other schools. By the late 1950s this movement had become the dominant academic force in most business schools. But the human relations school did not go much beyond the "case study" method pioneered by Harvard. Each case was considered on its own merits. No one developed a cohesive set of human relations principles that could be passed on. They thus became vulnerable to attack by management science, as recounted earlier.

Douglas McGregor of the human relations school made the distinction between autocratic and humanistic management styles that he dubbed Theory X and Theory Y. Theory X managers assume that most people are at heart lazy and shiftless. They respond mainly to fear and greed, to the carrot and stick. You cannot trust them. Theory Y managers, however, assume people want to do a good job and will do so provided management lets them alone. But McGregor did not make a distinction between social orders within an organization. In fact, after becoming president of his college, McGregor conceded some merit to Theory X in a bureaucratic environment. Forced to confront the ugly reality of bureaucratic turf battles, McGregor concluded that, in the end, someone has to prevail in such clashes, and that may require "kicking ass and taking names." One of the main points of this book is that different social orders motivate different kinds of behavior and those different behaviors call for different management styles. For example, if you insist on using slaves to harvest your cotton, you will probably need to apply the lash from time to time or at least empower your hired slave drivers to do so. Different strokes for different folks, as they say. Theory X, in short, also has its place.

But by far the most famous postwar management guru was and still is Peter Drucker. Drucker's fame began in 1946 with his book on GM, and he has remained the unofficial dean of management theorists ever since. He was a leading theorist when I entered college in 1947 and was still on top when I retired from Boeing in 1992. Despite his advanced age, Drucker remains prominent in 1997. I always find Drucker's views interesting, refreshing, and full of good common sense, often with sharp new insights (the knowledge worker for example) but sometimes repetitive. Despite his many insights, Drucker essentially takes the modern and Platonic view that managers should be an elite. And in a bureaucratic setting it is hard to see how it could be otherwise.

THE POSTMODERN THEORISTS

The first postmodern management theorist to make a big and lasting impact after the crash of the FPCC model was the late W. Edwards Deming. Slightly older than Drucker, Deming was all but unknown in the United States until 1980. Deming first rose to fame in postwar Japan, where in 1952 he began to work with Japanese firms to improve their product quality during the U.S. occupation. His ideas on TQM quickly took root and blossomed in good part because they were planted in fertile institutional soil. The Japanese did not organize bureaucratically. Employees were not paid according to the job, and so their job did not confer status upon them. Japan had no job evaluation, and did not do job performance appraisals. Japanese firms in effect promoted people in terms of their experience. All the regular employees (Japanese firms use about 15% hirelings) were de facto partners whose earnings rose or fell with corporate performance. The Japanese constantly refer to their companies as "family" and go on to organize accordingly, as confirmed by these policies.

Thus, Deming's urgings to get rid of waste and cut out non-value-adding work such as inspections and instead, "do it right the first time," were taken as suggestions that would help the firm as well as all within to prosper. In short, his ideas posed no threat and promised much good for the workers. If the firm abolished the job of inspector (as Toyota did in 1968), nobody hit the bricks. The former inspectors were cross-trained and redeployed to other work. Workers welcomed new technology that cut out drudge work because it meant they did less heavy lifting. The new technology did not put workers on the street.

These institutional realities were every bit as important to Deming's success in Japan as were his techniques. He seems to have understood this. In the summer of 1980, NBC did a documentary on Deming entitled, "If Japan Can Do It, Why Can't We?" In it, Deming excoriated the American approach to management. He condemned its top-down authoritarianism, its command and control, the lack of teamwork, fragmentation by function, and failure to motivate labor. Another American was telling us all this. Moreover, the Japanese freely credited Deming with helping them obtain a huge competitive quality advantage over American products. That NBC broadcast hit home like few other such documentaries have ever done. It can be taken as the beginning of the postmodern era of management philosophy in American business. It was the beginning of a radical and sudden shift away from modern management philosophy. Within a few years, the results began to register as big gains in American product quality and the checking of Japanese inroads into our markets.

Other theorists weighed in with other ideas. In 1993, Michael Hammer and James Champy wrote one of the best-selling business books of all time, entitled *Reengineering the Corporation*. Peter Senge proposed "the learning organization" in his best-selling *The Fifth Discipline*. Tom Peters and Robert Waterman wrote a huge best-seller, *In Search of Excellence*, in which they focus on some American success stories. Peters went on to give superb stage performances extolling and extending the new postmodern philosophy.

In one way or another the postmoderns were all saying much the same thing. Modern mechanistic management philosophy was dead as a stone. It may have worked in the age of steel and steam but it could not survive in the postmodern age of silicon and electronics. Each one had a somewhat different focus, their own spin. For example, reengineering urges dramatic changes while TQM stresses continuous and hence incremental change. Still, despite different strategies, they all painted a similar picture of postmodern management philosophy. The future was too uncertain for the old strategic planning part of FPCC to work. Forecasting was an art, not a science. It was dangerous to make firm plans for a turbulent and nonlinear future. Accordingly, organizations must replace rigid planning for tomorrow with flexibility today. The flexible organization, one that can respond quickly and effectively to sudden shocks and surprises, demands a dramatically different style of management. The old top-down command and control will not work here because it takes too long. Communications up and down are filtered out or edited and reedited. By the time the top has studied the problem, made a decision, spelled out the instructions for the various functions, and integrated it all into a coherent strategy, it may be too late. The Japanese may have already grabbed our markets or some new technology may have already made our product irrelevant. But not only the gurus were saying such things, so were top managers such as Jack Welch of GE, Frank Shrontz at Boeing, and Peterson at Ford Motor Co. Indeed, Ford, the prime innovator of FPCC, was among the first to ditch it and adopt the Deming philosophy.

Meanwhile, the common theme continues: The old adversarial relationship between capital and labor has got to go. It creates hardened positions and hence rigidity. The days when "labor" referred to common labor doing the heavy lifting has long gone. Brains have replaced brawn. The computer has replaced yesteryear's shovel. The typical job today requires knowledge and the processing of information. Moreover, unlike the past, computers now do almost all of the drudge work of data processing. This fact alone calls for a different style of management. Even in a stable environment we no longer need to pile layer after layer of middle managers on top of the work. The authoritarian style of management often relied on a tight control of information and that no longer works. Functionally divided bureaucracies, however, maintained control of their turf by maintaining control of information. Today's electronic technology based on the PC, along with the Internet and e-mail, demands the sharing of information to get the most out of it. But shared information eliminates the old need for all those layers of management.

This new technology and information sharing has also shifted management focus from function and the specialized division of labor by function to the whole process under control of crossfunctional and self-managed teams. Functional specialization is becoming an anachronism. Today's new work environment puts a premium on "bandwidth," the generalist rather than the specialist, and the person at home working in a variety of functions. Expert systems can provide generalists with specialized knowledge if needed, often at the click of a computer mouse. The old "cut and control" strategy is no longer appropriate in the days of e-mail and the Internet, as James Burke points out.[5] The Soviets learned that the cost of controlling cheap information in the age of electronic technology is too high, and if you are going to use that technology to advantage it is also impractical. To maintain an authoritarian management style, in ancient times or modern, depended for success on keeping much information confidential from subordinates and other departments. Cut and control, divide and conquer, play off one group against another, all these techniques of authoritarian and Machiavellian management were undercut or even destroyed by the miniaturized integrated circuit that now contains millions of transistors.

Yet, open information poses a risk of power struggles and turf battles in the bureaucratic format. This must change, they say. And, they add, this change will require a new atmosphere of trust within the organization, trust among employees, and trust between managers and employees. If we are to take advantage of the new technology and compete effectively in the global village we must learn to trust one another and work together as cooperative teams. Not all management theorists say all these things, but as a group they do. And most of them make many of these points. None of them argue in favor of the old mechanistic management, but, in common with Deming, they all say that the initiative for this change to a postmodern management philosophy must come from the top.

Moreover, the mechanistic bias in favor of reason and against emotion is changing. As Stan Davis puts it in a recent issue of *Forbes*, "In the old way of doing business, emotions never had a very legitimate place. The industrial age emphasized rationality and machines. . . . Make room for the new age of doing business. Information technologies are going to make emotions a regular feature."[6] Davis argues that as information becomes cheaper more of it becomes available. The more it is available, the more important it becomes to get people's attention. The best way to get attention is not through reason but through emotion, Davis argues. But, I would add, precisely the same thing applies to motivation. Moreover, trust is an emotional state, not one of reason. Reason and logic are important, to be sure, but they work in the service of emotion. That is especially true when it comes to trust and the motivation to work cooperatively. Even classical economists who put enormous emphasis on human rationality put forth a theory of rationality driven entirely by greed, their favorite emotion.

In the mid-1990s some critics began calling TQM a fad whose time had come and gone. (The most recent management fad is to decry management fads.) That is an odd assessment. In the first place, TQM stresses continuing improvement. Moreover, the huge stress put on quality did much to help American firms check Japanese penetration into our markets and even to reverse some of it. Directly because of TQM, Detroit today makes much better cars. Because of good-quality cell phones, the Japanese failed to dent this market. Software remains an American monopoly for the most part. Since the collapse of FPCC the easy pickings have ended for the Japanese.

One can compare the fate of Deming's TQM with an earlier version inspired by Philip Crosby, another quality guru. I refer to the "Zero Defects" campaign of the late 1960s. It was launched with great fanfare, many a CEO made speeches about it, and so on. Precisely nothing happened thereafter. Within a few months the campaign was quietly laid to rest. The difference was that Zero Defects took place in the same old bureaucratic environment. The whole responsibility was placed on the working level, with the management making no changes at all. FPCC was in full flower and that system all but prohibited much initiative for real change from the working level. Approval after approval was first required and then only after multiple reviews. In other words, the difference was not between the technical aspects of Deming and Crosby. They had much the same advice to offer. The difference was that Deming insisted that TQM would only work if management first changed its philosophy and then took primary responsibility. Most of the failures of TQM reflect the refusal to follow Deming's advice. Efforts to put either reengineering or TQM in place routinely fail for the same reason that the Zero Defects campaign did, namely for the lack of the appropriate management philosophy.

To sum up, most of the management theorists are in reasonable accord about what management in the postmodern world will be like, but not one of them completes the postmodern picture. None has seen that bureaucracy arises because of its policy to employ hirelings for the permanent staff. While nearly all of them talk a good deal about "partnering" with suppliers and with other firms to form "virtual corporations" (or, less pretentiously, joint venture projects), none of them comes flat out to suggest creating a partnership between the stockholders and the permanent employees. Downsizing, often touted as a way to banish bureaucracy, has misled many a recent guru to argue that permanent employment is a thing of the past. In fact, quite inconsistently, most of them call for more trust and teamwork on one hand, and on the other, more contingent (temporary) work. Some of these gurus, such as Charles Handy, seem to envision a workforce made up largely of self-employed itinerants jumping from one temporary job to another, and from one firm to another.[7] More people may well do that, at least for part of their career. In fact, many already are and have been for years. Such working goes back to the itinerant tinkers of the feudal era. It still goes on, whether by individuals on their own or through agencies such as Kelly Temporary Services, Manpower, Accountemps, and many others.

But self-employment is not going to become the standard way of working for most people. The reason is simple enough. Corporations that have a highly motivated permanent staff will tend to run competitive circles around those that do not. Such firms will attract better quality employees and gain and retain more advantages of the learning curve. Technology will not change that fact any more than it has in the past. Japanese experience suggests why. Japan never did buy into the modern mechanistic management philosophy, however many of the techniques they may have tried, even Taylorism.[8] But what Japan proved beyond reasonable doubt is that bureaucracy based on impersonal hired labor is always an inefficient social order. Even during the modern age of steel and steam, of mind-numbing assembly lines and of common labor doing mostly heavy lifting, modern bureaucracy was inefficient. After all, in the late stages of this very era, the Japanese began to capture our markets. For a time we had to stand by helplessly and watch it happen. Japan beat us in modern industry because they attacked our modern mechanistic format with an organic and family-like alternative much more in tune with human psychology. Thus they won hands down.

American theorists often mislead themselves into thinking that because silicon has replaced steel and small and powerful electronic computers have come into their own technology is driving the shift to a postmodern management philosophy. Of course technology is part of it, but let us be clear. The Japanese had won before the PC had time to show its stuff. Whether our technology is based on the stone axes of hunter–gatherers or the plows and reapers of a farmer, on the steel and steam of common labor or on silicon and electronic computers of knowledge workers, the organic will beat the mechanistic bureaucracy every time. The best format in not a function of technology, it is a function of our human psychology of cooperation.

In Part II we will discuss how and why the organic format, expressed as a corporate partnership between the firm and its employees, is the best and most natural way to work with any technology. But before looking at our solution, we need to look at the broader consequences of bureaucracy in our economy as a whole. The two worst consequences are inflation and unemployment. Inflation arises from a bureaucratic wage ratchet wherein wages are bid up in times of a skill shortage but cannot fall back in a later surplus. Unemployment comes by violating the precondition of flexible labor costs in Say's Law of Markets that enables free markets to balance supply and demand at full employment. The Great Depression was largely caused by that violation. In Chapter 6 we will look at the wage ratchet, and turn to the Great Depression in Chapter 7.

NOTES

1. Paraphrase taken from "Corporate Killers," *Newsweek*, 26 February 1996.

2. Exodus 17:21–26.

3. John Micklethwait and Adrian Wooldridge, *The Witch Doctors* (New York: Times Business Books, 1996), 99.

4. Allan Bloom, *The Closing of the American Mind* (New York: Simon & Schuster, 1987).

5. James Burke and Robert Ornstein, *The Axemaker's Gift: Technology's Capture and Control of Our Minds and Culture* (New York: G. P. Putnam's Sons, 1995).

6. Stan Davis, "What's Your Emotional Bandwidth?" *Forbes*, 7 July 1997, 233.

7. Charles Handy, *Beyond Uncertainty: The Changing World of Organizations* (London: Hutchinson, 1995).

8. William McDonald Wallace, "The Great Depression Reconsidered: Implications for Today," *Contemporary Economic Policy* 8 (2) 1995: 1–15.

Chapter 6

The Wage-Rate Ratchet

Wage rates in America's manufacturing sector rose by about 50 percent between 1933 and 1940. That rise took place in the face of an industrial unemployment rate that never fell below 20 percent. Moreover, prices hardly changed. That seemingly impossible set of circumstances set the stage for the postwar wage/price spiral, a spiral that remains with us. Since 1933, wage rates have increased at an average annual rate of about 6 percent. The rate of increase was less in the 1960s, when unemployment was hardly 4 percent. In the 1970s, when unemployment was often close to 10 percent, wage rates increased nearly as much, at about 9 percent per year.[1] In this chapter we will see how bureaucracy's dependence on hired labor drives this ratchet.

Rising productivity, of course, accounts for some of the wage-rate increase, but a higher wage rate is just one way of expressing increased productivity. It can also take the form of lower prices, as indeed it did in the period between the Civil War and 1900.[2] The reason wages began to ratchet independently of the demand for labor or for reasons of productivity after 1933 was simply that during President Roosevelt's New Deal, Congress passed a number of labor laws designed to empower organized labor to force management to pay higher wages. The logic was purely Keynesian. If workers earned more pay, they would spend more. That spending would increase aggregate demand, boost output, and thus cut unemployment. It did not quite work out that way. Not until World War II began, with its huge increase in defense production on one hand and a draft on the other, did mass unemployment disappear. The legacy of those labor laws was the wage/price spiral after the war. It was an institutionalized cost push inflation. Yet economists of the monetarist school adamantly deny the reality of cost push inflation to this day. At first this denial was a ploy to avoid wage/price controls. To concede wage cost push would have reinforced the arguments of those who advocated controls, such as John Kenneth Galbraith. Milton Friedman, then the dean of monetarism, so often and so adamantly proclaimed that "inflation is always and everywhere a purely monetary phenomenon" that monetarists actually began to believe it as revealed truth.

EMPLOYMENT POLICIES

Labor laws, however, are not really the point of this chapter. This chapter deals mainly with the institutionalized part of the wage ratchet. We will look at how the employment policies of bureaucracy help sustain the wage ratchet. Once underway, the wage ratchet takes on a life of its own. The subsequent decline of the trade unions that got it started attests to that fact. Using hirelings as permanent staff who must be paid a fixed wage rate is the main cause of the continuing wage ratchet. A contractually fixed wage rate, as we pointed out in the Introduction, is fixed mainly on the downside. Workers will almost never resist wage-rate increases, but, much as bondholders do, workers resist any unilateral cuts in the agreed rate of pay. In a sense, New Deal labor laws simply put hired labor on a par with hired capital. It was never legal for a borrower, having agreed to pay "hired capital" a particular rate of interest, to unilaterally cut that rate. After the New Deal it was no longer legal for an employer to unilaterally cut a hired employee's pay rate.

Some economists argue that given enough time and pressure, wage rates can indeed drop. That is correct, given enough time. But, as John Maynard Keynes is reputed to have said, "In the long run we are all dead." In this case, firms with wage costs that force up their prices beyond what the market will bear will go bankrupt if they cannot get those wage rates down quickly. From time to time firms close to insolvency can and have negotiated cuts in the wage rate. Those cuts were very rare, however, until the introduction of widespread Japanese competition in the late 1970s. Japan's stiff international competition provided sufficient pressure in a number of cases, including the automobile industry, to enable management to negotiate reductions, but that often takes much time. During this time they lose business. Firms that go into Chapter 11 can get relief from paying fixed rates of interest, but they must continue to pay fixed rates of wages. Still, Chapter 11 does not change the fact that a high ratio of hired capital to equity capital makes a firm financially far more vulnerable in a downturn. The firm with much debt (hired capital) is more vulnerable than the firm with mostly equity capital, because hired capital has a fixed cost while the returns to equity capital vary with performance. This dichotomy also applies to labor. Hired labor makes a firm more vulnerable than organic (equity) labor working as partners. The cost of any hired input is downwardly more rigid than is the cost of organic or equity inputs.

But interest rates do not tend to ratchet upward while wage rates do. One difference is that capitalist firms are already organic when it comes to capital. In general, hired capital is regarded as an adjunct to equity (organic) capital. The firm can pay off its debt and not replace it. The rate of interest is thus market driven. But another difference is New Deal labor law as amended and extended over the years. The same firm can pay quite different rates of interest to different blocks of capital doing exactly the same job. For example, in June a firm might lease a car for a salesperson based on an 8 percent rate of interest and then in July lease exactly the same model at a lower price based on, say, a drop in the rate of interest to 7 percent.

Within a firm, labor statutes mandate "equal pay for equal work" for hired labor. That law does not, however, extend to contractors who are also hired to do work. Even under the equal pay provision of labor law, a firm can pay different contractors different amounts for identical jobs. To illustrate, a company might hire out the detailing of the two leased cars mentioned above to two different detailers and pay each one a different rate. Was the lower-paid detailer treated unfairly? Not if that detailer got the work by virtue of a lower bid and was thus delighted to get the job. Between regular hired employees such pay differentials will not do. The lower-paid person could have a legal claim in most cases if paid a lower rate for identical work.

EQUAL PAY FOR EQUAL WORK

The "equal pay" provisions of the Fair Labor Standards Act and some "comparable worth" statutes such as in the state of Washington partly explain why wages ratchet for hired regular employees. Suppose that a firm launches a new product that proves popular, and suppose its manufacture requires new jobs and the company begins hiring people to do them. Production rises and sales boom. So the firm hires more people yet. Booming sales caused some wholesalers to order large amounts of the new product just before demand topped out. They are stuck with big inventories to work off so they quit ordering more. Soon, new orders to the company fall by 50 percent and it quickly fills all its back orders. Now the firm must either produce to inventory when no one is buying or cut production. With cash reserves too low to produce to inventory, the firm must lay off half the people they hired. Many of those laid off might be willing to work at a lower wage rate. No matter, the rate for those still at work remains the same—what the company agreed to pay.

Later, the wholesalers, having worked off their inventory, discover they cannot fill the new orders because retail sales are picking up again as the new product enters new markets. So the wholesalers place some big new orders for the product. The company now has to increase its production to fill these orders. To do that they must hire more production workers. The new boom in sales takes place in regions away from the plant. The plant itself is located in an area with a high rate of unemployment. The local unemployed workers are happy to work for $8.00 per hour, but our plant pays $10.00 to the existing labor and so that is what they must offer to the new hires.

The firm cannot hire the new labor at $8.00 without extensive negotiations with the union and they need the labor now. So they pay $10.00 in order to boost production and make those sales before their rivals can jump in.

More time passes. Sales continue to boom, but now reserves of unemployed labor have dried up. To get more workers to come aboard, the company soon finds it must offer $12.00 per hour. If it does, it will have to boost the pay of everyone already doing that job to $12.00, otherwise it will violate the equal pay for equal work law that is also a part of the labor contract. The cost accountants conclude the firm can still make a profit at $12.00, so they pay it. But then workers in other jobs demand a raise under the "comparable worth" provisions. For example, clerical office jobs were evaluated to be of comparable worth to the production jobs. The office staff thus gets its 20 percent raise as well. The accountants conclude that they can now make a profit only if they raise the price of the new product by about 20 percent to cover both their own higher wage bill and some rising material prices. At the higher price, the boom tapers off. Again the wholesalers are stuck with a big inventory to work off. Once again the company has to cut production and lay off labor. But it must continue to pay the now 20-percent-higher wage rate, and it must continue to charge the 20 percent higher price to cover the 20 percent higher costs or face bankruptcy. Thus has the interaction of labor law with bureaucratic employment policies created a wage ratchet that induces a price spiral.

THE WHIP SAW

Another systematic force behind the wage ratchet, again one related to the trade unions, is called whip-saw wage bargaining. It also depends on the equity principle of equal pay for equal work. When a firm attaches pay rates to jobs and not to the employees who do the jobs, the firm itself tacitly accepts that principle. Many jobs are grouped into trades under control of trade unions, such as carpenters, electricians, welders, plumbers, boilermakers, warehousemen, and so on. Unions demand that each job within its trade be paid exactly the same rate. To the union itself, the trade is the whole enterprise. The union official's main job is to get the best pay rate possible for that enterprise.

Despite pretensions of trade union solidarity, the various trades quickly divide into "us versus them" camps when it comes to pay rates. True, those holding unskilled jobs for the most part will accept the legitimacy of higher pay rates going to skilled jobs. But within the various skill categories fierce rivalry breaks out. Each skilled trade quickly comes to see itself as the "aristocrat" of the skilled trades. Electricians quickly convince themselves that their trade should earn top pay given the inherent danger of working with electricity. Carpenters, plumbers, and the like soon invent their own reasons why they should be the best paid. If the plumbers' union wins a higher wage, other unions demand, in the name of equity as they see it, that they too should be paid more. I have yet to hear of a trade or profession that claimed to be overpaid relative to others, not even athletes who often earn millions of dollars per year.

Even within a specific trade wage-rate rivalry can break out. For example, the policemen's union in Los Angeles years ago decided that its cops had the toughest police work in all California and thus should have the highest rate of pay. The San Francisco police, however, convinced themselves that they had as tough a job as any cops in the state and that they should be paid at least as well as those in any other city. Thus, if the Los Angeles cops got a pay raise that put them above the San Francisco cops, the latter would at once demand, in the name of equity as seen from a San Francisco point of view, a raise to bring their pay up to Los Angeles levels. If they got that raise, then the cops in Los Angeles would promptly demand a pay raise to assure that they remained the best paid police in California, and so on. While the whip-saw is perhaps not as potent a force as it was in the 1950s, 1960s, and 1970s, it remains in action and continues as a driver in the wage/price spiral.

JOB EVALUATION

These examples are more or less "union driven" as reinforced by labor law. But the unions by no means provide the only mechanism of ratcheting wages. Indeed, the wages of administrative staff can ratchet just as fast or faster. The wages of top management have ratcheted most rapidly of all in recent years. But even before the super-raises of the last ten years, a small consulting-services industry had arisen to facilitate this ratchet. Indeed, for a short time in the 1970s I was a part of it.

Job evaluation is perfectly logical given a workforce made up mainly of hired employees. In theory, of course, the market should evaluate the worth of jobs, but in practice that does not work out. The market could set wages directly if employers could rely on short-term workers hired day to day or even month to month. In that case the workers would bid for jobs, and through such bidding, pay rates would be established that could fluctuate with supply and demand much as is the case with some kinds of farm labor. In fact, that is sort of what the classical economists had in mind. Short-term employment, however, is not practical when corporations require long-service employees who must learn not only the work but how it fits in with that of others, the corporate management style, and the culture.

In short, the market cannot really set pay rates for jobs held by long-service hired employees. So how can equitable pay rates be established? Trade unions can negotiate those rates, of course, but less than 20 percent of the workforce belong to the unions. As for non-union employees, pay rates were at first negotiated individually, often with an owner–manager. In a small firm that worked well enough, but as small firms grew, individual negotiations began to produce chaotic wage structures. For one thing, the owner–manager had likely been replaced by a hired manager. By the 1920s, chaos was common. Pay-rate jealousies abounded as people doing similar jobs for similar periods of time began to discover big differences in pay. Something had to be done.

The answer was provided by some of the early advocates of scientific management. They explicitly likened the industrial organization to a machine. They argued that a job was akin to a machine part. They then used time and motion studies to redesign those "parts," hoping to make them more efficient. But how to establish a job's pay rate? The answer given by pioneers such as Emerson and Hay was a new analytical process by which a firm could "scientifically" evaluate the relative worth of each job or job category. That done, all jobs within a firm could be compared as to their relative worth to the firm. The process assigns so many points to each job. The jobs with the most points supposedly have the most worth to the firm. Certain jobs are regarded as "benchmarks" in terms of both pay and points. The other jobs are calibrated to those benchmarks. A graph is then made plotting the points the evaluation has given the job on one axis against the pay rate it now has on the other axis. Ideally, a relative straight line can be drawn through these plots as a "least squares" line. That is to say, the more points, the more pay. If some jobs come out with lots of points but less pay, those jobs are usually given a pay boost. For the job with lots of pay but few points, the job's pay rate is typically frozen at that rate. This "red-lining" policy avoids cutting anyone's pay to reduce the danger that employees who fear pay cuts might sabotage the process.

Immediately, of course, job evaluation induces a wage ratchet. It lifts the pay of those who are thought to be underpaid, but freezes pay for those thought to be overpaid. The freeze is supposed to last until inflation brings the red-lined jobs onto the least squares line. But this freeze policy is not the worst part of the wage-rate ratchet that job evaluation induces. Before discussing more serious problems, in fairness it should be pointed out that job evaluation actually did bring some order out of chaos. In the aftermath of years of individual negotiation, salary administration had grown well and truly chaotic. The "new order" nevertheless created and sustained a systemic wage ratchet that fit in with the ratchet introduced to wages by unions pushing wages up by whip-saw bargaining. Both of these effects began about the same time, during and just after the New Deal.

CONFESSIONS OF A CONSULTANT

Let me explain how it all works through a personal experience as a consultant in charge of the job-evaluation part of a larger consulting contract. The client was a middle-sized private–public utility. I was a subcontractor for the job-evaluation portion of the larger contract. I did not "sell" the business initially, but I took it over just after it was sold. And it was an easy sell, I assure you. The reason the client wanted a thorough job evaluation of all but unionized jobs was that the power company's CEO wanted a raise. But to get it he had to convince the board of directors to give it to him and, what is more, that raise had to look reasonable in the eyes of the public utility commission. All this was a common set of relationships, and, a common strategy had gradually built up to deal with it.

In my case it began when a consulting firm did a salary survey of the top jobs in various public utilities in both the public and private sector. (The form of ownership does not matter here.) Now, any such survey is bound to reveal statistical variation in the salaries paid for any given job. Some jobs will be paid higher, some lower, and some in between. Those holding jobs paid the top rate are never at a loss for arguments to justify that fact. Like the Los Angeles police, they will argue that their special circumstances explain their top pay. But those on the bottom will almost never accept the logic of their lower rate. Rather, they will argue as persuasively as they can that they have been shortchanged. Then they will look at the other benchmark jobs. These jobs too tend to fall in a lower quartile if the CEO's salary does. The CEO will point out this fact to the board and then conclude that the firm needs to conduct a comprehensive job evaluation for all jobs not covered by a union contract. That is the only way, he assures the board, to tell whether the entire firm is being fairly paid. To be objective, the CEO of course proposes that an outside consulting firm be brought in for an "independent" and "objective" evaluation. In fact, it will be the consultant who goes to the board and presents the evidence that the average pay in the whole firm (including the CEO, of course) is substandard, putting the firm's ability to attract good people at risk. The consultant thus shows the results of his job-evaluation survey and notes that most of the jobs are paid less than the statistical average and are thus "underpaid." The typical board agrees. It then authorizes the proposed adjustments in the firm's salaried payroll. This adjustment often means a 15 percent or so total pay increase, perhaps more than that for the CEO. Later, and armed with the same consultant's findings, the utility manages to convince the public utility commission to raise its rates.

To do this job, the consultant has to survey a large number of employees at various levels to discover what it is they do. That is a fascinating task. Everyone goes flat out to puff up the importance of the job he or she holds. They would be foolish to do otherwise, for much hinges on the outcome. Every job is broken down into what are sometimes called "compensable factors." Different systems identify different factors. Often to be found are such things as the level of training and prior education needed to do the job. Another common factor is the number of subordinates being supervised or, in a bit different guise, the value of the assets under the job's control. Another common item is how much money the job holder can spend without getting prior authorization. How much contact there is with customers or the public may also enter in. Part of the protocol of the process is to avoid confusing the job with the job holder. It is thought vital that analysts rigorously ignore the personal attributes of the job's incumbent. In order to get middle managers to buy into the scheme, however, a group of them is often formed to assign the points to the jobs. In the example cited, it was my task to describe the job in terms of the compensable factors. I then made up abstract descriptions and made my own estimate of each job's point value. The client committee then reviewed my estimates and made the final decisions. Except in jobs that had many incumbents, such as a file clerk or customer service representative, at least one member of the committee would sneak a look at and then reveal the name of the incumbent. If that person was well thought of, his or her job got more points. If not, that job got fewer points.

What this process of job evaluation never considered was teamwork and the importance of being able to work flexibly outside one's job description if the need arises. In fact, taking those things into account is to consider the attributes of the person holding the job and not attributes of the job itself. It soon struck me that the committee intuitively understood that fact. That is why they wanted to know who held the job in question. From practical experience they knew how important personal attributes and attitudes are to effective performance. They also intuitively understood that, as abstractions, jobs have no real meaning or existence. For example, some "jobs" I evaluated had been vacant for a time and the company was in the process of interviewing candidates for them. Still the department's work was getting done. Could we then say the job had no real importance? As an abstraction we most certainly can, but once a real person fills the job it takes on real importance. How much importance depends on what attitudes and attributes the new person brings to the job. Given a bad attitude on the part of the incumbent, some jobs, instead of adding value, subtract from it.

I also soon discovered that, to nearly any job description, most managers wanted to tack on a final appendage that said something like, "The incumbent performs other duties that may be assigned." Some supervisors would have been happy with job descriptions that contained that single statement, but that statement is not a job description as much as an expression of hope. After all, no machine part has the general property of "doing what is asked" beyond the specific mechanical functions designed into it. I cannot ask my spare tire to fill in for a broken fan belt. Job evaluation ignores interdependence among jobs that add real value. If the completed product requires some ten steps or jobs, even the simplest among them, if left undone or done poorly, can negate all the others. Breaking up the whole process into independently evaluated parts in terms of the relative importance of each one makes little sense. The effort itself can do harm. When people who thought they were making a valuable contribution learn that their job got relatively few points, they tend to feel put down. It does no good to tell them that the job, not their performance, was being evaluated. In that case, many people will feel as if they were being treated like the machine parts the process in fact has in mind. The whole system, of course, fuels the wage ratchet because people begin to systematically lobby for a higher evaluation. Junior managers clamor for more help, as in fact do middle managers who aid and abet the junior managers. People invent new tasks for themselves in hopes of getting the job's point total increased as a result of "the greater responsibility."

Cost-of-living adjustments (COLAs) are hard to avoid under a system of job evaluation. Even if a firm avoids a commitment to COLAs and tries to use inflation to reduce the earnings of "less effective" employees by holding down merit raises below the rate of inflation, job evaluation causes problems. Many managers consider this backhanded strategy sound, but it can backfire. After all, the pay rate is supposed to attach to the job and not the person. Before long, these jobs become "underpaid" relative to the others in the system. Pressure arises for a new job evaluation. Salaries are once again adjusted upward by 15 percent or so to correct the accumulated "inequities." And so it goes.

SKILL DILUTION

A related aspect of the wage ratchet comes into play when the market turns up and the firm must hire more people. If business is booming and many new people must be hired, they will take time to train. There is more to learning the job than just how to perform the operations. It also helps to know how the company operates, its culture, mores, and such. That takes time. In the meantime, people make mistakes while learning. Those mistakes must be corrected or else the work in process must be scrapped.

Skill dilution usually forces a firm to hire more people than it really needs to meet some level of production at acceptable quality. Hiring extra people puts upward pressure on wage rates. Of course, once people have been trained, have learned the corporate culture, and become productive, it takes fewer of them to do the work. In conventional economic wisdom, the newly created surplus gets laid off, but those layoffs do not reduce the wage rate for those remaining. That rate has already been contracted for. Meanwhile, for lack of any concept of operating reserves of labor, the cost of training skill-diluted workers is an investment that goes out the door along with the workers who embody the training. The downwardly rigid wage rates of hired labor, of course, inhibit a firm from looking at the idea of keeping reserve labor on the payroll. With hired employees, however, the cost may preclude having well-trained reserves on hand at the start of an upturn. Long-term advantages are moot if in the short run the firm goes bankrupt.

THE OVERALL EFFECT

Within a range of about 4 to 9 percent, nominal wage rates have risen an average of about 5 to 6 percent ever since 1933.[3] Before 1933, average rates would usually drop slightly in recessions, but not after

1933. The ratchet reached its highest rate of about 9 percent during the two OPEC oil crises, when unemployment rose to 10 percent, and was at its lowest rate of 4 percent during the 1960s, when the rate of unemployment was also about 4 percent. It is ludicrous for monetarists to claim that this ratchet is or ever was driven mainly by the money supply. True, if rigorous limits on the money supply were imposed, say through divine intervention, this ratchet could be constrained, but only by driving the unemployment rate to the sky. Recall that this ratchet began when industrial unemployment exceeded 30 percent. One could always roast the beef by burning down the barn, but that is hardly good policy. The wage ratchet simply is not a function of the money supply. It is a function of an employment policy that insists on using hired labor in preference to partners.

It is difficult to overestimate the economic damage done by the myth that hired labor is the natural employment relationship for permanent staff in our business firms. That myth, in the end, created the wage ratchet when combined with Depression-era labor law. The ratchet, in turn, when combined with OPEC oil price hikes and a misguided monetary policy, created the highest interest rates in our history and created the stagflation of 1973 to 1985. But the worst damage done by that myth by far was the Great Depression. That event changed the role of government and the way the economy works. It gave us very high tax rates and a welfare state that is now beginning to institutionalize a permanent underclass. To date, the Great Depression was the most traumatic event by far in the history of the U.S. economy. Chapter 7 takes a closer look at the Great Depression and the role that hired labor paid fixed wages played in bringing it about.

NOTES

1. Ronald Reagan, *Economic Report of the President, 1985* (Washington, D.C.: U.S. Department of Commerce).

2. U.S. Department of Commerce, *Historical Statistics of the United States, Colonial Times to 1970* (Washington, D.C.: U.S. Government Printing Office, 1985).

3. Ibid. for years up to 1970; Reagan, *Economic Report*, for after 1970.

Chapter 7

The Great Depression

America's GNP stood at about $104 billion in 1929. By 1933, it had collapsed to about $56 billion. (Both figures are stated in current prices of the day; multiply them by a factor of ten to approximate today's values.) No other industrial nation was hit that hard. Even by 1940, seven years after the low point, America's GNP had not quite recovered to its 1929 level. By comparison, between 1929 and 1933, Britain's GNP fell only by 10 percent; and, moreover, by 1939 it had risen well past its 1929 level. Germany, France, and Italy had similar experiences. One nation, however, was unique. That nation was Japan. Its real GNP actually rose by 6 percent between 1929 and 1933. Japan's only recession in the whole Depression era came in 1930, and its economy quickly bounced back.[1] Meanwhile, America's unemployment in 1933 stood at nearly 40 percent of the industrial workforce and 25 percent of the total workforce. Employment in the farm sector did not drop at all, and thus the industrial rate of unemployment was much higher than the total rate. Our industrial output collapsed by nearly 50 percent, while farm output actually rose 6 percent, or about the same as Japan's whole economy. This chapter shows that this similarity was no coincidence.

THEORIES OF THE DEPRESSION

Up to the Depression, so traumatic an event was widely regarded as impossible. Most economists believed that "supply creates it own demand." Known as "Say's Law of Markets," Say argued that the production of goods and services created enough income to clear the market of those goods and services. Thus, it was held, a market economy tended to stabilize at full employment. Except for workers between jobs (frictional unemployment), sustained involuntary unemployment was thought impossible. That theory was one reason the Great Depression came as such a great shock.

Say's Law, however, had a clear caveat. Supply creates its own demand if, and only if, production costs, and most explicitly wage costs, are elastic. That means that wage rates had to be flexible so that a firm could cut prices to sustain output in the event that demand softened. When the Depression struck, therefore, the first reaction of many economists was to blame it on labor for resisting wage cuts as they routinely did. That reaction proved highly unpopular. There were just too many people out of work and too much trauma. Before long, to voice that conclusion in a public forum was to invite harsh criticism. Even President Hoover, the New Deal's favorite scapegoat for the Depression, urged business firms not to cut wages. Soon the proviso of elastic wage costs that gave life to Say's Law was hardly mentioned. Instead, as Britain's soon to be Lord Keynes would argue, Say's Law was wrong because it neglected the role of savings.[2]

Say's Law was not wrong, as we shall see. It worked exactly as advertised, in that where costs were flexible prices fell and output and employment remained stable. Where costs were rigid, on the other hand, prices stayed high while output and employment plunged. That is exactly what the law predicts. Still, arguing that wage-rate rigidity was a cause of the Depression became what we now call a "politically incorrect" conclusion. Since it was politically incorrect in our

Depression-era culture to discuss the labor cost issue, the cause of the Great Depression had to become a great mystery.

Still, several partial theories later surfaced. The main ones are associated with the names of John Maynard Keynes, Gardner S. Means, Milton Friedman, Robert Bartley, Jude Wanniski, and, in my view the best of the lot, Joseph A. Schumpeter. Still, all these theories fail to explain why, between 1929 and 1933, the output of both the U.S. farm sector and the Japanese industrial sector rose 6 percent while U.S. industrial output collapsed by 40 percent.

KEYNES'S THEORY OF EXCESSIVE SAVING

John Maynard Keynes began by taking on the issue of downwardly rigid rates. Keynes noted that workers adamantly resist wage cuts. This is true. But Keynes failed to note that lenders of hired capital resist cuts in their agreed rates of pay as fiercely as workers do in theirs. Both resist for the same reasons. Neither hired factor shares in the upside gains and neither has a voice in policy. Neither is therefore prepared to put their rate of pay at risk. Like most economists, Keynes ignored the fact that the price the buyer agrees to pay for any hired input, be it land, labor, or capital, is downwardly rigid and logically so. This logic was and is accepted for hired capital, but was and is largely ignored in the case of hired labor.

Still, for anyone to suggest that such logic also applied to labor would have raised a big question: Should corporations depend almost exclusively on cost-rigid hired labor? The very question suggests its own answer, namely that corporations would be better off if they employed most of their labor in some form of economic partnership. After all, economists have always been clear that to depend heavily on cost-rigid debt or hired capital is to risk insolvency because in a slump interest costs cannot be cut. Thus, the policy prudent corporations follow is to use debt sparingly and to depend mostly on cost-elastic equity capital working in partnership. In short, prudent corporations depend mostly on stockholders and not bondholders.

Instead of invoking such logic with labor, Keynes claimed that workers suffered from an affliction he called "money illusion." Keynes meant that they could not tell the difference between real and nominal prices. In effect, he was saying that the working class as a whole was not very bright, in that they could not figure out that they were better off if prices fell sharply while their nominal wage remained constant. If any of that is true, then holders of bonds or other debt also suffer from money illusion, for they too resist cuts in their pay with a ferocity equal to that of workers.

Money illusion was, however, a secondary issue for Keynes. He went on to argue that even if workers gladly accepted employer-imposed wage cuts, Say's Law would not assure full employment. The villain, according to Keynes, was the "excessive" rates at which the wealthy saved from current income compared to the poor. Quite correctly he noted that, on average, people with high incomes will save a larger percentage of it than those who earn low incomes. It is also true, as Keynes pointed out, that the wealthy earn an outsized percentage of total income in relation to their numbers. (If they did not, they would not be wealthy in relative terms.) Normally, savings go to investors who use those funds for building new products, plants, or equipment, or for working capital. But if aggregate demand goes slack, according to Keynes, such investments will not take place. Therefore, the savings would remain idle. Spending then falls short, not only by the sum of the idle savings but also from lost spread effects of those investments. In that case Say's Law will not generate enough demand (spending) to keep the labor force fully employed. Involuntary unemployment thus ensues. Keynes went on to make a complex series of calculations that purported to show how excess savings could cause an economy to reach a balance between aggregate supply and demand at a substantial rate of unemployment.

Keynes's theory certainly sounds plausible, but purely as theory it has two problems. First, it ignores the fact that new technology can force new investment regardless of aggregate demand and in fact did so during the Depression. The airlines, for example, invested heavily in new equipment even during the 1929 to 1933 crash and continued to do so for the rest of the decade. Second, it also ignores the opposite fact, that when demand for a new technology matures, investment drops regardless of aggregate demand. This too happened in the auto industry at the outset of the Depression, as we shall shortly see.

Keynes published this analysis, *The General Theory of Money Interest and Employment*, in 1936. It made an enormous impact. His book was probably the most influential work on economic theory published in the twentieth century. It created a whole new branch of economics called macroeconomics. It put an end to laissez faire and justified aggressive government intervention through fiscal policy (taxing and spending) in the economy. In all this, Keynes did much to promote mathematical economics or econometrics and, indirectly, helped promote management science later on.

Keynes's analysis has sustained the logic of an activist economic policy by government ever since. Indeed, Keynesian policies had already been implemented by the New Deal. But those policies ran counter to established economic theory built around Say's Law and were highly controversial. Keynes did not invent the policies, such as welfare and public works, so much as provide the analytical justification for them. Here was a theory by a respected academician that "shot down" earlier theory in precisely the right way to justify what the New Deal was already doing.

Keynes was soon made a British Lord. He had, after all, given rise to a new liberal and secular ideology that demolished a crude social Darwinism that Calvinism's work ethic had spawned. The new ideology, of course, remained rooted in the mechanistic determinism of classical Newtonian physics, to be sure. It questioned the reality of "free will." In so doing, it put the onus of poverty and other social ills on "society," not the individual, and allowed the profit motive to play the major role in corrupting society. It thus tended to absolve people from much personal responsibility for their own condition. During the Depression that was a simple task. Anyone willing to look could see for themselves that mass unemployment was in great part involuntary. Few of the unemployed were victims of dysfunctional lifestyles that they themselves had chosen. Many a sober and oaken worker could be seen standing in line at a soup kitchen.

The idea of savings, previously a virtue with an almost quasi-religious (Calvinistic) aura about it, also became suspect. Excess savings, the specific vice of wealth in the new macroeconomics, had after all allegedly put millions of people out of work. Wealth, in fact, once again began taking on the attributes of immorality. That prejudice has always been implicit in Christian scripture, but since the Protestant Reformation and the rise of Calvinism it had largely vanished in the United States. Moreover, it was also quite clear on purely secular terms that the physical standard of living of all classes had risen by leaps and bounds over the previous century. Great innovators such as Tessler, Edison, and Bell created jobs for millions in the new electrical industry. So had the innovators of new processes, notably Henry Ford and his mass-production assembly line. Ford took the motor car from primarily a "toy of the idle rich" to a necessity of the working class. By 1929 there was one car for every five people, about one per family in those days. Henry Ford might be worth untold millions, but untold millions could also afford automobiles because of him. After all, they now had good jobs—some of them very well paid—making, servicing, and fueling those new motor cars.

But as the Depression settled in, expectations of more of the same to come collapsed. As President Roosevelt had said, "Our industrial plant is built." Suddenly the creation of wealth by the rich seemed a thing of the past. Instead, millions of people were now out of work. Moreover, the wealthy, according to the world's most respected economist, had much to answer for. They saved "excessively," perhaps because of what many came to regard as "excessive earnings." President Roosevelt, for example, would refer to the "malefactors of great wealth." For a while the word "plutocrat" became a popular putdown term for the wealthy. A new shift had occurred in America's social and ideological paradigm along a wide front.

Within the economics profession the focus of concern shifted from the creation of wealth through new production to the distribution of wealth. The question became one of how best do we carve up a pie that is no longer growing. Here, the issue of "fairness" tended to trump the issue of productive efficiency every time. The mere possession of great wealth suddenly became unseemly. Once again the ancient and sometimes correct suspicion arose that, in a no-growth economy, one person can gain wealth only at the expense of others. A new egalitarianism had emerged.

But what about Keynes's main thesis? Did excess savings bring on the Great Depression? Absolutely not. To be sure, Keynes was correct about the different marginal propensities to spend and save between rich and poor. But Keynes's main thesis was flat wrong. For all his complicated algorithms, Keynes had no data to support his thesis. He did not and could not show excessive rates of personal savings in the decade before the Great Crash. For example, in the 1920s, just before the Depression, the personal savings rate hardly averaged more than 4 percent, close to its long-term average before and since. No one has ever claimed that a 4 percent savings rate would unduly constrain consumer spending. It is hardly enough to replace worn-out capital.[3]

I do not say that savings cannot be excessive. Savings is subject to the law of diminishing returns like everything else. But "excess" savings did not cause the Great Depression in the United States. At 4 percent, our savings were simply not in excess. I do argue that rigid wage rates caused that disaster. I mean that if worker earnings had been flexible enough to permit price cuts by industry, no mass unemployment would have taken place. I also argue that, far from negating Say's Law, the Great Depression proved that when its precondition of flexible labor costs is satisfied it will indeed bring about full employment, otherwise not.

Here we can point to solid evidence. Mass unemployment in the United States hit only the industrial sector. The farm sector suffered none at all. Farmer earnings, moreover, are indeed flexible. They vary with output times market prices minus expenses. Thus, during the collapse from 1929 to 1933, farm prices plunged by about 50 percent and farm output rose about 6 percent. The drop in farm prices for the increased output offset the drop in aggregate income. Farm-sector performance was precisely in tune with Say's Law, and Keynes's theory cannot account for the difference between factory and farm. And what was true for U.S. agriculture more or less held up for farmers around the world.

Moreover, Keynes ignored Japan's industrial sector, which also performed about as Say's Law would predict. Prices fell sharply, thanks to the flexible earnings of Japan's more organic labor force, and so output held up. Not only that, but the rate of savings in Japan during the 1920s was far higher than it was in the United States. That

Japan's economy had largely escaped the Great Depression was well known at the time. Indeed, America's premier business magazine of the day, *Fortune*, devoted its entire September 1936 issue to how Japanese industry cut prices savagely to maintain output. *Fortune* even coined the term, "Japan, Inc." to describe it all. The editors wrote, often in awestruck tones, not only about how Japan's *zaibatsu* cut prices, but how they remained profitable doing so. Yet to this day Japan's performance is largely ignored by economists who purport to discuss the causes of the Great Depression.

Japan aside, and even before Keynes published his theory, many New Deal policymakers were deeply puzzled about why farm prices collapsed while industrial prices did not. For one thing, industrial price rigidity created great trauma for farmers. The prices farmers got paid for their output had fallen through the floor, while the prices they paid for inputs such as fertilizer, tractors, and spare parts remained high. This disparity in relative prices gave rise to farm subsidies and attempts to limit farm output to bring farm prices up. "Why," Roosevelt's Secretary of Agriculture Henry Wallace plaintively asked, "does supply set the price for farmers, while price sets the supply for industry?" A discussion of wage flexibility having become politically incorrect at the time, he had no answer.

MEANS'S THEORY OF ADMINISTERED PRICES

If Secretary Wallace had no answer, Gardner C. Means was soon to furnish one. In fact, Means advanced his theory before Keynes and it helped to get Keynes off the hook on the apparent confirmation of Say's Law in the agricultural sector. The disparity between farm and industrial prices, according to Means, was explained by the difference in competition. The farm sector, he correctly pointed out, was almost perfectly competitive in that no one farmer or group of farmers could set the price on anything. They were forced to take a market price or sell nothing. Not so with the industrial sector. As a rule, a business firm does not confront auction prices in the way farmers do. A business produces goods and then sets prices on them. People buy at that price or they do not, but the initiative for setting the price remains with the firm. Moreover, according to Means, many business firms were oligopolistic. Being relatively few in number, they could indeed "administer whatever price they liked." According to Means, business firms routinely set the price high to "protect their profit margins." Like Keynes's theory that was soon to come, Means's was a great hit. It salvaged the notion of competition as a positive good but at the same time fingered the wealthy as the villains of the piece. To this day it remains the primary textbook explanation of the difference between farm and industrial prices in the Great Depression, and, indeed, between purely competitive and oligopolistic prices in general.[4]

Means did not, again perhaps because it was politically incorrect, make much reference to the relative difference in the elasticity of labor costs between farm and factory. In fact, it is easily demonstrated that the cost difference was the key. For example, in the many instances where raw-material costs were a large part of the industrial output price, that output price fell when the input price did. For example, the price of wheat collapsed and so the price of bread fell sharply. The price of cotton collapsed and so the price of cotton textiles fell nearly 30 percent. The price of crude oil collapsed and so the price of gasoline fell. Again, where industrial costs fell, corporations "administered" price cuts on their own output. Industrial prices fell, on average by about 15 percent, and that drop roughly accounts for the disappearance of the very profit margins that Means claimed motivated "high administered prices." During the collapse between 1929 and 1933, corporate profits for the whole of industry fell below zero, to become a loss. There were no profit margins to protect.

Means's theory collapses when we broaden our scope to include Japan, because in Japan his central premise falls apart. Concentration was far greater in Japan's industrial sector than was true for the United States. In Japan, just four *zaibatsu* firms—Mitsui, Mitsubishi, Yasuda, and Sumitomo—dominated Japan's entire industrial sector. The term *zaibatsu* translates roughly as "financial clique" and was a synonym for oligopoly. These were legal in Japan, for it had no antitrust laws and the government supported oligopoly as being in the best interests of the nation. So why, if Means's theory of administered prices is correct, did the *zaibatsu* slash prices by about 40 percent on top of a 50 percent devaluation of the yen? Was this business altruism? Hardly. As *Fortune*'s editors took great pains to point out, *zaibatsu* price slashing proved profitable. And while the devaluation of the yen helped the Japanese to sell abroad, it was a double-edged sword. After all, devaluation boosted the price of Japan's imports, again as *Fortune* took pains to point out.

THE BARTLEY–WANNISKI THEORY OF THE SMOOT–HAWLEY TARIFF

Not only does Japan's performance falsify Means's theory, it also negates another theme promoted by the *Wall Street Journal*'s editorial page editor, Robert Bartley, and a previous writer, Jude Wanniski. Their theory blames the Depression on America's Smoot–Hawley tariff that took effect in June 1930. It supposedly triggered a "beggar thy neighbor" trade war that converted a nasty recession into a general world collapse. Imposing high import duties on foreign products supposedly triggered a series of retaliations that brought world trade to a virtual standstill. Worse yet, according to this theory, the Depression that followed brought on World War II. Where Europe is concerned, Smoot–Hawley no doubt impeded trade, but it most definitely did not impede Japanese exports to America. In fact, Japanese exports to the United States and other nations exploded during the 1930s and, as a result, Japan's industrial economy boomed. As *Fortune* pointed out, unlike Nazi Germany or fascist Italy, defense spending played a minor part in Japan's Depression-era prosperity, driven as it was mainly by foreign trade.

The only way it can be said that the Smoot–Hawley tariff contributed to war in the Pacific was to prove to the Japanese army that the *zaibatsu* were fully competitive. They needed no great empire, as the army argued, to compete with Britain, France, or the United States. The *zaibatsu* had shown that, despite Japan's paucity of raw materials, they did well even in the face of high raw material prices brought about by the devaluation of the yen. Japan had no unemployed masses clamoring for resettlement overseas, as the army had often claimed as an excuse for imperial aggression.

So frustrated did army officers become by *zaibatsu* success that they contracted out for the assassination of various *zaibatsu* officials, including the managing director of Mitsui in 1931. Not until 1937, however, did the army get enough control of the government to launch Japan on the road to World War II by attacking China and deliberately sinking the U.S. Navy gunboat *Panay* in Chinese waters. (Cooler heads forced an apology for this sinking, complete with reparations.) By 1937 it was clear that Japan had escaped the Great Depression, in part, as *Fortune* pointed out, by its aggressive export policy based on price cuts so deep that they enabled Japan to jump right over Smoot–Hawley tariffs as if they were not there. With Japan, Smoot–Hawley failed to do the job Congress had in mind when it passed the law.

As a young child I clearly remember these Japanese imports, for they included many of my toys. I also remember listening to adults complain about these imports taking jobs away from Americans. And finally I recall the explanation for their success, a myth I believed up to the beginning of my doctoral research on Japan's early economy. Japan's success, I was told, was possible because they paid "slave wages" and Japanese workers were little more than "indentured servants" working long, hard, and exhausting hours for a handful of rice. In fact, the "slave wage" part seemed plausible if one converted a devalued yen into strong dollars and then presumed American prices. But, of course, the base wage ignored up to half the pay that came as a bonus, and Japanese workers paid Japanese and not American prices.

In fact, a study commissioned by the U.S. State Department (cited by *Fortune*) concluded that, after paying for necessities, the typical Japanese industrial worker had more cash left over than his American counterpart. To be sure, the American worker likely owned a car, while the Japanese worker did not. Still, the "slave wages" hypothesis was little more than self-serving propaganda. It served mainly to let us avoid looking at our own way of dealing with labor. Indeed, *Fortune*'s surprisingly objective look at what was going on was not repeated. Little was learned from it. But once the army took over and Japan invaded China proper, that was not surprising. After Japan attacked Pearl Harbor four years later, we were even less willing to learn, while after our victory we thought we had nothing to learn from Japan.

MILTON FRIEDMAN FINGERS THE FED

In his monetary history of the United States, published in the early 1960s, Milton Friedman fingered the Fed as the instigator of the Great Depression.[5] Indeed, the Fed raised the rate of interest at the worst possible time, when the economy was sliding into a deep recession. (Friedman concedes a serious and preexisting recession.) Higher interest rates "caused" the money supply to contract, he argues, converting recession into a disastrous Depression. I do not for a minute defend the Fed's action. To increase the rate of interest in 1931 was gratuitously wrongheaded policy. It could only make things worse. But blaming the Fed does not come close to explaining the crucial issue, namely, why industrial prices did not fall far enough to clear their markets at full employment while farm prices could and did.

Moreover, the farm sector felt the full lash of the Fed's higher interest rates, much more so than industry. After all, as industrial output plunged and layoffs soared, many firms could live off accumulated inventory. Disinvesting, they needed less working capital. So instead of borrowing money, they paid off previous loans. As they did, the money supply contracted. The typical farm family, however, could not disinvest. It had to continue to borrow money, not only to plant the next crop but to live until that crop came in. Still, despite the Fed's blow to farmers, Say's Law worked anyway. That is, farm markets cleared at full employment in the short run, when it counted, and not in the long run when we are all dead.

Again, the evidence is clear. Given elastic labor costs, markets can and do clear at full employment. It helps if all costs are elastic, but labor costs are crucial and as a practical matter elastic labor costs requires organic labor. Farmers used hired labor to harvest the crops, but the cost of that labor fell because it was hired day to day. This year's wage did not depend on last year's, and so the wages of temporary farm labor were in fact market driven. But note that farmers faced rigid (and in the case of borrowed capital) even rising costs of their purchased and hired inputs, except for casual labor. Yet despite those constraints, the farm sector still cleared all markets at full employment. Farm employment even rose a bit during the Depression.

Let the money supply and aggregate income collapse at the same time; farm prices collapsed right along with them to clear the markets at full employment. What more evidence does one need that Say's Law works when labor costs are flexible?

Milton Friedman and his monetarists, together with a more recent school of thought called "Rational Expectationists," have spent the entire postwar period hiding from the cost issue. They just will not concede anything to supply-side costs. They will not recognize that markets clear in the short term, where it counts, only if those costs are elastic. They speak of markets clearing "in the fullness of time." That may well be true, but Say's Law has the markets clearing here and now when unit labor costs are elastic.

I have a private theory of why the monetarists so avoid facing up to the implications of downwardly rigid wage costs. First, Professor Friedman was perhaps intimidated by the prevailing notions of political correctness during the Depression when he was a student. To talk about elastic labor costs was to suggest union bashing. If one wanted to support the free market, which requires elastic labor costs to work efficiently, then one had to work around this social obstacle to free expression. So if one can argue that markets clear in the long term, that is "good enough for government work" (and the government's work is, in the end, the real issue here). Second, Friedman developed a related fantasy that if only one controlled the money supply, all would be well. That one lever would be good enough. All the rest sorts itself out in the long run. Third, Friedman became fearful that the logical response to accepting business-sector insistence on the reality of a wage/price spiral would be to see the wage/price controls of World War II reimposed.

Certainly John Kenneth Galbraith, the most widely read American economist from about 1956 to 1976, did all he could to stoke those fears. Ever nostalgic for a return to his glory years as the top wage and price controller during the war, Professor Galbraith in all his books was quick to suggest that we reimpose those controls. After all, during each postwar recession the average wage rate continued to rise in the face of higher unemployment. Prices dropped slightly in 1949, but not thereafter. Galbraith was also a great believer in Means's theory of administered prices, where large firms can charge what they like. He had also convinced himself that large business firms can "manage aggregate demand." They do so, according to Galbraith, through advertising (consumers cannot resist).

If wage and price controls were beloved by Galbraith, they were anathema to Milton Friedman, but Friedman found himself boxed in. His own past monetarist rhetoric had cut him off from looking at the cost problem brought on by overdependence on hired labor paid downwardly rigid but upwardly ratcheting wage rates. So he had to use his genius to convert the wage/price spiral into his fanciful price/wage spiral. Business did not fight him as hard as they might have on this issue. They too were in horror of a new government czar that would control wages and prices. Again, Galbraith kept the specter of those controls front and center for at least two decades, and apparently convinced President Nixon, who imposed such controls temporarily during the first OPEC oil embargo. Professor Friedman was almost frantic. But in concocting his price/wage spiral he had to ignore the fact that in the seven years from 1933 to 1940 wages rose by 50 percent, 20 percent above their 1929 level. Prices, however, rose hardly at all, a mere 7 percent over seven years, and, by 1940, remained about 20 percent below their 1929 level. Friedman just blandly ignores the fact that the wage ratchet had a full seven-year lead on the price spiral.

SCHUMPETER'S TRIPLE CYCLE THEORY

Joseph Schumpeter advanced yet another theory of the Great Depression in 1939, when he wrote a two-volume book entitled *Business Cycles*. He argued the Great Depression in the United States happened because three differently timed cycles had all turned down by 1929. These were (1) a short-term inventory business cycle of about three years, (2) a seven-to-ten-year construction cycle, and (3) a "long wave" cycle of thirty years or so. This last long-term cycle was first identified by a Russian economist, Kondratieff, who did not specify a cause. His communist bosses were pleased at first, until he pointed out that this long-wave downturn appeared to be self-correcting. Self-correcting capitalism was a politically incorrect conclusion to reach in the Soviet Union, so that conclusion cost Kondratieff his life. He died soon after in a Siberian prison camp. Kondratieff's long-term cycle can be explained by the maturation of new industries. Briefly put, during the dynamic growth phase of any new industry output goes first to new demand and second to replacement demand. If new demand vanishes (if the market is suddenly saturated), the output necessary drops to replacement-only demand.

The auto industry from 1900 to 1929 illustrates this process as one trigger of the Depression in the United States. In 1900, the industry employed almost no one. By 1929, autos had become the largest industrial employer in the United States. Moreover, the new auto industry greatly expanded the demand for sheet steel, rubber, glass, upholstery, and electrical and petroleum products. Road building boomed, as did suburban housing construction. In the early stages of any new industry, rising demand is almost pure growth. Very few sales are for replacement. But after a while the original surge of new products begin to wear out and a replacement market opens up. Replacement is also driven by a rapid pace of product improvement such as we have seen in personal computers in the last decade. Rapid improvement also took place in the emerging auto industry as electric lights and self-starters, enclosed cabs with heaters, much better brakes and tires, and far greater reliability were added. The main thrust of growth, however, came not only because the auto got better but also because it got cheaper. A new Chevrolet cost $1,700 in 1920, but a far better version could be had for $700 by 1929.[6] Automakers could cut prices that much for three reasons. First, both process and product technology got better. Second, as demand soared, economies of large-scale production came into play. Third, the industry learned how to make economies as they gained experience, thus taking advantage of the "learning curve" in how best to make and distribute the product. By 1929, all these sources of cost reductions had reached their limit for that time. Better cars then began to cost more, not less. When prices quit falling, demand tends to mature. The product might well continue to improve, as indeed the auto did after 1929, but it also began to cost more. Here, instead of compounding each other's stimulus, higher prices offset the stimulus of better quality. Growth then comes mainly from rising aggregate income, much as the Keynesians thought, but at much lower rates.

In 1929, annual output of motor vehicles had reached about five million per year, roughly half for net growth and the other half for replacement. When the growth ceased in 1930, total output plunged by half, falling to two-and-a-half-million replacement vehicles per year. A similar shock hit glass, rubber, electrical products, and sheet steel. Mass layoffs began to take place. Despite protestations that "prosperity is just around the corner," involuntary unemployment began to soar. There being no safety net in place (no unemployment pay, etc.), aggregate income began to plummet followed by aggregate demand across the board.

Now add in a normal short-run inventory downturn. Then add a slump for new housing (thought by many to have been a delayed reaction triggered by ending free immigration in 1924). Given all three downturns, one has, as Schumpeter points out, the makings of a bad depression. Indeed, Schumpeter had by far the best explanation of that Depression if one takes a hired labor force paid rigid wage rates for granted. I added the analysis about the maturity of the auto industry, which only became clear much later. Conventional wisdom held that auto demand plunged 50 percent in 1930 because aggregate income fell about 10 percent in that same year. I put it the other way around. Aggregate income plunged 10 percent because the auto industry matured and thus lost 50 percent of its output. Neither excessive savings, tight money, the Smoot–Hawley tariff, nor administered prices taken separately or together played much part in that maturity. It was cost/price-driven, pure and simple.

One might argue on the issue of administered prices, so let us take a more detailed look. True, the auto industry administered its prices, but it had been doing so since its inception. Moreover, for the previous twenty years, indeed since Henry Ford invented his assembly line in 1909, the auto industry administered its prices steadily downward for an ever-improving product. By 1929, the auto industry cut prices by more than half, about as much as they could. Auto production had been reasonably stable for the whole decade of the 1920s at about four million vehicles per year. That output went almost all for growth at first, but by 1929 about half went for replacement. The economies of scale and learning-curve improvements were accomplished. As those costs came down, the industry "administered" corresponding price cuts. But contractually rigid wage rates had risen to much higher levels and stayed there. Any further price cuts would have required labor-cost elasticity, and there was little of that. Therefore, the auto industry and its suppliers had to cut production and lay off labor as output dropped abruptly by 50 percent to meet replacement demand without any growth. Many small auto firms went bankrupt.

Now suppose that the auto industry generally had employed organic partners rather than hirelings. If so, instead of paying rigid wage rates they would have had cost flexibility through bonuses tied to corporate performance. Automakers could then have done what the Japanese did: cut prices to keep output going. After all, they had been doing just that through economies of scale and learning for the past twenty years. Output would have continued to remain stable. As prices fell, growth would have continued but replacement would have become an ever-greater part of total output. There would have been no Great Depression and thus very likely no New Deal. Tax rates would likely have remained low. The welfare state, at least in anything like its present form, would not likely have emerged because an organic partnership handles welfare for its members—taxpayers do not need to get involved.

PARTNERSHIP AND PRICES

One of the major tenets of contemporary economics is that prices are truly responsive to market forces only under conditions of pure competition. Oligopolistic prices are held to be administered by individual firms outside the market because they are big enough to get away with it. I believe the evidence is clear, however, that given elastic costs almost any degree of market rivalry forces prices down, even for oligopolistic firms. My corollary is that given rigid costs, even perfect competition cannot force prices below operating costs once profit margins are gone. We have already seen how the auto industry cut its prices continuously as economies from technology, learning, and scale brought down costs. We are now witnessing the same thing in computers and other electronics.

Or consider the railroads. In the 1880s, the Santa Fe Railroad extended its lines to Los Angeles, a Southern Pacific monopoly before that. When the Santa Fe opened passenger service between Los Angeles and Chicago, they did so by charging $10.00 less than Southern Pacific. Southern Pacific promptly matched that cut and then cut another $10.00 itself. Before this price war ended, such cutthroat competition between the two carriers drove the price of a passenger ticket from Chicago to Los Angeles down to $1.00. In the process, the population of Los Angeles shot up from five thousand to one hundred thousand.[7] Such ruinous predatory pricing drove Congress, during the heyday of laissez faire economics, to create the Interstate Commerce Commission. Its job was to regulate price competition for the railroads, and Congress later extended such regulation to trucks and airlines.

With capital intensive common carriers, any rivalry, even with just one other firm, is enough to drive prices below the full cost of capital recovery—as with Southern Pacific and Santa Fe. When Congress laid the Civil Aeronautics Board to rest in the late 1970s, the same thing happened again with the airlines. The danger in such competition, of course, is that only the strongest survive it. Having swept the field of weaker rivals, the financially strong dominate their markets and set monopoly prices. If the cost of entry is low, new rivals will appear under cover of high monopoly prices. They charge less to gain market share, forcing all prices back down. But if the capital or other costs of entering a new market are high, new entrants become scarce. They know that the monopolist could bankrupt them by slashing prices before the new entrant could get established.

The main point I want to make here is this: If the firm depends on partners (organic labor, if you will), labor costs will be elastic. If a market downturn comes, any rivalry at all will be enough to force the firm to cut prices to maintain output. That is exactly what happened to the *zaibatsu* firms during the Depression. They were not being altruistic. They simply did what they had to do given their organic employment policies. The *zaibatsu* could not lay off their

members, but the bonuses they earned were tied to corporate performance so that the firms could safely risk cutting prices. Indeed, that
was the most rational course they could take. To keep prices high
would court disaster. Their best hope of remaining profitable was to
administer prices down enough to keep output up and probably gain
in market share. That is just what the *zaibatsu* did and it worked. As
Fortune's editors so breathlessly pointed out, despite Smoot–Hawley
and other protective tariffs, Japan's share of world trade shot up.

CULTURE AND THE COMMODITY
THEORY OF LABOR

Culture per se did not blind the West to the value of organic labor.
That blindness was much more induced by the commodity theory of
labor. As noted earlier, the commodity theory was in part an artifact
of Britain's Enclosure Movement. Recall that this movement had so
demoralized the original labor pool from which Britain first recruited
factory labor that it would have been surprising had factory owners
not excluded workers from organic partnership. Since they had no
counterpart to Enclosure, the Japanese had no hang-ups about bringing labor into factories as organic members of an extended family.
That was the natural and logical thing to do, assuming a labor force
that factory owners believed would respond to an organic employment policy as loyal productive members of the firm.

It is understandable why Britain, and thus the United States, did
not "go organic" at the outset of the Industrial Revolution, but the
demoralization of the workforce that Enclosure entailed is now ancient history and need not inhibit our thinking any longer. Let us
junk the mechanistic commodity theory of labor that was an artifact
of Enclosure. Based on solid empirical evidence, we can easily replace it with a theory of organic labor that has naturally elastic costs.
An organic theory of labor allows for teamwork, esprit de corps, and
similar social values. Yet such cooperation within the firm in no way
negates the value of competition between firms. Not only that, organic esprit de corps enhances teamwork and hence the competitive
thrust of the organic firm. An organic theory of labor is thus fully

compatible with market competition in a market economy. Organic labor makes such competition both the most efficient and most humane way to allocate scarce resources between rival claimants. I submit that this point is the most important lesson we can learn from the Great Depression.

So what would happen if we dropped our modern mechanistic view of organization and, for the postmodern era, adopted organic employment policies in the form of a corporate partnership between money and knowledge, between stockholders and permanent employees? We turn to that question in Part II.

NOTES

This chapter first appeared in a slightly different version in "The Great Depression Reconsidered: Implications for Today," *Contemporary Economic Policy*, April 1995: 1–15. Published by permission of Western Economic Association International, www.weainternational.org.

Centuries (New York: Weatherhill, 1974).

2. John Maynard Keynes, *The General Theory of Employment, Interest and Money* (New York: Harcourt Brace and World, 1965).

3. Ronald Reagan, *Economic Report of the President, 1985* (Washington, D.C.: U.S. Department of Commerce).

4. Paul Wonnacott, *Macroeconomics* (Homewood Ill.: Irwin, 1974).

5. Milton Friedman and Anna Schwartz, *A Monetary History of the U.S., 1867–1960* (Princeton, N.J.: Princeton University Press, 1963).

6. Alfred P. Sloan, *My Years with General Motors* (New York: McFadden, 1965).

7. David Halberstam, *The Powers That Be* (New York: Alfred A. Knopf, 1979).

PART II

PARTNERSHIP

Chapter 8

Corporate Partnership

Reality arises from relationship. A different relationship creates a different reality. The relation of partner–partner between the firm and its permanent staff creates the reality of a relationship that integrates the interests of stockholders and employees. Partnership thus dissolves the harsh reality of the adversarial relationship between capital and hired labor that is implicit when employees must work for hire if they are to work at all. Corporate partnership, of course, does not guarantee success. All sorts of things can still go wrong. But where other things are reasonably equal, partners will compete much more effectively in the market than will hired hands. The chances are that the partnership will adjust to new technology and other market shifts more quickly and effectively and in general prove more resilient in surviving surprise shocks compared to a bureaucracy.

The flexibility that a partnership acquires comes from its inherently elastic costs. Every partner's income will vary with the firm's performance. Not only does variability make labor costs flexible, it also motivates the partners to behave flexibly. Elastic costs and flexible working enables a partnership to withstand recessions or match price cuts by competitors. Or, on the other side of the coin, the partnership is also better able to initiate price cuts, perhaps to enlarge its market share. Bureaucratic rivals are especially vulnerable to such attack. Arie de Geus, a retired Shell Oil executive, makes a similar point in his recent book on "living companies." They are much longer lived, he argues, than are "economic companies," his label for the mechanistic bureaucracy.[1]

All these advantages reflect the fact that the policies that create a partnership work well because those policies create a stable internal social order. It is insulated from all but the most severe shocks from the outside. Therefore, a partnership works with, rather than against, autopoiesis. Autopoiesis, remember, drives us as individuals to preserve our identity and status in the face of environmental change. We can and will respond very flexibly, and indeed accept all sorts of change, if by making those changes we can better preserve the integrity of our own identity and its status. We will change jobs, learn new skills, accept less money, and even cooperate with people we may not especially like if it helps preserve the integrity of our identity. Working with individual autopoiesis explains why a partnership can respond far more flexibly and effectively to a broad spectrum of challenge compared to bureaucracy. Partnership offers stability to the individual where it counts, and so the partners respond flexibly to the partnership where it counts. The bureaucracy does not do that; it undercuts autopoiesis by allowing all sorts of outside shocks to put the integrity of the individual's identity on the line. Individuals respond by fighting any change that poses a threat.

THE TERMS OF MEMBERSHIP

Partnership can emerge by a natural process of subconscious bonding between people working together to achieve a mutually desirable goal. Because it is subconscious, we do not need a theory to tell us about bonding as partners. Why then are partnerships not common in large firms in the West? Mainly because our culture gives high regard to theory and, when it comes to large organizations, modern conscious theory suggests we forget about partners and use hired labor impersonally and organize it mechanistically. So argued Max Weber, who believed that bureaucracy was the most efficient way to organize large-scale operations of any kind.[2] Partnerships, according to Weber, may work out in a small firm, but not in large ones. Japanese industry proved Weber wrong, but we are still stuck with his theory embedded in our personnel policies. Thus we need to bring the case for partnership out from the subconscious and make that case explicit. The first principle of employment policy is that the employee is a member of the firm and not a hireling. He or she has entered a family-like setting, with all that setting implies. We fall into family-like relationships when we work toward common goals. Not for nothing does the Mafia organize into families, or do members of both churches and underground terrorist groups refer to themselves as "brethren." Even a bureaucracy, in periods of reasonable stability, tends to think in family terms through bonding. Such bonding wants to happen. Put in the right policies and it will happen, even in the face of turbulence.

When a person is made a partner, he or she is no longer a hired hand and is no longer thought to be in that impersonal and market-driven exchange of time for money to be paid at some set rate so beloved by economists. Still, a business partnership need not be forever. The key word is *goal*. For partnership to work, the firm needs a common goal, one in which all partners freely share. Making money (for all of them, of course) works, but that alone is not enough. The goal must also include a business mission or purpose, usually to provide some specific goods or services. That business purpose can be a project with a definite life and an ending point. When the project is completed, the partnership dissolves and there are no hard feelings. In fact, project partnerships can take place within a firm. That happens all the time, according to Warren Bennis.[3] People are brought together to complete some task. Perhaps the mission is to design new technology, write new software, do a research study, build a road, or create an advertising campaign. Just this sort of thing is one reason we hear more and more about "partnering" between a firm and its suppliers, who must work closely together to get the project done, whether in the context of a joint venture, a "virtual corporation," or risk sharing between the designer of a new commercial jet and the firms that build major components of it to the designer's specs. But, again, when the goal is achieved, the partnership dissolves and the partners go on to other things.

In this chapter, I focus on the ongoing firm and its permanent staff that expects to be in business indefinitely. Here, policy must make it clear that the partner is a member of the firm as if family. That membership is independent of the job the partner does. Rather, the partner does any work that needs doing where he or she has the skills. That proviso does not exclude specialization, but it does exclude erecting boundaries that exclude all others from the specialty or that insulate specialists from ever doing any other work. (Exceptions may occur where state licenses are required for certain work, such as to practice medicine.) The division of labor can survive, but not as a way to allocate pay, because that creates a socially toxic caste system of status based on who does what.

THE TERMS OF COMPENSATION

If not by the job, then how is a partnership to decide on who gets paid how much? In much the same way as stockholders: according to one partner's investment relative to the other partners. In a bureaucracy, the general principle of pay equity is equal pay for equal jobs, more pay for more important jobs, less pay for less importance. In partnership that principle can be stated as equal pay for equal investment, more pay for more investment, and less pay for less investment.

But before a firm can allocate pay shares to the partners, it needs an acceptable way to divide the total net revenue between the working partners and the stockholders. I define net revenue as the funds that remain after paying for purchased supplies and raw materials, rent, interest on loans, taxes, and for contract or temporary hired labor. In addition to outside purchases, deductions must be made for depreciation charges taken for capital equipment and for the base pay of the partners. In either case, the principle is the same, a cost incurred to insure renewal of the resource. Net revenue would be divided between the stockholders and the working partners, to be paid out as dividends and bonuses, respectively. Bonuses and dividends would rise or fall together, to integrate the economic interests of the two groups to the advantage of both and to the disadvantage of neither. How would this net revenue be divided? Any division that both sides agree is equitable will work, and that means it is negotiable.

What advantage does partnership have over an ESOP? The problem with most ESOPs is that the employee–stockholders may still work under bureaucratic terms of employment. If so, owning a few shares of stock rarely changes much; the incentives of dysfunction remain in place. As hirelings, they are still usually paid by the job. The caste system therefore remains, as do bureaucratic turf battles and power struggles. In other words, an ESOP does not really correct the main causes of bureaucratic cost and deployment rigidity.

Real partnership, however, creates a much more flexible structure of *unit* labor costs. This cost flexibility enables the partnership to survive hard times without resorting to layoffs. The greater the proportion of bonus to base pay, of course, the sharper the sales slump the firm can weather without layoffs. Come a slump, the bonus may drop, but the hired worker faces the loss of job and thus all wages. The risks of new technology to each category of employment are also similar. Hired workers risk the loss of their job, partners merely run the "risk" of redeployment. Partners therefore do not resist new technology as much as hirelings who fear it could put them out of work. Indeed, partners may also welcome the new technology if it means eliminating drudge work and offering them a chance to do something more interesting. It will not matter how many jobs the new technology threatens to cut, as a working partner you would train to learn other skills and thereby increase your relevant investment.

Stockholders own capital in general and individual stockholders have no specific claims to specific items of capital equipment or other assets. They earn dividends as a function of the performance of the whole enterprise and not from the performance of particular parts. So it is with working partners; their pay depends on the performance of the whole enterprise, not on the job they may or may not do. Just as with stockholders, a partner's relative claim to pay will depend on the level of investment, but of relevant time and effort rather than cash.

To put this point into better perspective, consider the problems a company could create for itself if it tried to tie stockholder dividends to particular items of capital equipment. In that case, a firm would have bureaucratized its capital. Endless debates would then ensue about the relative contribution to the bottom line of this machine compared to that. One might use lease rates of similar items of equipment, but in that case it gets paid a fixed rate just like that of the hired worker who operates it. There would be no gain and much harm for bureaucratizing the stockholders terms of compensation, and that is equally true for employees.

RELATIVE PAY AND PROMOTION

Again, for both stockholders and partners the pay equity principle states "equal returns on equal investments." If the firm tries to violate this principle it will undercut trust. Thus, subjective judgment should play little part in deciding relative investment levels. It will not be quite as clear-cut as with stockholders. For them, every share (at least in a given class, such as common stock) is paid exactly the same, down to a fraction of a cent, and it does not matter how much that share of stock cost when it was purchased. The formula for working partners should point in that direction to obviate favoritism or prejudice in allocating pay. When either favoritism or prejudice appears, so does suspicion and fear. Trust then often makes a quick exit. The person who cannot, upon reflection, convince themselves that they deserve something extra if judgment begins to play a significant role in deciding who gets how much is rare. The bright ambitious employee will then try to influence such judgments with the classic techniques of office politics. They begin to curry favor or subtly try to make other people look bad so they can look better.

Purely objective measures of investment should apply to partners whenever possible. The easiest of these will be "time invested," that is to say, seniority. Seniority is a necessary but by no means a sufficient measure. The "quality" of that time is also important. For example, time spent learning a skilled task would count for more than in learning unskilled tasks. The level of education achieved could also count as relevant investment, but the point is that whatever counts should be made clear and stated as objectively as possible. As for education, if a college degree counts as an investment for pay-rate purposes, it should count the same for everyone. If degrees from some schools are to count more than others, then that should be clear up front, not after the fact. Subjective judgment can be tolerated in deciding what should count and by how much, but once these decisions are made, they should be clear and apply equally to all.

The precise definition of investment should be tailored to fit the circumstances of the partnership itself. Almost anything can work, provided it is clear and has been agreed upon. What counts as relevant investment for purposes of pay rank can vary from one firm to another. It could well change over time, as the partners themselves might decide. But once counted as an investment, the investment remains even if the item in question is deemed no longer to be relevant and removed from consideration. The stockholder model applies again. For example, if a firm issues new stock to buy some equipment but later technology makes that equipment obsolete, the money collected to buy it still counts as an investment. We would not penalize a stockholder whose investment purchased the obsolete equipment. All the firm's stockholders would suffer any losses equally. The other side is equally true. If that new money happened to be used in such a way as to turn a huge profit, all the firm's stockholders would gain, not just those who put up new money. In effect, the stockholder model, as a matter of holistic principle, never relates dividends to the contribution to net profit made by any particular block of capital.

The issue here, broadly speaking, is *relevant* experience. The more one has acquired, the more one has invested. Experience can be thought of as a volume having length, breadth, and depth. The length can be measured by the amount of time served, or seniority, if you prefer. Depth, however, refers to the degree of skill or knowledge one acquires about a specialized trade or subject. Breadth, of course, refers to the variety of skills or subjects with which one has some functional competence but not that of an expert.

In practice, a partner capable of performing only a few unskilled tasks after ten years would have accumulated credit only from seniority. A person who developed a special skill or knowledge in great depth would accumulate credit along both the length and depth dimensions. If, in so doing, that person also became a jack of several other trades as well, that person would accumulate investment credit along all three dimensions. One technique for measuring the total increase in a partner's invested volume of experience is to index the increases along each dimension. Crossmultiplying the indexed changes to calculate the total increase in the volume of invested experience leverages the pay of partners who invest depth and breadth as well as length. Their base pay and relative claim to the bonus would rise rapidly compared to the classic "time server," who could claim only greater seniority.

Moreover, the bureaucratic pathology of people seeking out well-paid jobs for which they have no real talent would have no point. Those jobs would have no pay rate. That fact would also reduce the trauma of abolishing a job or job category because, say, technology made it irrelevant. The more that status and pay attaches to the job, the more traumatic job abolition becomes, as does the transfer of someone not doing it well. The fear of the side effects of such trauma has a chilling effect on removing incompetent performers or abolishing jobs that no longer add value. The bottom line is that the partnership which compensates the volume of experience rather than the job would make it easier to match people to the jobs they can do well. It would also dissolve the Peter Principle, wherein bureaucratic employees "tend to be promoted to their level of incompetence." The Peter Principle is a specific bureaucratic malady of paying the job, not the person.

A MERGER OF INTERESTS

Fair pay is the key to an effective partnership because only if pay is fair does a real merger of economic interests among the partners, as well as between stockholders and working partners, take place. They are no longer adversaries who play a zero-sum game with each other. The tendency of employees to sub-optimize around functions and specialties also vanishes. With such partnerships a strong motive naturally arises to cooperate toward the common economic goal. Partners with big egos also find it more profitable to participate as cooperative team players. Esprit de corps tends to arise spontaneously, something that people, as social animals, tend to prize for itself as a kind of psychic payoff for teamwork and cooperation. Ask anyone who has enjoyed such an experience.

Meanwhile, for partners, the firm's customers become every partner's effective "boss," just as with a self-employed person. In effect, those who provide the revenue, namely the customers, largely decide whether or not the partners get "merit increases" in the form of larger bonuses and dividends. Every partner therefore has a direct and personal stake in keeping the customers satisfied. Internal efficiency also affects pay, and so every partner has a personal stake in reducing waste, in keeping non-value-adding work to a minimum, and in optimizing around the enterprise as a whole and not its parts. This attitude requires no sense of self-sacrifice for the partner, but it does for a hireling who, by helping to cut out waste, may cut out his or her own job and income as well.

PARTNERSHIP PAY RANGES

An effective compensation plan, however, will have a comparatively narrow range of pay grades and rates from top to bottom. The now common huge ranges raise serious doubts about fairness. According to Peter Drucker, a range of about of 35 to 1 would be a reasonable spread in a large firm. That is to say, the top-paid person would get about thirty-five times as much as the lowest paid. The U.S. military does very well with a much more compressed pay range of about 12 to 1. During Desert Storm, for example, General Colin Powell, chief of all the armed forces and toward the end of thirty years of service, earned only about twelve times as much as an eighteen-year-old recruit who had just entered basic training. General Powell earned only about three times as much as a senior master sergeant with about the General's same number of years of service. Such a compression in range of earnings did not seem to compress the quality of American officers relative to other nations, nor in comparison to their industrial counterparts in the United States. One could argue, of course, that "duty, honor, and country" motivated those making the regular army a career. No doubt patriotism plays a part, but that is far from the whole story. The huge earnings multiples many CEOs now enjoy are new in American industry. Such multiples did not exist when the United States reigned supreme in the industrial world before 1965. Drucker's 35 to 1 worked then and it no doubt could do so now.

The real question here is how to motivate those executives now making multiples of up to 300 to 1 to agree to cut back for the general good. Not many people earning one hundred or two hundred times the firm's entry-level income would happily cut back to a multiple of a "mere" thirty-five. And yet no voluntary shift to partnership is likely without top-level cooperation and, indeed, leadership. Still, if the entry-level annual earnings come to $20,000, the top level would earn $700,000 per year, a sum that hardly suggests taking vows of poverty. Bill Gates, for example, pays himself a sum in that ball park.

Indeed, Gates illustrates another issue here. Entrepreneurs, the founding fathers or mothers of a firm, can get rich by owning stock in their creation, as did Bill Gates. Indeed, Gates's net worth (in 1997 an estimated $35 billion) is so huge that his actual salary and bonus is spare change. Of course, he came by his wealth because he owns so much stock in the company he helped create. Yet Gates shared his wealth, as evidenced by the fact that out of sixteen thousand Microsoft employees, about three thousand of them have become millionaires through company stock options. Thus, the type of partnership agreement outlined here hardly precludes one from getting fabulously wealthy as an entrepreneur. Moreover, those who work for such firms rarely resent wealth acquired in that productive kind of way, because they owe their employment to the company thus founded. What employees deeply resent is to see a manager rise up, take control, and then use the company and its employees as a vehicle for acquiring great personal wealth, often at their expense. The CEOs who earn big bonuses through big layoffs are deeply resented, even by those who keep their jobs. Such CEOs become known as the Chain Saw Als of business.

The pay-rank system proposed here, however, would compress the range of partnership earnings, but only as a partner, not as a stockholder. I can think of motives why CEOs might accept a compressed range of partnership earnings. First, consider the case of the CEO who has already become independently wealthy. In that case, the marginal value of additional wealth as such is relatively low. At the same time, the possibility of great public notoriety is relatively high. As many a CEO has already found out, with outstanding new wealth comes outstanding, often unwelcome, and usually adverse new publicity. To back partnership, however, could do the reverse. Instead of standing out as an icon of greed gone gross, he or she could be celebrated for selfless high-mindedness.

A variation on this same theme are the aging entrepreneurs who want to leave behind an enduring legacy. By helping to convert their firms into corporate partnerships they would much improve the chances of enduring success. Moreover, they would not, as is now the case, have to give away their stock to make the employees the owners. They could still leave the stock to children or charities without fear that either would run the company into the ground for short-term gain or simple short-sightedness. The working partners on the board would make sure that a founder's progeny could not dictate destructive policy.

If the alternative to partnership is bankruptcy, a 35 to 1 multiple looks a lot better than nothing. Thus, the threat of bankruptcy, either through a sudden crisis or a slow relentless slide, could well cause a greedy CEO to reevaluate. It is trite but still true to point out that most people will not make drastic changes in their way of living unless forced to do so by circumstances. Market competition could easily create the necessary circumstances and become the forcing function here. Indeed, the shift that has already taken place in TQM or reengineering was market driven.

Meanwhile, the individual partner would have a good deal of personal control over how much of an investment he or she wanted to make in the partnership. Partners would not need to curry favor to get promotion when that issue depends on the subjective judgment of others. Partners could decide for themselves how to allocate their own time and effort among life's competing claims. The firm might become the all-consuming passion for some partners and they would tend to invest the most. For others, family considerations might come first. Church or other spiritual activities might take top priority with others. Sports, gardening, or other do-it-yourself projects might take the lead with others. Then, too, individuals might change their priorities over time. What would emerge would be a distributed but largely self-selected bell curve of sorts regarding relative pay rank for any given age group. A few would reach the top. A few would rise only a little. Most people would fall somewhere in the middle as they decide for themselves how to balance the competing demands of family, recreation, and other activities with their desire to rise in relative status at work.

WHO DOES WHAT?

Again, the actual job being performed would not determine one's relative pay grade. The job might count toward either breadth or depth, but would itself have no pay rate. In any event, jobs would rarely come with precise job descriptions outside of which one was not to work. To be sure, it may be necessary to spell out the duties of some jobs in detail, but detailed job descriptions would be unusual. Job rotation, however, would be the norm and would count toward broadening one's average skill base. The specific content of most jobs would vary as conditions changed.

Critics often point out that even if they perform well in previous jobs, neither the seniority nor the performance necessarily assures competence in a more responsible job. But in partnership promotion is in relative rank, not job. Seniority counts toward promotion in that rank, it does not confer rights to particular jobs. People would do the jobs they could do well. If it became apparent that some job was beyond a partner's ability, he or she would be transferred to another job or given additional training. Such moves would not involve promotion or demotion, merely transfer. Systematic job rotation and cross-training, meanwhile, would create a profile for each partner of the kinds of jobs they could do well and the kinds they could not. We must remember that the ability to do a job well comes from a complex mix of natural talent, including physical, intellectual, and emotional attributes as well as desire, training, and experience.

THE CYCLICAL PARTNERSHIP

Can a corporation in a cyclical industry such as capital goods assure the employment security implied by partnership? After all, the sharp swings can be as much as 50 percent from top to bottom. The answer is yes, indeed. Moreover, the firm would be much stronger for it because by avoiding layoffs it also avoids the skill dilution typical in a cyclical industry when business turns up. To begin with, the skill dilution makes the swings far sharper because the firm must overhire to compensate for the dilution of skills that comes with a rapid buildup. Instead of hiring more people, the firm simply redeploys partners from reserve duty to operations. Reserve duty can include such activities as cross-training, longer-term maintenance projects, or new business development. On the upturn of the cycle, therefore, the partnership would outperform the "hire 'em fire 'em" bureaucracy every time. Instead of green new hires fed into operations who make scads of mistakes while learning, well-trained partners could hit the ground running. It is true that partner bonuses might take a hit during the slump, but that is not the only way to reduce costs. Temporary periods of short work weeks, or "vacation shutdowns" can also act as a cost buffer. Some reduction in headcount comes through normal attrition, perhaps 6 percent or so per year as people retire, quit, or die. In the peak of a buildup, a judicious use of contract labor also provides another buffer. As their contracts end, the people leave. Moreover, many people might volunteer to work part time for a while, mothers or fathers with small children, say, or those with elderly parents to care for. Others might take voluntary leaves of absence to complete a college degree.

One major aerospace firm did a staff study on this very issue. It had just gone through a major downturn with big layoffs a few years earlier. Then, quite unexpectedly, the market turned around sharply. New hires flooded in. Before long a horrendous amount of skill dilution became evident by the fact that nearly 50 percent of the shop floor man-hours had to be spent on reworking mistakes. The firm was forced to hire far more people to compensate for the skill dilution than it would need once the new hires had enough on-the-job training to do their jobs well. The accountants had not factored in the cost of that extra labor when calculating the "savings" to be had by the layoffs during the cutback. No one calculated the cost of lost customer goodwill from so many production mistakes. The study retrospectively simulated the previous downturn, presuming a no layoff policy had been in effect. It then presumed the existence of all of the buffers described, along with a few others, and assumed a 10 percent rate for the bonus. Taken together, these buffers cut costs roughly equivalent to the layoffs themselves. Had these buffers been in place to facilitate the study's no layoff policy when the downturn came, no skill dilution would have taken place on the subsequent upturn. Huge costs of extra labor and rework would thus have been avoided. Customers would have been happier. In short, a no layoff policy combined with the proper buffers can pay huge dividends.

PARTNERSHIP: THE ULTIMATE SHARK REPELLENT

During a debate over stakeholder versus stockholder capitalism, a clever argument surfaced. It seemed to take Wall Street money managers off the hook as the leading instigators of massive layoffs. Yes, these managers put pressure on stock prices to be sure, but mainly because the nation's employees, as a group, force their hand. Employees, the argument continues, are the major cause of their own layoffs. How? Why? Because so many corporate employees participate in 401K investment and retirement plans. After all, the employee–participants, not the firm's management, select the plan they invest in. Those in 401K plans thus can and often do change from one plan to the other, usually based on its performance. If they do not like a plan, they get out, its price drops, the fund managers sell bad stocks, and the CEO panics and perhaps lays people off to cut costs to get the price back up. Since these retirement funds control huge blocks of stock, in total they overwhelm the influence of individual investors. Thus, the argument goes, 401K employees have only themselves to blame for layoffs.

Most CEOs could resist such pressure if that was all there was to it. Most boards, after all, are hand picked by the CEO. They typically remain loyal to him if he has done nothing really wrong. But board loyalty is no help against the next implicit threat, namely, an unfriendly takeover. Financial sharks, such as T. Boone Pickens, are always on the lookout. They are looking, among other things, for companies whose market value drops below the sell-off price of the firm's assets. For an amusing example, I refer to Danny DeVito's portrayal of "Larry the Liquidator" in the 1992 movie, *Other People's Money*. The moment Larry gets out of bed in the morning, he consults his computer, programmed to spot potential takeover candidates. When one shows up, Larry begins buying up stock, and when he gets enough, he announces his intent to take over. He then proposes to sell off the assets or profitable divisions of the firm, close it down, and distribute the proceeds to the stockholders. That sum usually comes to much more than the current market price of the stock. If the stockholders like the deal he offers, they vote it in. Out goes the CEO and all the employees.

Given that kind of threat, almost anyone could ethically justify big layoffs now to prevent even more massive layoffs, including one's own, later on. That proposition is, as they say, a "no brainer." But is that the only option? Not really, when we remember that the takeover threat arises almost entirely because the employees, as hired hands, have no voice in corporate affairs. Make partners of the employees and give them representation on the board of directors and the threat of unfriendly takeovers simply vanishes. Unless the working partners also vote to deconstruct the corporation, the shark cannot make it happen. Thus would an agreement to form a corporate partnership prove to be the ultimate "shark repellent." Moreover, it would have a major advantage over the present repellents, often called "poison pills." These "pills" usually involve incurring a great deal of debt, perhaps for a preemptive bribe to the stockholders once the shark announces his intent to takeover. Another alternative is so-called greenmail, a bribe paid to the shark as a higher than market price for the shark's accumulated stock. Either way, the corporation is weaker because of the debt, which added no value of any kind.

In sum, the CEO's stereotypical short-term financial view that so many people complain about is driven by real, if pointless, bureaucratic necessity given the threat of unfriendly takeovers. Partnership can defuse that threat. Off comes the pressure to take that short-term financial view. So does the temptation to give a phony stimulus to profits right now in order to get the stock price up. No longer does a CEO need to cut back on vital training, safety, maintenance, or other prudent investments that pay off later just to placate Wall Street's money managers here and now. The partnership is free to focus on longer-term issues.

SUMMARY

Corporate partnership confers greater flexibility, resilience, and ability to survive, primarily because it confers more flexible labor costs. Flexible costs confer greater price flexibility both defensively or offensively. Flexible costs also express a unity of economic interests. That unity dissolves the adversarial relationship and at the same time motivates esprit de corps, better teamwork, and more flexible deployment. Partners become adept at adapting to change in a way hirelings rarely do. Those flexible costs also focus attention on the customers who keep the partnership in business and, as a further result, focus the attention of the partners on the whole and not just on their part. Finally, flexible unit costs let the partnership avoid layoffs on a downswing and hence the cyclical skill dilution on the upswing that usually follows. As a result, it preserves its investment in training and thus in the intellectual capital distributed among the partners. But getting there from here can be tricky. So we turn next to making that transition.

NOTES

1. Arie de Geus, *The Living Company: Habits for Survival in a Turbulent Business Environment* (Boston: Harvard Business School Press, 1997).

2. H. H. Gerth and C. Wright Mills, eds. and trans., *From Max Weber: Essays in Sociology* (New York: Oxford University Press, 1958).

3. Warren Bennis and Patricia Ward Biederman, *Genius: The Secrets of Creative Collaboration* (Reading, Mass.: Addison-Wesley, 1997).

Chapter 9

The Transition to Partnership

When a crisis strikes, most of us become willing to consider making changes we might otherwise dismiss out of hand. If things seem okay as they are, we may resist change, even for the better. The transition from bureaucracy to corporate partnership obviously entails considerable change. Thus we can expect resistance despite the clear advantages of such a shift. Resistance can be reduced, however, if the firm first makes some comparatively simple changes in the wage and salary structure. For nonunion employees at least, top management can, and often does, revise the wage and salary structure. This revision should be made before partnership is even suggested.

THE FIRST STEP

The first step is to create a new structure of personal pay grades clearly divorced from job content. These grades must attach directly to the employee regardless of his or her job assignment. No change in pay takes place nor does any change in whatever job title the employee has, but the connection between them has been severed. If it is already in place, the transition to partnership will be much smoother. Moreover, personal pay grades have big advantages entirely on its own merits. When pay grades attach to persons rather than jobs, people become less job defensive and more flexible. Such grades also reduce the bureaucratic fragmentation of the organization. It becomes easier to assign people to the jobs they do best. It is also easier to define job content more flexibly. A job's content can be redefined as conditions change without having to reclassify the job and its pay rates. Employees will be less tempted to resist requests to do work outside their usual job because such requests will not imply a change in status. People who deserve a promotion in pay grade can be promoted without waiting for a "job to open up." When pay grades are divorced from the job's title and its content, it becomes much easier to form teams willing to work flexibly in response to changing conditions. Personal pay grades survive even radical shifts in technology, job content, skills, and new demands for training. Such grades are very stable, giving them an enormous advantage in times of change. People who know they have a secure and stable status are psychologically free to cooperate in making those changes work. Again, the big reason people resist changes in the bureaucratic job is not because they love the job as much as they love its formal status. Pay-grade stability thus makes it much easier to rotate people among a variety of jobs to broaden the skill base. If personal pay grades are put in place before partnership is formally proposed, it will ease the way. Some firms will already have the essence of that system in place.

DESIGNING PERSONAL PAY GRADES

The structure of job-neutral pay grades can be designed to fit the special circumstances of the firm, and of course pay grades are already common. But one practice that reduces the firm's ability to make good use of them is, typically, a large pay overlap between grades. The high end of, say, grade 3, might pay as much as the midpoint of grade 4 and low end of grade 5. Such overlap defeats the purpose of using differences in pay grades to clearly define differing levels of prior investment. To illustrate the point with stockholders, one with one hundred shares will always receive more dividends than one with only eighty shares. While perhaps not absolutely vital, keeping each pay grade (and steps within it) different makes it clear: One's rank is a measure of the level of one's *prior* investment akin to the number of shares a stockholder owns. Moreover, a clear separation does away with the need for merit raises, most of which are disguised cost-of-living adjustments. Under this new structure, a partner's base pay goes up in steps as his or her level of investment rises. A partner is not given merit money for doing a good job. Doing one's best should be the normal expectation of a partner.

CUSTOMER-DRIVEN MERIT RAISES

Giving supervisors the power to grant or withhold individual merit increases converts the supervisor into the partner's real customer, deflecting his or her attention from the firm's customers. Subordinates, at least subconsciously, will tend to court the favor of the supervisor in hopes of getting a raise, regardless of the effect on the whole enterprise. In my experience, only the unusual supervisor will not favor subordinates who behave as if the supervisor was indeed the real customer and will award pay increases accordingly. In fact, a major power that customers have over some suppliers is the power to pay a higher price or "tip" for the services rendered. In many cases that power does no particular harm. What serves the supervisor may also serve the enterprise well. But often enough supervisors will pursue personal goals that poorly serve the enterprise. If so, supervisors can punish subordinates who pursue goals that benefit the enterprise but undercut the supervisor's personal interests, but a bureaucracy has only its own policies to blame.

In partnership, its customers will decide how much merit money to pay out, and they do this for the partnership as a whole, not for individuals. Happy customers will buy more as a rule. Thus, if the partnership keeps its costs in line, greater sales increase the bonuses for partners and dividends for stockholders. To eliminate the buyer–seller relationship between supervisor and subordinate is of course a sharp departure from standard practice and traditional theory. But old practices, together with the theory behind them, poorly serve the needs of the whole enterprise because those practices have a strong tendency to divert employee attention away from what is best for the whole firm. The compensation and promotion policy suggested here, however, provides a strong incentive to keep all the partners focused on what is best for the partnership as a whole, because that focus best serves their own interests. When a firm's external customers control merit increases for everyone, everyone takes a holistic point of view.

TOP MANAGEMENT'S PAY

Initially, top management grades could be kept separate and then fitted later to the broader structure once the partnership negotiations are underway. Still, the question remains of how much more the top grade gets relative to the lowest. The bigger the organization, the broader the range can be, up to a point. Any pay range the partners agree on might work, but the wider it is, especially beyond about 30 or 35 to 1, the more divisive a big range is likely to become. So too with a very narrow range: As one's investment in time and effort rises, so must the formal recognition of that fact as codified by the range of pay grades. Failure to create a meaningful promotion ladder has been the bane of many a worker-owned cooperative.[1]

For the sake of argument, assume the top management of some corporation recognizes the advantages of inviting employees to become partners. Further, assume that the firm is not at risk of bankruptcy and is financially stable. Let us also assume that the present salary and bonus ratio of the top management's pay is 80 to 1 or higher. The fairness issue will at once come into play. Those who achieve the high end of such a range probably did so in good faith, and the system they worked for rewarded them according to its rules. Is it really fair abruptly to change the rules? True, the super-multiples poorly serve the partnership's sense of equity, but abrupt abolition is also unfair. We must remember that people of all ranks almost instinctively defend whatever status level they have achieved. The best way to deal fairly with this issue is to make it an opportunity rather than a crisis. Opportunity abounds. One way to exploit it is to offer those with inordinately high pay multiples a deal. In exchange for the discounted present value of future wage claims (up to retirement) at existing multiples, offer them stock of equivalent value. Treat these managers fairly and they acquire a huge incentive to do everything they can to make the transition work, for success will likely improve the price of their stock. Moreover, if they continue to hold the stock, the benefits persist even after they retire. Thus, instead of resisting the change to corporate partnership, they acquire a strong incentive to make it work out in the long run. If their stock goes up, so will the bonuses of all the working partners, including themselves. Nobody gets laid off. Everyone in the enterprise wins. Making this exchange of high earnings multiples in the future for stock in the present before a partnership agreement is proposed defuses a highly sensitive issue in advance.

SPECIAL ISSUES

Having detached pay grades from jobs and having established an equitable range of base rates from bottom to top, a proposal of partnership can now be made. Before discussing how, a few other issues need to be addressed. For example, is the firm unionized and, if so, how many are there to deal with? How many operating units or profit centers are there? A large conglomerate that encompasses many different businesses and sells in different markets presents special problems. Should the business centers be approached one at a time? Should each center be a separate partnership? If so, how and in what way should they be linked? As a confederation? A federation? Obviously, such questions are best answered case by case. Still, the passion for spinning off and downsizing over the past ten years has made these issues somewhat less complicated. Nearly anything might work as long as those who form the partnership agree to it. Just as with an airplane, a remarkably wide range of specific designs can fly, and fly well.

THE PROPOSAL

The process for a proposal of partnership can best begin by forming a task force charged with exploring the concept. The task-force members should come from all pay levels, functional areas, or other groups eligible for initial partnership. The task force would study the problem and then make a specific proposal within the general guidelines and definition of partnership, but taking full account of the specifics of the corporation. The proposal should then be informally circulated for review and comment. After the review and necessary changes, the proposal should be presented to the board for final approval. Only then should the proposal be formally presented to those eligible for inclusion. It need not require a vote. People as individuals would simply be free to accept or reject the proposal for themselves.

THE CRUNCH ISSUE

Whether most employees accept or not will depend heavily on the issue of compensation and especially the relation between the bonus and base pay rate at the time of transition. Hired workers know what their rate of pay is, but partners will not be sure until after the fact because the bonus will vary with corporate performance. A definite base pay must attach to each of the various pay grades, but if the bonus is to be a significant source of partner income, the base rates of the different grades must be less than existing pay rates. Ideally, the bonus would comprise about half a partner's earnings. As a rule, it should be at least 20 percent to confer meaningful cost flexibility. The pay grades will also determine the relative shares of the bonus under the principle of equal pay for equal investments.

Moreover, guarantees against layoffs in hard times or from big changes in technology must be proportional to the degree of downside income risk the partners are willing to accept. If no downside risk is acceptable, then employment security must be less. Unless the proposal addresses this issue head on, the cynical employee will be tempted to suspect the proposal for partnership is just a trick, a cleverly packaged scheme to con employees into accepting wage cuts. Thus, the employment security provisions of partnership must be welded to, and made an explicit function of, the ratio of the bonus to the base pay rates at the time of transition. The precise ratio will, of course, vary from year to year after the agreement takes effect.

Meanwhile, plenty of precedence exists for taking a smaller base pay in order to become eligible for partnership, or even for a bonus without partnership. Associates in public accounting or law firms often take a cut in base pay upon becoming partners eligible to participate in partnership earnings. But in most such cases those cuts are a long- and well-established part of the professional culture. Not so for the firm making a transition to partnership. While one could certainly point to established precedents in the largely professional service partnerships and a few others, care must be taken to defuse suspicion that the object is a clever ruse to cut wages. Even though the upside earnings' potential is better, the big bonus comes later, if ever, while the "pay cut" comes now and for sure.

EMPLOYMENT SECURITY

The good news, however, is that better employment security also comes now. That provides a much better incentive to put one's current income at risk than does the prospect of a big bonus later. Such security has cash value today, here and now. This cash value has grown in recent years because of mass layoffs at IBM, AT&T, and other firms long regarded as pillars of bureaucratic employment security. No more. Employees now hear more and more that "employment security is a thing of the past in this day of rapid change."

That statement is, of course, true for hired workers, but it need not apply to a partnership. Still, that claim points up a basic truth. A presumption of security despite fixed wages can no longer be sustained. New technology, new organizations, new laws, new foreign competitive threats, reengineering, and TQM have all helped destroy the old bureaucratic job security. If workers prize employment security, they will have to accept a downside earnings risk, just as do stockholders, the self-employed, and other forms of partnership. That is simply a fact of life and is implicit in an organic relationship. By the same token, one cannot demand a partner's employment security and also expect the assured wage rate of the hireling subject to layoff. Here the truth should be faced up front. A partner's bonus, and hence total earnings, might initially drop compared to what he or she had been earning as a hireling, but then secure employment comes with a variable rate of pay.

Individuals should, of course, have free choice in this matter. Come aboard as a partner if you prefer employment security with the po-

tential for upside gain rather than fixed pay rates, no upside potential, and the risk of layoff. Otherwise, you are free to remain a hireling, assured of your certain rate of pay, but you will have no claim
on employment security come reengineering, better technology, or
softness in our markets. Many who are near retirement and already
vested may well elect to finish out their careers as hirelings, but they
will soon be gone and, not much later, forgotten. Still, a choice must
be made here, and the different choices come with a different set of
risks and opportunities. These risks and opportunities are, in principle, exactly the same ones that employee–investors who participate in 401K plans must make. They must choose whether to put
their 401K money in bonds paying fixed rates of interest or in stocks
paying variable rates of dividends. Given a partnership proposal,
they have another choice, only now their investment choice involves
their time and effort rather than their money.

Meanwhile, trade union negotiations often center on employment
security. Most unions have shown willingness to trade employment
security for money. It must be remembered, however, that employment security is not the same thing as job security. Jobs can come or
go; employment does not depend on a designated job when the end
of a job simply implies redeployment, either into training or another
job. It does not mean the end of an income, provided unit labor costs
are flexible up and down. Again, that is the crucial tradeoff: assurance of employment at variable rates or no assurance of employment
but with assured rates when employment is available.

BASE TO BONUS RATIO

The issue of what ratio to target between base pay rates and the performance bonus can be approached in several ways. The higher the proportion of earnings received as a bonus, the greater the employment
security. The more paid out as a bonus, the greater the cost and price
flexibility the company achieves and thus the greater the shock it can
survive without need for layoffs. In theory, base pay rates should assure
survival of the individual partners, but not much more. That might mean
starting out at or near the minimum wage. If that is not practical, it is
possible to achieve the target ratio, whatever it is, in stages.

Here inflation can be put to use. Use existing pay rates as the base, but then freeze that base. No cost-of-living adjustments or merit increases will be made, at least until the target bonus ratio is reached. Meanwhile, the money that would have gone into cost-of-living adjustments and merit raises would go into a growing bonus pool, so to speak. It would grow until a substantial portion of a partner's pay came as a corporate performance bonus. If inflation averaged 5 percent, all else equal, the bonus would reach a significant 28 percent in five years and 63 percent in ten years. Of course, employment security in the first three years would be tenuous in the event of a serious sales slump.

But other strategies can improve that security. Even with an early recession, those who choose to remain hirelings would be the first to be laid off. A temporary reduction in the number of hours worked per week or month is another option that avoids layoffs for the partners but still cuts costs. Leaves of absence for partners can also provide a layoff buffer. For example, a partner might be allowed to return to college to finish a degree on half of base pay. Mothers or fathers wanting to stay home with infant children for a year might be given a similar option. Taking early retirement provides another buffer.

If those who chose early retirement were given options to become members of a sort of "ready reserve" and return to handle temporary assignments, the attractiveness of that option might increase. Such a "ready reserve" could also solve other problems. Instead of using permanent staff to handle peak loads, early retirees might be used to handle those peaks. In effect, the partnership would have created a sort of cadre and reserve system that in some firms could reduce permanent staffing by 40 percent or more. The cadre and reserve system much improves flexibility to expand and contract. It could also reduce the need to employ hirelings as short-term replacements for partners on temporary assignment, out sick, or on vacation.

Still, best practice would reduce base pay from current wage rates by an amount large enough to allow the bonus to become a significant amount, perhaps 15 percent of total pay, from the outset of partnership. The variable bonus will be the most visible sign and substance of the unity of interests shared by the partners and stockholders. The more paid out as bonus rather than as a base, the more unified those interests are. Still, at the transition inflation can be used to expand the bonus portion gradually until the desired ratio is reached. The fixed-rate option will undoubtedly serve the needs of some people best and there is no reason why a corporate partnership could not employ some hired labor. For example, a firm with highly seasonal sales could hire temporary workers to meet the seasonal peak, as do most retail outlets during Christmas rush or food-packing plants during the harvest season. Some firms also have a weekly or even daily peak load for which hired part-time workers might work out. In some cases, highly specialized experts might be hired on a contract. Partners, however, will make the best permanent staff.

WHO IS ELIGIBLE?

In the transition, the offer of partnership ought to be open to everyone considered to be permanent staff. For new employees, a probationary period, say, a year (at most two) of continuous and satisfactory service, can be specified. Once a corporate partnership has been established, categories of membership can be defined. For example, those still in a probationary period could be called candidate partners. The candidate later becomes a regular partner after a satisfactory probationary period. Many firms already have a similar policy for hired employees reaching "permanent" status.

For the regular partners, the personal pay grades can be easily converted to partnership rank, stated as such. The advantage of doing this is that a personal rank instantly defines one's established status and reinforces the separateness of rank from job. For example, the pay grade O-3 is used by the army, but the rank "captain" that goes with it is much more prized. Moreover, our culture does this all the time, not only with the military, but with the faculties of most colleges and universities and with students. A high school senior is also a "grade 12," but we use the word "senior" much more often than the number twelve. The rank of captain defines a status, not a job, the rank of professor defines a status and not the courses taught, and the rank of college junior defines a status and not the course of study. In professional partnerships, a distinction is usually made between junior and senior partners. In a large corporate partnership, six levels of rank would probably suffice. For example, one might begin with "candidate partner," go on to "junior partner," then to "assistant partner," followed by "associate partner," then by "full partner," and ending with "senior partner." An additional rank, "general partner," might be reserved for those in the top positions who have "general" experience across the whole enterprise. Again, such ranks are kept separate from the coordinating chain of command in which the various job titles might be found. For example, the job title "plant manager" or "chief accountant" might well remain, but such titles would not designate the incumbent's rate of pay. Either job might be held by an assistant, associate, or full partner, depending on his or her ability. The experience acquired in such jobs would count toward further promotion and hence higher pay later, but would not determine current pay. Still, a loose relationship would exist between a job's level of responsibility and prior experience needed and the rank of the person holding the job.

THE UNIONS

Where trade unions are present, the proposal of corporate partnership must obviously take them into account. For the sake of argument, let us assume that they adamantly resist the idea. After all, once employee interests are integrated with those of the stockholders, they are "members of the firm," so why would they need unions? Indeed, unions arose to protect their members in good part because hired employees, in practice, could not be partners. Union officials thus have a motive to resist a plan that undercuts their job.

In that event, proceed with the nonunion employees. Then invite local union officials or their representatives to sit in on the partnership negotiations anyway. They would be tempted to accept. For one thing, unions have been losing members for years and many union officials recognize that conditions have changed drastically from the early days of union strength. Moreover, for almost two decades the unions have had to recognize the need to cooperate with management to hold off foreign competition. If they do not, they risk losing everything. Thus, many union officials tacitly admit that the union movement needs to reinvent itself, and the question becomes this: Is there a useful place in a corporate partnership for either trade or industrial unions? It largely depends on whether the unions can adjust to the concept of partnership. If they can, the unions could find a useful place, perhaps initially by playing a major role in negotiating the agreement. After the agreement, unions could play a major role in training and crosstraining. They might also become the personnel agency through which temporary or part-time hired workers were recruited. But there is little room in corporate partnership for the unions in their old role as protectors of hired workers against a predatory management, since both groups would be dissolved and reformulated as common partners with common shareholders in a common corporate enterprise. Unions, in short, would be in much the same position as the Polio Foundation after the development of the polio vaccine. The foundation had to find new diseases to conquer.

DIVIDING THE PIE

We have addressed the issue of how the working partners divide their share of net revenue for both base pay and bonuses according to pay grades. Now we come to the issue of how to fairly divide the pie between the common stockholders and the working partners. In broad outline, the formula by which the pie or net revenue is calculated is simply that sum which remains after paying the bills. The bills, however, will include base pay for partners and its equivalent, capital depreciation, for stockholders. The bills also include taxes and any hired or contract labor, including fees paid to professional law or accounting firms. But, however calculated, the question of how to divide net revenue between the two groups, stockholders and partners, remains. That question can be best settled by negotiation in light of conditions. It will make a difference whether the firm is capital intensive, knowledge intensive, or labor intensive. Retrospectively, one can calculate the history of the past division going to capital and labor and use that record as the point of departure. For the economy as a whole, about 75 percent of the national income goes to hired workers and, while it has varied widely in recent years, something like 8 to 15 percent has gone to corporate profits. The remainder goes to net interest, rent, and proprietors income (the earnings of farmers, other self-employed, and professional partners). The 75 percent share going to hired labor, however, overstates its portion in the business world, because the wages of civil servants, the military, domestic household help, and nonprofit private firms (charitable groups, private schools, hospitals, etc.) are also included. A fifty-fifty split, however, is a reasonable point from which to begin negotiations.

THE NEW BOARD OF DIRECTORS

How many board members are elected to represent the interests of the working partners can best be decided by negotiation. Whatever both sides agree on could work, but again a fifty-fifty split might be a reasonable place to start. Without knowledge of special conditions, a fifty-fifty split between stockholders and working partners empowers both sides. Neither side could run roughshod over the interests of the other. The new board, however, could no longer be a CEO's tame lapdog. Another approach would be a forty-forty split, with outsiders, neither stockholders or partners, holding the remaining 20 percent. The outside interests might include members of the community where the firm is located, the major lenders such as banks, other major suppliers, or customers. Among those groups care must be taken to avoid conflicts of interest.

How would representatives of the working partners be selected? The obvious method would be by majority vote of those partners. It might be decided that a partner must have reached a certain minimum rank to become eligible to serve or perhaps even to vote. As to voting, it might be well to follow stockholder practice. Stockholders have never gone for the "one stockholder, one vote" theory. Instead, they have followed the "one share, one vote" theory. I have never heard anyone claim that rule to be unfair. The equivalent for working partners would be, say, one vote per level of rank, again recalling that rank represents, roughly at least, a partner's level of investment. Thus the partners who have invested the most time and effort would have the greatest voice. That is a well-established principle of equity for equity investors. Otherwise, the investor of one dollar would have the same voice as the investor of a million dollars. The greater the stake, the more the say. Questions of whether membership on the board is to be a partner's main job while serving or simply an honorary duty might vary from case to case. Again, whatever the negotiators agree on could probably work.

WHY SHOULD STOCKHOLDERS SHARE POWER?

The short answer to this question is that they will be better off. A major reason why that is true has already been discussed, namely the need to create an identity of interests among all investors. Today, stockholders, by virtue of their control of the board, also force the employees to remain in subordinate status as hirelings. The stockholders have thus, implicitly at least, set up an adversarial relationship. Yet they have also turned the actual working control of their assets over to people who have their own ax to grind. Regardless of what theory says they ought to do, hired workers will in fact put their own interests first in the event of conflict, and why shouldn't they? In fact, the theory of stockholder control is a polite fiction. Whoever does the actual work of production and distribution has de facto control of the assets. The central question for stockholders becomes this: Do I want to continue handing over the working control of my assets to people whose own best interests are different from mine, or would I prefer that people who share my interests have that working control?

Another aspect of this fiction is that the CEO often has control of the board, often with little equity interest, because he appoints the board members. But again, having control of the board does not necessarily translate into effective working control over the assets. These assets will get used most efficiently for the interests of the whole enterprise only if those who work with those assets have a good motive to optimize around the whole and not the parts. Real partners have that motive. They earn more when they optimize their efforts around the whole. Hirelings rarely have that motive, and the policies by which they are employed give them strong motives to optimize around the parts. Keeping their jobs may depend on it.

PARTNERSHIP AS AN EXTENDED FAMILY

One incentive to facilitate transition would be to offer such services as child care, possibly preschool, and in some cases perhaps even elementary school for the children of partners. Some firms are already moving in this direction, and it makes organic sense. Human families evolved in extended groups, not in isolation. Moreover, the extended family also evolved as a means of "earning a living," not just as a way of rearing children, and it provided a "social safety net" for its members. All three functions combined holistically in early human communities, and that made sense. Later we assumed that, with the Industrial Revolution, its age of reductionism, and bureaucratic compartmentalization, we should separate these three functions. But now we see that assumption was wrong. Partnership offers a realistic opportunity to once again combine these functions into an integrated whole with suitable adjustments for current conditions.

Child care, meanwhile, has become a huge problem for working parents. If the whole family worked together, however, much of the problem would disappear. Given incentives to eliminate work that adds no value, it would be possible to free up partners to spend some of their time taking care of the kids, including their own. Obviously this proposal would be more appropriate in some settings than others. Child care also requires appropriate facilities to make it practical, but where conditions are appropriate it could pay a big dividend, not only to parents, but to the whole partnership. Today, the efficiency of many an otherwise good employee is constrained by the stress of this issue in terms of both time and cost. Absenteeism is greater and worry can distract attention from the job at hand. The problem can be acute when both parents work. Under this system, working mothers would be able to work, see to the care of their children at the same time, and not have to leave promising careers to care for the kids. As the old African saying goes, it takes a whole village to raise a child. An organic corporate partnership could provide a major part of that "village," because it can provide a real sense of community with a common purpose.

A FURTHER TRANSITIONAL INCENTIVE

Congress has before it a proposed "R" corporation, meaning *responsible corporation*. This proposal suggests reducing tax rates for those firms that conform to its definition, such as no more than a 50 to 1 ratio between the top and bottom earnings. My suggestion is simply to abolish the corporate income tax for corporate partnerships.

This would in no sense be a subsidy so much as quid pro quo. We saw earlier how our bureaucratic firms played the major role in converting a 1930 recession into the Great Depression. We also saw that Japan, after consciously rejecting our bureaucratic form of capitalism, escaped that Depression with almost no unemployment. Japanese firms could cut prices where ours could not because the Japanese had elastic labor costs of partnership. Through such price cuts, Japanese corporations maintained output, employment, and even profits and thus saved the Japanese government enormous expense.

We see today the continuing consequences of those different employment strategies. The United States, unlike Japan, driven by mass unemployment in the Great Depression, was forced to create a huge welfare state. Today, welfare has taken on a life of its own. It has created a growing body of "tax eaters," people dependent on entitlement to public funds. They are allied with a growing number of civil servants whose careers depend on those entitlements remaining in effect. Finally, a Congress that seeks the votes of both groups has a strong motive to continue funding them. Members of Congress are also concerned with "job security."

True, a major backlash against welfare has emerged. But in nearly every case those who would do away with welfare are vulnerable to the accusations of being coldhearted and lacking all compassion for those less fortunate. Liberal defenders of the current welfare mess, and it truly is one, correctly point out that many people dependent on welfare got there through no fault of their own. Of course many others, even a majority perhaps, get on welfare for such reasons as drug or alcohol abuse. Yet even if most welfare recipients have only themselves to blame, it remains true that a large minority seemingly does not. That fact makes the "compassion card" compelling to many voters who do not like welfare. In the end it is unrealistic to expect to solve the welfare mess unless we can also fix the circumstances that gave rise to it.

Meanwhile, the so-called Keynesian safeguards (unemployment insurance, welfare entitlements, social security, and such) have so far prevented another Great Depression. But these safeguards have ever-mounting costs of their own. Meanwhile, it was never true that as individuals we had to create our own safety net. For centuries the extended family acted as a safety net. But our Industrial Revolution, one that adopted bureaucratic capitalism under the commodity theory of labor, largely destroyed the extended family and did not replace it with anything better. Thus, given the crisis of the Great Depression, something had to be done. The government, urged on by the voters, stepped in to create a welfare state to preserve our system of bureaucratic capitalism. That was doubtless a much better choice than a far worse Marxist alternative, but it was a poor solution nonetheless in that it relieved symptoms but did not solve the problem. Thus we are now suffering the side effects of prolonged "symptomatic relief."

The bottom line is that the government (that is the taxpayers) clearly have a big financial stake in how we organize our business enterprises. Big government, many regulations, the welfare mess, and high taxes are all prices paid, at least in good part, to sustain the old and anachronistic bureaucratic format. Change the format to organic partnership and the demands on the welfare state begin to decline. So does the demand for big government with its high taxes and excessive regulation. Corporations organized as organic, family-like enterprises, that is, as corporate partnerships, can take over much of the responsibility for individual welfare, in tune with ancient tradition. From the dawn of humanity up to the Industrial Revolution, the family was as much a unit of production as it was a unit of nurture. The fragmentation that followed the Industrial Revolution is not "natural." It is a dismal experiment in a "dismal science" that failed dismally.

Thus, the taxpayers have every reason to encourage corporate partnerships. The more of them there are, the less the government needs revenue to finance welfare. The best way to encourage formation of corporate partnership is to abolish the corporate profits tax on them, as a quid pro quo. The profits tax is paid before stockholders pay yet another tax on the dividends paid from profits, but one can argue that double tax is fair if profits arising in corporate bureaucracies help create conditions that require a welfare state. By the same reasoning, if those corporations transform themselves into partnerships that take over a big part of the welfare role for their own members, there is no logic whatever to a double tax. All that logic supports abolition of the corporate profits tax.

LEGAL CONDITIONS

What conditions should corporations meet to qualify as a tax-free corporate partnership? To begin with, implementing a formal partnership agreement that includes some minimum percentage of regular employees, perhaps 80 percent, to qualify for tax relief. Furthermore, that agreement should specify that the risk of layoff has been replaced by variable earnings related to the performance of the enterprise. The agreement should also specify the maximum multiple between the highest earnings as a multiple of the lowest as called for by the law allowing for tax relief. (Drucker's 35 to 1 would be reasonable.) The agreement should clearly state the appropriate principle of pay equity for partners is "equal pay for equal investments." A maximum probationary period should also be specified, perhaps two years. In short, the requirements needed to legally qualify as a corporate partnership should be a real. They should not be loose enough to encourage creating an empty form without real substance as a tax dodge.

Once such enabling legislation takes effect, the motive to create corporate partnerships would increase sharply. Partnership's more flexible labor costs, greater spirit of internal cooperation, and higher esprit de corps would create such a powerful competitive force that it would be difficult for the corporate bureaucracy to withstand it without some compelling technological superiority. The management of those bureaucracies would thus come under intense pressure to transform their firms into corporate partnerships in order to survive. Meanwhile, the loss of tax revenue would be offset by the reduced costs of unemployment. In short, a general transition from modern bureaucracy to postmodern partnership would have major macroeconomic benefits. Our next and final chapter provides a brief overview of how such a postmodern economy might look in light of those benefits.

NOTE

1. Taken from personal interviews in the 1970s with several plywood cooperatives in the Puget Sound region of Washington. Some are now defunct, in part from the tensions created by the lack of a promotion ladder. Older employees resented the fact that new employees received almost identical pay without nearly the same experience.

Chapter 10

The Postmodern Economy

What would an organic postmodern economy look like after shifting from bureaucracy to corporate partnership? First, and at long last, such a shift would enable the free market to fulfill its early promise of full employment without inflation. That promise would keep even during periods of dynamic change. If made up largely of organic partnerships, an economy does not require a stable equilibrium. It can handle dynamic change. Business firms would, through enhanced powers of self-organization, achieve longer life. Social harmony would much improve. We would privatize much of our welfare. As a nation we could cope with international competition much more effectively. Finally, and also at long last, we cease vain attempts to compensate for problems created by bureaucratic organization with policies that at best provide symptomatic relief. No longer would we need to endure the side effects of those policy distortions. Needlessly high taxes, welfare dependency, huge budget deficits, and socially divisive civil rights laws that impose unfair obligations on some to create entitlements for others could all become history. Let us look at some of these issues in more detail.

FULL EMPLOYMENT

The free market has not delivered on the promise of full employment so far because of the systemic cost rigidities that bureaucratic industrial organization entails. From the outset, Say's Law held that rigid labor costs prevent supply and demand from balancing at full employment. The Great Depression proved that proposition, of course, but that event also provided clear, if widely overlooked, proof that Say's Law works as advertised even in adverse conditions—when labor costs are flexible. Given organic cost flexibility, the free market will indeed assure full employment. Only organic enterprises provide labor with the right incentives to accept flexible earnings. The main incentive is employment security—while the firm remains solvent—and, second, the right to participate in upside gains. The straightforward way to achieve full employment is through employment policy in our corporate enterprises. That strategy does the job without fuss. We would not need Keynesian fiscal policies of tax and spend, elaborate planning, and the "fine tuning" of monetary policy and its endless and disruptive changes in interest rates.

SELF-ORGANIZED CORPORATE LONGEVITY

Secure employment does not mean, as it does for a tenured judge or professor, a fixed income. If the partners slack off, their bonuses will fall. Slack off more yet and insolvency follows. Thus, organic partners have a motive to work both hard and smart while taking a holistic view of their enterprise. Organic partners will respond to market incentives cooperatively, often with great élan. They too are guided by Adam Smith's "invisible hand," which we now can know as a specific application of a much wider process of self-organization found throughout nature. Markets, inclusive of the enterprises that make them up, depend on self-organization to survive and evolve in an environment that is subject to constant change. Researchers such as Dr. Stuart Kauffman or Robert Wesson insist that a similar form of self-organization drives biological evolution much more than does natural selection of random mutation. The old Darwinian formula, based on natural selection of random mutation alone, is now seen to have astronomical improbabilities. The three-billion-odd years since life appeared on earth is not nearly enough, according to these students. It would take trillions of times longer. Though not completely understood, self-organization explains biological evolution far better. Indeed researchers such as Dr. Kauffman at the Santa Fe Institute have learned how to simulate self-organized evolution of growing complexity with computer models.

Meanwhile, human evolution has shifted mainly to cultural evolution and that is clearly moving at a rapid and largely self-organized pace. If we cannot observe that process at work in the biological past, we certainly can do so now in culture. We can observe the process most easily and accurately in human organization. We can also show that organic enterprises self-organize both better and faster than bureaucracy. Organic enterprises can respond to unexpected shocks and surprises far more effectively than their bureaucratic counterparts modeled on a machine. A crucial difference between real machines and real organisms is that organisms can self-repair, but machines cannot. Human organizations reflect that difference. The organic enterprise has much improved chances of survival over the long run because it can self-repair. In the United States and much of Europe, one industrial bureaucracy after another has become extinct either through bankruptcy, dismemberment, or absorption by other firms. Most of the change in the economy comes through creation of new enterprises that kill off the old. Joseph Schumpeter called that process "creative destruction," and he saw it as implicit in capitalism. New firms are often based on innovative technology, something that cumbersome bureaucracies resist. Yet if the creative new firms organize bureaucratically, what goes around comes around. They too grow old and rigid. They too resist innovation. Unable to adapt quickly to change, they too fall victim to yet newer firms with better products or processes and die off.

While serving on a Boeing task force looking into this issue, we ran a drill on the turnover of the firms that make up the Dow Jones industrial average. Few of the firms from the original list of about thirty remained. Others came and went. Yet, as pointed out earlier, the Mitsui Company, the largest business enterprise in Japan by 1750, retains a top spot in terms of sales revenue, not only for Japan but worldwide. Mitsui's history spans the entire time of the Industrial Revolution. In fact, it was founded about the time the Pilgrims landed at Plymouth Rock. Despite all the enormous technological and competitive changes since, changes that drove so many bureaucracies to extinction, Mitsui survived at or close to the top in its own environment and despite all the new firms that have come along since then. From its formation, Mitsui designed itself as an extended organic family, along blood lines at first. It later dropped the blood requirement but retained the family format, a decision that was crucial to its longevity. Again, organic enterprises respond far more effectively to environmental change than do their mechanistic rivals.[1]

American firms, organically formatted, could do as well. Indeed, they could do better in the "global village," given our cultural diversity. Diversity makes us more comfortable in an international setting. It also brings a broader point of view to business enterprise. As a nation we have grown in strength, in part through diversity. We met and successfully overcame many challenges and surprises such as the War of Independence, the Civil War, Pearl Harbor, and mass immigration. But our bureaucratic business enterprises have not enjoyed the same success. America, of course, is good at creating new enterprises and diversity has helped here too. The innovations coming from new firms (many started by immigrants) have provided much of our economic dynamic. But again, after becoming successful, if the new firm becomes bureaucratic it grows old, ceases innovating, and later dies off. That is simply the *tao* of bureaucracy. Its employment policies constrain autopoietic self-organization and, hence, the capacity for self-renewal that is implicit in family-like organic enterprises.

SOCIAL HARMONY

Full employment through a quantum shift to organic partnership would much improve our social harmony among diverse ethnic groups. Some of our present disharmony arises from the thinking implicit in the bureaucratic ethic of fragmentation. Here the fragmentation is into ethnic groups. Activists reject the traditional "melting pot" goal. They argue that ethnic groups should be "protected" against natural and largely self-organized evolution "in the name of diversity."[2] The freedom to intermarry dooms that goal from the outset. But more to the point here, organic enterprises would tend to reduce tensions between diverse groups. The reason those tensions fade in organic enterprise is that all members will have the same economic goal. If people, even with different values, tastes, and outlooks, all agree to pursue a common goal, they tend to put their differences aside. They can best achieve the common goal by cooperating with each other. With cooperation comes social bonding. Then camaraderie and esprit de corps breaks out. Despite their differences, they begin to think of each other as members of the same extended family. Such family-like cooperation is but another, and widely overlooked, aspect of Adam Smith's invisible hand of market competition. The competition between the enterprises helps bring about the cooperation, bonding, and esprit de corps within. Competition between rival enterprises, provided they are organically formatted, much enhances the cooperation within them. The reverse is equally true: Organic cooperation within greatly sharpens the competitive spirit. The consumer ultimately benefits, but then so do the producers. This cooperative side of the invisible hand (spontaneous self-organization) is powerful. It can even work in bureaucracy at times, but in bureaucracy it is more fragile and not nearly as effective as in a partnership. This spontaneous drive to cooperate in achieving common economic goals can only reduce racial, ethnic, and related tensions among the members. That outcome might well conflict with the goals of the activists of fragmentation, but it would happen anyway.

It is necessary that American corporate partnerships be ethnically diverse. If business firms organized along racial or ethnic lines, competition between them might exacerbate ethnic tensions much as when ethnic groups identify with particular "homelands." No longer would it be a case of Ajax Company versus Acme, Inc., but of one ethnic group versus another. Thus, if social harmony is a goal, corporate partnerships must include diverse races and ethnic groups. Such partnerships would become our most active and effective melting pots.

Given the enabling legislation to charter corporate partnerships outlined earlier, the nation could, with little risk of discrimination, dispense with affirmative action regulations beyond entry level. Once aboard, promotion is based on one's investment of time and effort, not in terms of a better job. Most of the arguments over affirmative action regulations deal with who is best qualified to get what job, because the job defines the bureaucratic employee's corporate identity and, as measured by the job's pay rate, his or her status as well. Thus the question of who gets what bureaucratic job is very sensitive, even at the entry level. It is an issue pregnant with potential for conflict. But jobs do not carry the freight of identity, status, and pay in the corporate partnerships discussed here. Those jobs are instead more loosely defined, subject to change, and are often rotated. Moreover, we have a half century of experience in the military, since the integration of blacks shortly after World War II, to prove it. Promotion in rank for those objectively eligible simply is not as sensitive an issue. It generates far less internal controversy than does promotion in job. The organic firm can thus place people in jobs they do well with little fuss. The practice of job rotation and cross-training informally reveals who does what best. If it turns out that "white men can't jump," then fewer white men will be placed in jobs that call for much jumping skill. Of course, the white man who could jump well could still be placed in a job calling for that skill—the placement decision would not be based on color or other group identity, but rather on individual ability. Moreover, job "placement" would often consist simply of an informal, sometimes self-selected change within a self-managed team. The content of stable jobs would also tend to change to reflect new conditions.

STABLE PRICES

Another outcome of organic employment is much improved price stability. If business firms generally were to become corporate partnerships, the Fed would be off the hook. Its job would be much easier, indeed routine. Its actions would cease being front-page news. The reason is clear. After the shift, organically flexible labor costs will allow prices to do their job, to strike a balance between supply and demand at full employment and without inflation. Otherwise, bureaucracy's sticky prices prevent or upset that balance. The Fed has spent over sixty years proving that it cannot compensate for sticky bureaucratic prices that arise from rigid wage rates. Replace those rigid wages with the flexible bonuses on which partnership depends, and the end of the wage ratchet and its companion the price spiral will be at hand. So will the bureaucratic suspension of Say's Law of self-organized markets. From the perspective of the twenty-first century, that suspension will be seen to have been the main economic aberration of the twentieth century and the greatest flaw in neoclassical economy theory. It proclaimed the glories of the self-organized markets, but then went on to keep it in hobbles with the commodity theory of labor. It then adamantly refused to recognize the cost-push implications for monetary policy.

In an organic economy, however, the Fed could control the money supply without much fuss through low and stable interest rates. Low rates would force lenders to lend cautiously. Low rates would, in fact, force lenders to veto leveraged speculation because it would entail too much credit risk for the lenders. Low and stable interest rates, however, would encourage real investment by reducing the opportunity cost (roughly measured by interest rates), part of the "hurdle rate" that any new investment should achieve to make sense. Investor interest would then tend to shift from bonds to stock, making it easier to finance new investment from equity rather than debt. Meanwhile, low rates would cut debt service costs on the federal debt. A balanced budget becomes practical. Tax rates could be cut. In the twenty-first century, the Fed's economists could admit that their twentieth century forebears blinded themselves to cost-push inflation driven by a bureaucratic wage ratchet. Future economists will understand why: The people at the Fed dared not admit the wage ratchet because that admission would undercut the Fed's power. The Fed's chairman would have had to admit that monetary policy could not stop cost-push inflation because it arises not from monetary but from human resource policy. Paradoxically, much of the Fed's clout, especially since 1965, has come from its inability to stop cost push, wed to its denial of that fact. As William Greider pointed out in his massive history of the Federal Reserve, *Secrets of the Temple*, the Fed managed to delude Congress into thinking that monetary policy was deeply mysterious, accessible only to the "priesthood" within the Fed's "temple."

Thus, in the 1980s the Fed was able to argue that (1) low interest rates in the form of usury limits would constrain bank credit to low- and middle-class borrowers. Then, with a slight shift of context, the Fed went on to argue that (2) low interest rates also spark runaway credit demand and hence inflation, driven mostly by these same middle-class people to whom the banks would refuse to lend money because low rates entail high credit risk. The real mystery is why Congress, four administrations of both parties, and most economists could believe both propositions to be true at the same time. I suspect the reason was, subconsciously at least, fear. Most of the people involved in this issue perhaps feared that the price of exposing this logical contradiction would have been to concede that monetary policy could not stop wage ratchet. To concede that much, however, is to suggest that wage and price controls may be the only practical alternative in our bureaucratically organized economy to control cost-push inflation. Between the two, living with that logical contradiction was perhaps the lesser of two evils, but this is now. We do not need wage and price controls; they do too much harm. We need elastic labor costs, and the only way to get them is through corporate partnership.

WELFARE

We addressed welfare in the last chapter, but, once again, the organic corporation recreates an extended family-like enterprise that takes over from the state the primary responsibility for the welfare of its members. For the members, hard times and tough competition may mean lower bonuses, but they will not mean unemployment. The failure to establish this relationship at the outset of the Industrial Revolution, as pointed out earlier, helped bring about capitalism's instability, culminating in the Great Depression and, subsequently, the welfare state.

Of course, it will take time to wean people off welfare dependency. Organic enterprise by itself will not make it happen. Organic partnership will, however, reduce the unemployment that creates much of the need for welfare. Of course, other problems will remain, such as drug and alcohol abuse. Some teenage girls may well continue to insist they have a God-given right to give birth to children out of wedlock and that God has also imposed a duty on the taxpayers to pay those girls to exercise this "right." I occasionally receive term papers from students who, in effect, argue just that. My informal monitoring suggests that most of these papers come from two groups: (1) welfare mothers under twenty-five, and (2) men and women who work for the state welfare agencies that are headquartered near the town where I teach.

These ancillary problems, however, can be addressed much more easily in an environment where secure employment at variable rates is standard practice. For one thing, a precedent would emerge. If the taxpayers can acquire employment security only if they accept a variable rate of income relative to funds available to pay them, how can welfare recipients expect more? The taxpayers could insist that welfare entitlements are limited by the funds available to pay them. If tax collections drop, so do welfare payments. Otherwise, as the income received by taxpayers falls, their tax rates must go up to maintain a constant level of payments to welfare recipients. There is no equity in that proposition.

FOREIGN COMPETITION

Corporate partnerships (CPs) can, of course, cope with foreign competition better and, indeed, preemptively. That is, if a CP sees that another firm, foreign or domestic, is attacking its markets, the CP could cut prices before the attack gets a firm foothold. Had American firms shifted to partnership after World War II, Japan could never have cut so deeply into our markets. (It is, of course, an ill wind that bears no good. Those market gains quite likely kept Japan out of the Soviet orbit.) A corporate partnership, faced with foreign competition, might choose simply to vacate some market because it could do better putting its resources elsewhere. If the CP decides to build plants abroad, it will not lay off its members in the process, but will shift them to other activities and perhaps allow the firm to downsize by normal attrition.

ECONOMIC POLICY

The manifold problems created by bureaucratic capitalism over the years has, in one way or another, driven most of our nation's economic policies. These problems gave birth to the easily corrupted fiscal policy of tax and spend, which includes welfare, deficit spending, and much more. The Fed's refusal to recognize the source of these problems badly corrupted monetary policy. Bureaucratic capitalism has also created a crisis in trade policy. By insisting on free trade despite our institutionalized labor cost rigidity, our economy becomes highly vulnerable to newly emergent, cost-elastic organic competition from abroad. That competition will only continue to get more intense. A free trade policy is viable in an organic economy, but can be ruinous if it is bureaucratic.

Thus I have argued throughout this book that we should replace bureaucratic capitalism with organic free enterprise. In that way we can strengthen the greatest self-organized human institution ever to have evolved, namely the free market. Then we can return to rational economic policy, fiscal, monetary, and trade, by rejecting the commodity theory of labor and adopting a human resource policy based on organic rather than mechanistic relationships. Moreover, through improved longevity and better social stability and health, our postmodern organic partnerships would enable America to quit fragmenting races and ethnic groups through policies that encourage divisiveness, however well intended.

SUMMARY

Given an organic free enterprise economy, unemployment and budget deficits drop, cost-push inflation driven by a wage ratchet disappears, and class conflict coupled with ethnic strife dissipates. The old caste or functional distinctions between management and labor become muted in self-managed organic process teams. Our business enterprises would cope with change far better and thus survive much longer. Of course, economic change is inevitable, but the suffering, such as involuntary unemployment, is not. Our business enterprises need only adopt the flexible organic format. The transition they began about 1980 will then be over, a true quantum shift.

NOTES

1. Data on Mitsui taken from John Roberts, *Mitsui: A Record of Three Centuries* (New York: Weatherhill, 1976). See also Arie de Geus, *The Living Company: Habits of Survival in a Turbulent Business Environment* (Boston: Harvard Business School Press, 1997).

2. Arthur M. Schlesinger, Jr., *The Disuniting of America* (New York: W. W. Norton, 1992).

Partnership and
Postmodern Science

The mechanistic model, whether applied to the universe as a whole or just to business firms, has three great problems. First, the model dehumanizes people into machines or commodities. Second, and related to the first, the model's materialism makes no room for immaterial entities such as esprit de corps that motivates cooperation and good teamwork. Third, it assumed a deterministic, hence a linear predictable future. All these failings are embedded in the Newtonian science that gave birth to the mechanistic world view and its application to modern organizations. One variant of that model, FPCC, failed utterly in a competitive market test with Japan's organic alternative and nearly brought ruin to the economy.

The new sciences of quantum physics and chaos theory do not have these failings. They allow for human consciousness and spirit on their own terms and not as a epiphenomenon of matter. In these sciences people can be people, not machines, and they can have a spirit. Finally, both quantum physics and chaos theory stress that the future is uncertain, and not, in the usual definition of the term, deterministic. These are truly dramatic shifts in point of view. Therefore, it seems reasonable to provide the reader with a nontechnical overview of how quantum mechanics and chaos theory demolished the mechanistic model and at the same time offer support to the organic alternative that experience suggests is far more effective.

The mechanistic model of the universe began to unravel early in the twentieth century with the emergence of quantum physics. This new science began when physicists gradually came to see that atoms were not indivisible bits of matter akin to tiny billiard balls. That image had dominated thinking about atoms since a Greek philosopher, Democritus, hypothesized the atom over two thousand years ago. By about 1900, puzzles began to emerge in the classical or Newtonian physics. Try as they might, Newtonian scientists could not explain these puzzles. This story that has been told often and well and I need not repeat it all here.[1] But a crucial finding by Britain's great scientist Earnest Rutherford was that atoms were not solid. They had an outer ring of tiny electrons surrounding a nucleus (later discovered to consist of protons and neutrons) and, in-between, well over 99 percent of the whole atom was simply empty space. Postwar experiments later showed that the protons and neutrons were made of something smaller yet, dubbed "quarks" by the American physicist Murray Gell-Mann. Quarks and electrons seem to have no actual substance. They appear to be dimensionless bits of energy spinning this way or that, with either a positive or negative electrical charge.

These "empty atoms" suggested that the "rock-solid" matter of our senses was simply an illusion. The appearance of solidity, say, of the chair I am sitting on, is an illusion created by the electromagnetic field in which like charges repel each other. The electromagnetic field thus assures that the electrons in the outer ring of the chair's atoms repel those of my body. That nonmaterial repulsive force makes my chair feel solid to my body, but to a neutrino, which has no charge, the chair might as well be a vacuum through which the neutrinos pass with a vanishing small probability of a collision with either electrons or quarks. That passage can be compared to a spaceship passing through the solar system, so little space do the electrons and quarks take up.

Thus, instead of tiny indivisible solids as basic units of matter, experimentation revealed an atom of largely empty space inhabited by a veritable zoo of subatomic particles. Moreover, these particles can change into each other, or so the experiments by increasingly powerful particle accelerators suggest. The very notion of "matter" became somewhat problematic at the outset, after Einstein's famous formula that $E = mc^2$. It states that matter converts into energy and vice versa, and the formula was soon confirmed by atomic bombs, both fission and fusion (hydrogen) bombs. None of this boded well for a mechanistic world view of the universe. Indeed, in Newton's day energy had no integral relationship with matter. Now it seemed pure energy was the "real" or underlying reality, with matter just one form of it, and an illusionary one at that. Worse findings yet were in store for the mechanistic model. By 1927, Denmark's Neils Bohr and Germany's Werner Heisenberg discovered that matter, such as electrons with some mass, and energy, such as photons with no mass, had a dual existence, a split personality. Each one could manifest itself either as a wave or a particle, depending on how we observed it, and in the absence of observation it had both characteristics at the same time.

This puzzling duality has been demonstrated time and again by what is called the "double slit" experiment. If photons are dispatched toward a panel with two slits in it, and behind those two slits an experimenter places a screen, that screen detects a "wave interference pattern." That is to say, the photon has gone through both slits at the same time as if it were a water wave, creating two waves on the other side, one from each slit. The screen behind the panel then picks up the interference of these two waves as a series of dark and bright lines, dark where the two waves cancel each other out, and bright where the waves doubled to enhance their effect, exactly as water waves do. Thomas Young first did this double slit experiment in 1810 to "prove" that light was a wave rather than a "corpuscle," as Isaac Newton had thought.

If the experimenter substitutes a particle detector called a photo-multiplier tube for the wave detecting screen, the tube will see no wave at all. Instead, it will record light as particles, or what we call photons. But as photons, the light has only gone through one of the slits, not both, and so no interference pattern appears. If we start with the screen detector and see light waves, then add the particle detectors, the wave interference pattern disappears. Suddenly we get only photons.[2] The light seems to "know" what we are looking for and then it obliges us. Even stranger experiments have been done involving "non-locality." Non-locality refers to events that seemingly transcend space, time, and motion and can happen instantaneously across great distances. In one experiment, in a pair of polarized particles going in opposite directions, one will instantaneously register its effect on its twin miles away. More commonly, electrons seem to jump from one energy state and "orbit" around an atom's nucleus to another without "traveling" between orbits. They are in one or the other, but never in between, not even in transit. Einstein rejected such ideas. He insisted a proper experiment in non-locality would prove him right. The exact opposite happened. In 1982, a team of French physicists led by Alain Aspect was able to conduct the very "thought experiment" Einstein and some colleagues designed. Aspect and colleagues proved Einstein wrong. Non-locality apparently is real. Action can apparently occur at a distance independently of time and space.[3]

HEISENBERG AND THE BUTTERFLY EFFECT

According to Werner Heisenberg, one of the founders of quantum mechanics, the act of observation will distort either the position or the velocity of a subatomic particle. One can fix position only by disturbing its velocity, and one can fix velocity only by disturbing its position. This phenomenon gives rise to the Heisenberg Uncertainty Principle. We cannot know both the velocity and the position of a particle at the same time. That fact demolished the determinism based on the billiard ball metaphor of atoms that lay behind the mechanistic model of the universe with its mechanistic determinism. Both were stone dead after Heisenberg, but it took time for that realization to spread. The mechanistic model also required the atoms that make up matter to be like miniature and indivisible billiard balls. The position and velocity of all matter had to be known simultaneously to predict the future by using Sir Isaac Newton's three laws of motion and universal laws of gravity. Indeed, the mechanistic model was reasonable enough if atoms were solid particles whose position and velocity could be known at the same time, but Heisenberg's Uncertainly Principle of quantum physics ruled out that possibility, at least in the realm of the subatomic.

The implications of that finding spread quite slowly at first, and for decades stayed mainly within the realm of subatomic physics. But even after the 1960s when, combined with other findings, the implications began to spread, it seems that managers and economists were again among the last to get the word. It took the new science of chaos theory, more often now called complexity theory, to extend Heisenberg's principle to the macro world where we live. My personal enlightenment came from a part of chaos theory called the "butterfly effect" in weather forecasting.[4] Reading about the butterfly effect convinced me that quantum physics had relevance in the world in which we live. I had heard of Heisenberg's principle for decades, but it took James Gleick's book on chaos, telling of how Edward Lorenz stumbled across the butterfly effect (which contends that a butterfly flapping its wings at the right time in Brazil can cause a tornado six months later in Chicago through positive feedback), to drive home to me the inherent uncertainty in my kind of forecasting. Never again could I believe that a forecast based on extrapolations from a turbulent environment could be accurate, except perhaps by dumb luck. If the environment was turbulent, then relationships between the dependent and independent variables could be nonlinear. That means a small change in an initial condition could cascade, sometimes explosively, into much larger changes in the outcome. Turbulence was a standard condition, not something rare, in the political, social, and economic arenas.

To be sure, the butterfly effect refers to a different kind of uncertainty from that which Heisenberg described, but some of the implications are the same and the butterfly effect in weather forecasting illustrates it well. According to Gleick, to get enough information to make an accurate six-month weather forecast, MIT scientists calculated they would have to put sensing instruments in every cubic meter of airspace on the globe. Only then could one track all the butterflies, a metaphor for all movement, including every human sneeze. But with such a mass of sensing instruments would room remain for butterflies or humans? Enter here Heisenberg's Uncertainty Principle.

Such a mass of instrumentation would drastically distort the very weather we wanted to forecast. From a different route we return to Heisenberg's point that observation can change what is being observed. Only now we see this to be true in the macro world, and not just in the subatomic. We too can change behavior by observation. That fact does not sit comfortably with the ideal of the scientific method, in which a detached outsider objectively observes the results of some experiment without in any way influencing those results. While such influence can be trivial (watching the moon through a telescope, for example), in others it is decisive.

One can think of many examples from daily life to illustrate how observation can change behavior in order to illustrate the uncertainty principle. Highway traffic tends to slow down when motorists know they are under radar observation. People are less likely to shoplift if they know that the store monitors the aisles with closed circuit TV. According to one study, people are more likely to wash up after using a restroom when other people are present. To turn on the TV cameras in front of a crowd often elicits a demonstration when none was going on before the cameras arrived. Many an activist group makes the presence of the TV camera a condition for the demonstration. Indeed, the act of observation can itself become that small change in initial conditions triggering a cascade toward an explosive outcome, as for example the chance observation of the beating of Rodney King as recorded on a private citizen's TV camcorder. That chance initial event was the small change that clearly set in motion a cascading chain of events that ended in the Los Angeles riots a year or so later.

This cascading phenomena is also a standard feature of life. According to Bill Gates, a mothers' rummage sale that aimed to buy a primitive computer for young Bill's school set in motion the chain of events that cascaded into the founding of Microsoft by Gates and his fellow classmate Paul Allen.[5] Part of the lore at Boeing, where I spent twenty years, concerned a similar example. In 1915, an itinerant pilot came to Seattle offering joy rides. A wealthy lumber man in the area paid $5.00 to go up. He was fascinated by that flight. In fact, he decided he could use his experience in the lumber business to build a better airplane and, with a partner–friend, proceeded to do so. The lumber man's name was Bill Boeing, and the new company soon became the Boeing Airplane Company of Seattle, with its rain and cloudy weather, was about as unlikely a place as one could think of to become the home base of the world's largest producer of commercial aircraft. Such cascades from trivial events are the bane of linear analysts, but such cascades are nonetheless the factual basis of much creation and many innovations. Those cascades also explain why we cannot predict all the effects of our innovations, which routinely have unintended consequences.

We can note the same phenomenon in social and political affairs. Consider how a wrong left turn in Sarajevo, Bosnia, triggered the outbreak of World War I in August 1914. On June 28 of that year no one in Europe had the least idea that six weeks later the whole of Europe would be embroiled in the bloodiest war of its history as a cascading consequence of a limousine driver's wrong left turn. Drivers, of course, make wrong left turns every day. But every now and then it happens at a "bifurcation point," where the most trivial of changes can change the world. In this instance, a would be Serbian assassin named Gavrilo Princip sat dejectedly at a sidewalk cafe in Sarajevo, cursing himself that he had failed in his mission and contemplating his return to Belgrade, Serbia. His target was to have been the Archduke Ferdinand of Austria–Hungary, of which empire Bosnia was a part. Many Bosnians were ethnic Serbs and they wanted to be part of Serbia, an idea that multi-ethnic Austria–Hungary resisted. Hence the plot to assassinate the Archduke. Meanwhile, a block or so away, the Archduke and his wife were driving from their hotel toward city hall in their limousine. The driver was unfamiliar with the streets and took a wrong left turn onto the very street where Gavrilo sat dejectedly at his sidewalk cafe. History records the wrong left turn as the crucial incident, but that is somewhat arbitrary. It could just as well have been the driver's discovery of his mistake just as he approached the sidewalk cafe. Indeed, he stopped right in front of Gavrilo. It was an open limousine, and the Archduke was well known. Someone pointed out who was in the car. On hearing that, Gavrilo jumped up, pulled out his pistol and shot the Archduke and his wife dead.[6]

This assassination, however, might have remained merely of local significance except for two things. First, relations between Serbia and Austria–Hungary had been strained for some time. Transcending that

fact was an even more important one: It was specifically the Archduke who was determined to settle the dispute diplomatically. On
this issue he was locked in a struggle with General Hotzendorf, the
Chief of Austria–Hungary's General Staff. The General wanted war
with Serbia, the Archduke was determined to avoid it.

To General Hotzendorf the assassination was a gift from the gods.
The main obstacle to his plans had been taken out in the best possible way to dissolve all opposition to his goal of making war on,
and thus subduing, the troublesome Serbs. The General quickly sold
the aging emperor, Franz Joseph, on the idea that retaliation was the
only right thing to do. Hotzendorf thus issued a set of demands to
Serbia that effectively relieved the small nation of its sovereignty.
Serbia apologized and agreed to many of Austria's demands. Still its
government balked at some demands that ended sovereignty. Having already mobilized his army, General Hotzendorf used that resistance as an excuse to invade Serbia.

The invasion might have remained a purely Balkan crisis except
that Serbia had a treaty with Russia that called on Russia to come to
Serbia's defense if invaded by the Austrians. Czar Nicholas of Russia decided he had to honor his treaty obligations and so mobilized
to fight Austria. On learning of Russia's mobilization, Emperor Franz
Joseph pointed out to his friend, Kaiser Wilhelm of Germany, that in
the event Russia mobilized against Austria–Hungary a treaty between
itself and Germany called for Germany to come to the aid of the Austrians. The Kaiser too, decided to honor his treaty. When Germany
ordered mobilization, however, the Czar called up the French to re-
mind them of their mutual treaty that if Germany mobilized against
either one the other nation would also mobilize. France decided it
had no choice, and anyway France had a major resentment against
Germany for having seized Alsace-Lorraine in the Franco–Prussian
War of 1870. The general staff of the German army, for its part, had
anticipated the French reaction and regarded France as a more dangerous adversary than Russia. Accordingly, the German general staff
had worked out detailed contingency plans for a war with France.
Known as the Von Schleieffen Plan, it called for an end run around
the French army in hopes of wrapping up any war in about six weeks.
The strategy was brilliant, but unfortunately it could be implemented

assassination and thus change the course of human history. The specter is that by merely stepping out of our time capsule we become that tiny, tiny change in initial conditions that cascades into our own oblivion. Suppose you get out of your time capsules and merely walk across the street. That simple act causes someone to pause for a half second to let you by. That person is hardly aware of you, but that half second may be just enough to prevent the chance meeting he or she might otherwise have had with a friend. But for you, they would have stopped to talk. They might then decide to join others in a nearby cafe where this person meets his or her future spouse. After marriage, they conceive one of your great grandparents, but because of you that marriage never happened, and thus of course neither did you. The point is that each of us owes our personal existence to the history of nearly everything that took place exactly as it did before our conception. Even the most trivial change, say, five hundred years ago, could result in an entirely different cast of characters making up the population of today's world. An old proverb well captures the unpredictability of our nonlinear world, and was for years known not as the butterfly, but as the "horseshoe nail" effect:

> For the want of a nail the horseshoe was lost
> For the want of the horseshoe, the horse was lost
> For the want of the horse the rider was lost
> For the want of the rider the battle was lost
> For the want of the battle the kingdom was lost
> And all because of the horseshoe nail!

QUANTUM CONTROVERSIES

Many fine books have been written for the general reader about the rise of the postmodern sciences and the radical shift in world view they helped bring about. Some of these books focus on history and development, others on the contributions and personalities of the people who played prominent parts. The scientists most frequently cited are Albert Einstein and his debating partner Neils Bohr, Irwin Schroedinger, Werner Heisenberg, Wolfgang Pauli, and Paul Dirac. These and other scientists all played crucial roles in the early years to establish quantum mechanics. In more recent times, the names of Murray Gell-Mann and Richard Feynman, John Bell, David

only by attacking France through the neutral nation of Be
invading Belgium, Germany induced the British to honor th
to guarantee Belgium independence. Thus the United Kin
tered the war on the side of France and Russia. Though si
pared to the French and German armies, the British Expe
Force was able to slow the German attack just enough to e
French to defeat the Germans at the Battle of the Marne ir
gust. In October, the war bogged down into trench warfare t
over four bloody years.

This cascade of events all took place in six weeks. It came
plete surprise, for on June 28 no one in Europe expected
summer. Moreover, no one really wanted it, perhaps Gene
endorf aside. Britain's King, Germany's Kaiser, and Russ
were all cousins personally fond of each other. Each mona
own way tried to stop the cascade. They all talked to each
telegraph trying to stop it, but they failed for technical reas
ordered, military mobilization was almost impossible to sto
days until it had run its course. And once it did, fighting
broke out. But as Germany's Kaiser put it when informed
his general saff, "Gentleman, you will live to regret this w

The outbreak of World War I is simply a dramatic exam
nonlinear turbulence of chaos theory in action in human a
cascades happen all the time. For example, chance meeti
often set in motion events that later led to marriage. The cl
such a marriage owe their very existence to the accident of th
meeting (not to mention untold millions of other chance
Consider the fact that the chance of any one male sperm c
with the female egg after copulation is about eight hundre
to one. Each of those other eight hundred million sperm ce
have led to a different person if it connected with the san
slight change in the time of orgasm would likely mean tha
ent sperm would unite with the egg. Each of us owes our
to an incredibly unlikely past chain of chance events, in w
link was itself improbable.

Science fiction writers sometimes point this out. A time
that allows us to go back in time raises a terrible specter. It i
we could change the outcome of, say, a major battle or pr

Bohm, John Wheeler, Roger Penrose, and Steven Hawking, among others, figure prominently.

So dramatic was the shift itself that some of those who helped bring it about could never quite adjust to it. The most famous example is probably Albert Einstein. It has been reported that he just could not bring himself to abandon classical determinism in favor of quantum probabilities and uncertainty. He summed up his doubts in a famous (if apocryphal) quip, "God does not play dice with the universe." Late in his life, Schroedinger said that he was sorry he had anything to do with quantum mechanics, yet his probability equations of the wave function were vital to it. David Bohm insisted up to his recent death that determinism remains embedded in what he calls the "implicate order." This order, Bohm claimed, contains hidden variables that determine the specific outcomes of what we can only predict as quantum probability in the "explicate order." But this implicate order is of course safely beyond the possibility of observation. Bohm's friend of his student years, Murray Gell-Mann, reports that, as a Marxist in his youth, Bohm was actually attempting to salvage the historical determinism embedded in Marxist ideology.[8] Yet in 1951 Bohm wrote one of the best of the early textbooks on quantum physics. He went on to become something of a New Age cult figure as a result of his theories.

Among the first to discuss the new philosophical implications of quantum mechanics was a physicist by the name of Fritjof Capra. In 1976 Capra wrote a book entitled *The Tao of Physics*. It related the new and, in the view of some, mystical findings of quantum physics to the older mystical views of the universe that had characterized the Eastern religions, such as Taoism, Hinduism, and Buddhism. Capra's book helped popularize the shift from the mechanistic world view of Newtonian physics.[9] Shortly after it was published, the mechanistic paradigm came into serious question, especially in business. The dysfunctions of mechanistic bureaucracy were becoming clear because it could not compete effectively against Japan's organic alternative. But once pointed out, the relationship between Newtonian science and mechanistic bureaucracy seemed glaringly obvious. At the same time, it was obvious that the Eastern world view that rejected the mechanistic metaphor had much to offer. At least in the form taken by Japanese firms, the Eastern organic alternative was a clear winner. Those organic firms were running competitive circles around our mechanistic bureaucracies.

Whatever the practical failings of the mechanistic view, many scientists greeted Capra's thesis with contempt.[10] They wanted to exclude from physics anything suggestive of a nonmaterial spiritual reality. They feared, not without reason, that later on religion might hijack science and subject its experimental findings to theological tests of "truth." Again, in light of history, this is not an unreasonable fear, but it has little to do with the existence or nonexistence of a spiritual reality apart from matter. But other and perhaps less fearful or tradition-bound scientists welcomed the discussion. Many jumped into the fray, and some physicists came "out of the closet." They confessed to a belief in a higher power or creative force that was fully compatible with quantum physics. For example, Edgar Mitchell, who has a doctorate in astrophysics and was one of the only people to walk on the moon, had a spiritual experience on the return journey. It so moved him that he spent the next twenty years researching the relationship between science and spirituality. Mitchell published the results of his findings in 1996 as *The Way of the Explorer*.[11] In it, he posits a new "dyadic" model that rejects both scientific and religious determinism, and yet allows for a nonmaterial and universal mind of which we are all part. Another physicist, Amit Goswami, wrote a similar book in 1993.[12] By a somewhat different route and with a somewhat different model he calls "monistic idealism," Goswami reaches conclusions not unlike those of Mitchell. Both authors express views that are fully compatible with the dominant "Copenhagen Interpretation" of quantum physics, both give non-locality a major role, and both argue that quantum physics, by positing the need for intelligent observation to "collapse" the wave function of matter, necessarily requires that the mind creates matter rather than the other way, as conventional Darwinism argues.[13]

Other scientists have also entered into these debates, but, broadly, the postmodern philosophies coming out of quantum physics relate to the Copenhagen Interpretation. It is and has been the dominant view since 1927, the year that quantum physics coalesced as a coherent science with Heisenberg's principle. "Copenhagen" was a term given in honor of Neils Bohr, whose views prevailed to set the tone of the new science. Albert Einstein strongly objected to Bohr's interpretation, but he lost every debate he had with Bohr on this issue over the next decade.

Despite Einstein's defeats, many practicing physicists continue to share Einstein's same doubts. They depend on the Copenhagen Interpretation's mathematics, but feel an often acute discomfort at the growing trend, inside and outside of science, to create what they fear is a "new mysticism" akin to that of ancient Eastern religions. One Nobel Laureate, Leon Lederman, refers to such philosophers as "the dancing mu shu masters," a put-down of Gary Zukav's book, *The Dancing Wu Li Masters.* Zukav also pointed to the similarities between quantum mechanics and Eastern religions. Murray Gell-Mann, who is also a Nobel laureate, dismisses such philosophizing as "quantum flapdoodle" in his recent memoirs. A less well-known physicist and professor, Victor J. Stenger, wrote in 1995 *The Unconscious Quantum* to rehabilitate the mechanistic and deterministic view. His is a good overview of the controversy and makes some valid points, but Stenger ignores a vital issue. He simply does not address the fact that, outside the rather narrow field of mechanical engineering and its relatives, the mechanistic world view has failed dismally in practice. The FPCC model in business is a classic example. Stenger betrays not the least hint of these failures. He sticks with narrowly scientific issues, and time and again simply claims his non-Copenhagen interpretations, being less mystical, are to be preferred.[14] He is not convincing.

SCIENCE AND PHILOSOPHY

Consider the major way around Copenhagen, namely the "many worlds interpretation" (MWI). Some physicists prefer it because it uses exactly the same math as Copenhagen but does away with the mysticism that matter can be both particles and waves at the same time and, even worse, potentially in different places at the same time. MWI restores Newton's mechanistic universe, but at a horrendous cost of unbelievability which strikes me as mysticism raised to an infinite power. MWI has the world splitting into different universes every time a quantum probability comes along. Never mind that this assumption trashes the principle of conservation of energy. If this interpretation were true, our meta universe would consist of an infinity of noninteracting parallel universes, the number expanding at an infinite rate every second as each new universe immediately divides at every quantum probability event, and so on ad infinitum.

Each of us, in this view, supposedly has billions of clones of ourselves in these superimposed parallel universes. Still, Stenger likes it, because he says, "The cosmology of many universes is more economical if it provides an explanation of the origin of the universe that does not require" God.[15]

Meanwhile, most physicists simply ignore these philosophical issues and get on with it, using Copenhagen math. But, as to the role of philosophy in science, it can only become more significant. Modern science, after all, came out of natural philosophy and, according to some observers, is about to return because it is now becoming too expensive to conduct experiments at the leading edge of physics where new theory is confirmed, denied, or revised. The cancellation of the superconducting supercollider in Texas illustrates that fact. Experimental cutting-edge physics has gone about as far as it can go, given any technology in sight. It has hit a brick wall of costs, as illustrated by string theory, a recent concept that attempts to integrate the four forces of nature into one grand theory. Michio Kaku calculates it would take more energy than we could likely ever produce to demonstrate string theory and its related concept of a "hyperspace" of eleven dimensions. The reason is that it would take a "particle accelerator" one thousand light years long to test the concept. (The solar system is one light day across.)[16] John Horgan concludes that physics is now entering a postempirical phase. Horgan calls this new phase "ironic science."[17] By that he means physics has pushed its hypotheses past the point where it is possible to test them in the framework of the traditional scientific method. Thus, Horgan argues, the leading edge of physics stands on the brink of ending where it began, as a branch of "natural philosophy."

FROM REDUCTIONIST KNOWLEDGE
TO HOLISTIC WISDOM

Those who want to continue to compartmentalize science and keep it separate from other areas of life are on the defensive. So are those who argue that reductionism is the only road to the "Truth." Many well-regarded scientists now question reductionism. That method is now on the defensive compared to a newer view that we can understand the parts only if we first have a grasp of the whole. The holistic view is gaining ground not only within science but outside as well. For example, the word "culture," as applied to a business firm, was rarely heard until about twenty years ago. Then it became a buzzword that implied a corporate ethic that was best understood as a whole. Moreover, even with machines, the whole emerges first in thought, and only then are the parts designed.

Reductionism, of course, remains a useful method of improving our understanding of machines and mechanical processes and how machine parts fit together. But in many areas, such as culture, a holistic understanding can vanish if overanalyzed. A good defense attorney, in my view, relies on that fact. Simply break the testimony of each witness down into as many separate pieces as is possible. Then raise questions about the accuracy of each bit by the simple device of asking if the witness can state with absolute certainty that things happened exactly as said, and beyond all other possible explanations. Witnesses rarely can do that, of course. Viola, the defense attorney, has planted the seed of doubt in the jury's mind as he or she deliberately undercuts a holistic understanding of the testimony. As a defense attorney, autopoiesis drives you to create reasonable doubt in the jury's mind even when you know the defendant is guilty as charged.

HOLISTIC PSYCHOLOGY

Much of the growing body of "self-help" literature was always suspicious of that form of psychological reductionism known as Freudian analysis. Many people have spent their whole lives in expensive Freudian analysis (Woody Allen comes to mind) and still manage to live dysfunctional lives. Entirely on our own, many of us can fall into the trap of endlessly analyzing a problem, going around and around, mentally plowing the same ground over and over, and stopping only at the point of mental exhaustion. In my own experience, this compulsive and futile exercise in reductionism rarely resolves the issue. And so says a growing body of what might be called "self-help" psychology. I would summarize the thrust of this more holistic approach to mental health as follows: (1) Quit analyzing the "problem"; (2) shift your focus to visualizing what you believe to be the best solution; (3) keep that solution near the center of your thoughts; (4) pray for it, or perhaps affirm it, and above all visualize your solution as being real here and now, and let your feelings reflect that "fact"; and (5) quit worrying and go on about your life. The theory holds that if you consciously "reprogram" your subconscious mind through such "self-talk" and focused visualizations, your subconscious self will soon after guide your behavior intuitively toward your goal.[18]

Another more or less destructive form of reductionism, according to this same line of thought, is to analyze the "sins" of our adversaries in great and searching detail. For one thing, analysis on our part rarely if ever translates into change by others. It will not matter if our analysis is right on. Indeed, even if both accurate and objective, this analytical process can still hurt us if it diverts our attention from the task of correcting our own defects or pursuing solutions to our own problems. A negative focus on the faults of others often holds us back from making the changes we need to make in ourselves. "We won't achieve salvation by confessing the sins of others," someone once said. Or, "Why give rent-free space in your head to people you don't like?" We can spend that same time far more productively if we work toward achieving solutions to our own problems.

It is perhaps no accident that these more holistic and less reductionist approaches to mental health evolved almost entirely outside academic mainstream psychology. Long dominated by a dispute between Behaviorists and Freudians, both schools, despite their different theories, emulated the reductionist methods of mechanistic physics. With a few exceptions in special circumstances, neither school did much to improve mental health. In fact, neither school had much room for self-help. You had to hire expensive psychiatrists to follow Freud, and few people could afford their prices. If you preferred the theories of behaviorism, however, you simply had to put yourself on the receiving end of "operant conditioning" by those who had power over you, such as teachers, parents, bosses, and those who could apply the carrot and stick to you. Thereafter, you trusted to luck that the people doing the "conditioning" were working on your behalf rather than on their own.

Into this vacuum of real help, a large and variegated cottage industry of more holistic self-help counselors arose, complete with inexpensive books, tapes, and videos. Of course, many people who read, listen, or watch these messages fail to follow through. On the other hand, the testimonials of those who have tried to implement such messages is very large. Despite the many differences in detail of the various schools of thought, within this "cottage industry" runs a remarkably consistent thread. This thread has remained surprisingly self-consistent since the self-help movement based on the subconscious mind began in the United States during the 1830s, when the phenomenon of hypnotism became known here.[19]

FROM A MECHANISTIC TO AN
ORGANIC UNIVERSE

The shift from reductionist knowledge toward holistic wisdom is part of a broader shift from the mechanistic to the organic view of life. Few physicists now push the clockwork view of the universe, a mechanism consisting of separate parts working together as if a machine. Today the universe is more often seen as an organic whole, a view that owes much to the wave/particle duality of matter, the fact that subatomic particles seem able to convert from one to the other, and the various forms of non-locality.

Biologists, however, have staged a last-ditch defense of Darwin's mechanistic view of life itself. Life evolved, according to Darwin, by the simple mechanism of natural selection of the "fittest of random mutations of heritable characteristics." Those few that promoted some plant or animal's ability to reproduce more effectively survived. The great majority, of course, did not and those simply died out. Over the three-odd billion years of evolution, this trial and error of blind chance supposedly forced otherwise inert matter to evolve into ever more complex molecules and from this complexity life spontaneously emerged. But now researchers are having massive second thoughts that life could actually have evolved from blind chance and natural selection alone. Based on computer simulations at the Santa Fe institute, Dr. Stuart Kauffman estimates the probability that blind chance created life as we know it at something on the order of 1 in 10 to the 30,000th power.[20] When one recalls that the universe is only twelve-odd billion years old (1.2 times 10 to the 10th power), and a generous estimate of the number of atoms in the universe is something like 10 to the 90th power, Dr. Kauffman's 10 to the 30,000th power is a number too vast even to imagine.

To the combination of random accident and natural selection, Dr. Kauffman adds the power of self-organization to explain evolution in terms of what he calculates to be much more realistic probabilities. Self-organized evolution, argues Kauffman, occurs at the edge of order and chaos, and he insists that complexity itself gives rise to the powers of self-organization in purely natural terms. Perhaps so, responds Dr. Stephen C. Meyer, fellow of the Discovery Institute of Seattle and a professor of philosophy at Whitworth College. But even adding self-organization does not do away with astronomical levels of improbability. Something is still missing, in Dr. Meyer's view.[21] To Meyer, the missing element is information. The medium is not the message, he insists. A news story in the *New York Times*, Meyer points out, contains information that is not implicit in the newsprint and ink. The information in the story comes from a source independent of the media that carries the message. So, he says, is true of the information contained in the genetic code, because the information is not just a question of the proteins involved but of their sequence, their open order which can contain either information or nonsense depending on that order. So it is with letters forming words, and words forming sentences and paragraphs. It may be that the infinite number of proverbial monkeys pecking away at an infinite number of typewriters would ultimately type *Hamlet*, but we must remember the improbabilities involved are also close to infinite. That is to say, those monkeys would also require an infinite amount of time. Put another way, during the period of time this universe has been around, it is highly unlikely any of our infinite monkeys would have yet typed the first few paragraphs of *Hamlet* in correct order. Since the genetic code contains something like one hundred thousand words, according to Meyer, it would take trillions of times longer than the estimated life of the universe to get it right by chance alone. Here it is well to remember that in playing the Lotto one's chances of picking a mere six right numbers out of forty-eight in any order is 7,000,000 to 1 against. If those numbers had to be selected in a proper order as well, the odds against would rise enormously, and in the one hundred thousand words in the genetic code the correct order is the difference between nonsense and information.

Meyer argues that self-organization, important though it no doubt is, does not overcome this sequencing problem. As Rupert Sheldrake, a British biologist, puts it, "The genes dictate the primary structure of proteins, not specific structure of a duck's foot or lamb's kidney or an orchid. The way proteins are arranged in cells, the way cells are arranged in tissue, and tissues in organs, and organs in organisms, are not programmed in the genetic code which can only program protein molecules. Given the right genes and hence the right proteins, and the right system by which protein synthesis is controlled, the organism is somehow supposed to assemble itself automatically. This is rather like delivering the right materials to a building site at the right times and expecting a house to grow spontaneously."[22]

This debate relates to the evolution of organizations as well. First, we know that evolution takes place and that chance events can change organizations. We also know that such events in particular circumstances might prove beneficial by conferring a competitive advantage, all right out of Darwin. But we know from experience that, in a crisis, self-organization often takes place to transform the organization. Here I mean self-organization not directed by some central authority. I argue that self-organization takes place much more effectively through an organic format of human organization, compared to the bureaucratic.

As I use it, the word "organic" has a different meaning from the distorted meaning it had in the mechanistic era. Under the impact of communism and fascism, the term "organic" was often used to mean a political state, as in the "organic state," meaning totalitarian. A totalitarian state clearly threatened modern Western notions of the importance of individual freedom. In the Western view, the state derives its importance from the individual and exists mainly to serve individual needs. According to Thomas Hobbes, Edmund Burke, and other Enlightenment philosophers, states were formed mainly to protect individuals from a brutal anarchy of "all against all." States derived their powers from the "consent of the governed." The American Republic was founded explicitly on such premises, in the minds of such founding fathers as Thomas Jefferson, James Madison, and others.

As used here, however, the term "organic" leaves no room in theory or in practice for dictatorship or totalitarianism, nor does organic as used in biology imply anything of the kind. Your body, for example, is an organic whole and yet it has no dictator in charge, not even your conscious mind. If our bodies depended on our conscious minds for control, we would die in seconds. Our subconscious mind is spread over the whole body and coordinates the trillions of biochemical actions that go on each minute to keep us alive. Consciously, we would be unable to direct even a tiny fraction of 1 percent of the total activity. We have no conscious awareness of most of what goes on within our bodies, and few of us have much idea of how it all works.

As for organization, we see an irony here because, unlike politics, where the mechanistic model of the state made individuals of supreme importance, the modern mechanistic model of organization gave individuals short shrift by reducing them to impersonal commodities. Business firms often operated as dictatorships within their limited sphere, and some still do. Freedom for the individual was found outside, not within the firm. The postmodern organic view renounces dictatorship in favor of employee empowerment and participation. Employees are now urged to take ownership and work together toward a common goal in cooperative teams for the benefit of all. The main obstacle to this vision, however, is the policy of denying people the opportunity to do this as partners and as members of a common enterprise. It instead forces them to work for hire or not at all, unlike capital that can work under either option at its own choice.

FROM STARS TO TEAMS

For centuries we have looked to stars and superstars as "saviors." Whether it was in winning the big game, turning the tide of battle, making the great discovery, writing the great novel, closing the great sale, or winning the election, we traditionally sought out some star to carry the day. We have by no means made a complete shift here, but we are well underway. Moreover, we increasingly see that we often fabricate our stars in order to enhance their drawing power. Hollywood has long used publicity machines for that purpose and so have most political parties.

That tradition dies hard. For one thing, academia is still organized around the star system. The 4.0 student is still lionized. Until quite recently he or she was expected to shine based on individual ability and effort. Teamwork plays almost no part in this approach to scholarship. The ability to work harmoniously with other people to achieve some goal hardly matters. Students might sometimes work together on projects or help each other study, but the academic system rarely encourages this approach. Sometimes an instructor might also promote such methods, but again, with a few exceptions such as the debate team, it was not expected or encouraged. The idealized goal that academia sought was "to teach our students how to think."

What was missing from this idealized goal was the fact that interaction with other people can be and often is a great stimulus to thinking. Academia is slow in getting the word, but in the business world this view has gained so much ground that it is close to becoming the accepted doctrine. Business leaders are beginning to chastise business schools for the old focus on stars instead of teams, and for the failure to include team projects in the course of study and thus denying students practical team experience. Given the traditional division of labor in academia and the fragmentation of disciplines along mechanistic lines that we call the "liberal arts," making this transition is easier said than done. The traditional system has enormous inertia. It is difficult to acquire factual knowledge outside the fragmented context of the liberal arts. In graduate school the whole aim is to produce rather narrow specialists. While division of labor was successful for centuries, particularly in science, when it first evolved this division of labor was also quite reasonable. The undergraduate student would be broadly educated in the liberal arts to provide a reasonable overview of human knowledge. If the student went on to graduate school, he (rarely she) would tend to specialize in one of the professions, such as law or medicine, and then go out and practice. Otherwise, the graduate specialized in one of the disciplines, be it science, literature, or philosophy, in hopes of teaching it to others or doing research in it.

In science itself, the resources needed to push the experimental envelope to its frontiers long ago left the individual scientist behind. Now it often takes large-scale organizations to conduct experiments, as pointed out earlier. The Manhattan Project that built the atomic bomb during World War II provides the classic example. Here, big egos and stars tend to get in the way, except perhaps as the leading visionary. As Bill Gates put it, "It will be hard to deal with me unless I'm in charge."[23]

Meanwhile, it has been demonstrated experimentally time and again that when people cooperate with each other in teams they almost always reach better solutions to the problems they face than do individuals. Put another way, a group of motivated people possessed with but average talent often devises better solutions compared to the lone genius. After all, a group of people will differ in their talents. Thus, the range of talents within the group usually exceeds that of the lone genius. Moreover, they will generate a broader range of ideas by "sparking off" each other. Two heads, as they say, are better than one.

FROM SECULAR MATERIALISM TO SPIRITUALITY

The wave aspect of the wave/particle duality is real but amorphous and somewhat mysterious. The same can be said for force fields, space, and time. It is thus more difficult to dismiss the spiritual aspects of life as unreal or illusionary. We noted earlier that physical matter, once regarded as reality, is now seen to be an illusion created by electromagnetic force. What appears solid is almost entirely empty space, well over 99.999 percent so. Take away the electromagnetic field which causes electrons to repel each other and what seems like solid matter vanishes from view. But what exactly is that field? We do not really know what it is but we know how it works.

When René Descartes spoke of a mind–body duality, he tried to compartmentalize the immaterial and perhaps spiritual aspects of life from the "solid substance" of science. Before long, scientists were beginning to dismiss the idea of an immaterial mind and, in fact, some still do. Earlier in this century, Gilbert Ryle dismissed Descartes's immaterial mind as "the ghost in the machine," the body being the machine in this case. Human thought and consciousness on this reading arises purely from molecular interactions in the brain. Yet a new view is arising. Paul Davies expressed it well when he noted that Gilbert Ryle was correct in dismissing the ghost in the machine, "not because there is no ghost, but because there is no machine."[24] In organizations, "ghosts" are everywhere. They make up immaterial relationships, corporate culture, traditions, and esprit de corps. None argue that these items have material substance, but all are aspects of organizational reality. Moreover, these nonmaterial aspects can have real financial value, as measured by stock prices when they substantially exceed the book value of assets and cash on hand.

FROM BUREAUCRATIC CAPITALISM TO ORGANIC FREE ENTERPRISE

Capitalism has long been condemned as a curse and praised as a boon to mankind. If we cut right to the chase, we can say that the free market part of capitalism has been a boon because it forces industrial enterprises to compete with one another. But capitalism as a bureaucratic and hence authoritarian method of organizing the factors of production has often been a curse, even within a competitive market environment. Without the market, of course, the authoritarian bureaucratic method of organizing an economy becomes the tyranny of a command economy as it takes over the distribution side as well as production. That indeed was the lesson of the experience of the late Soviet Union.

This book proposes to bring capital and labor together into an organic partnership within each competitive enterprise. Such a partnership would dissolve bureaucratic capitalism. It would metamorphose itself into organic free enterprise. This shift would preserve the free market, the sanctity of the individual, and retain the positive aspects of competition between firms while avoiding the negative effects of competition within them.

NOTES

1. For a good account, see David Lindley, *The End of Physics: The Myth of a Unified Theory* (New York: Basic Books, 1993). See also John Gribbin, *In Search of Schroedinger's Cat: Quantum Physics and Reality* (New York: Bantam Books, 1984).

2. Danah Zohar, *The Quantum Self* (New York: William Morrow, 1994).

3. Ian Marshall and Danah Zohar, *Who's Afraid of Schroedinger's Cat? All*

the New Science Ideas You Need to Keep Up with the New Thinking (New York: William Morrow, 1997), 64–67.

4. James Gleick, *Chaos: The Making of a New Science* (New York: Viking, 1987).

5. Bill Gates, *The Road Ahead* (New York: Viking, 1995).

6. Frederic Morton, *Thunder at Twilight: Vienna, 1913–1914* (New York: Charles Scribner's Sons, 1989).

7. Ibid.

8. Murray Gell-Mann, *The Quark and the Jaguar* (New York: W. H. Freeman, 1994).

9. Fritjof Capra, *The Tao of Physics* (New York: Bantam Books, 1976).

10. See also Gary Zukav, *The Dancing Wu Li Masters* (New York: Bantam Books, 1979).

11. Edgar Mitchell, with Dwight Williams, *The Way of the Explorer* (New York: G. P. Putnam's Sons, 1996).

12. Amit Goswami, with Richard Reed and Maggie Goswami, *The Self Aware Universe: How Consciousness Creates the Material World* (New York: G. P. Putnam's Sons, 1993).

13. David Darling, *Zen Physics* (New York: HarperCollins, 1996); and Michael J. Behe, *Darwin's Black Box: The Biochemical Challenge to Evolution* (New York: The Free Press, 1996).

14. Victor J. Stenger, *The Unconscious Quantum: Metaphysics in Modern Physics and Cosmology* (Amherst, N.Y.: Prometheus Books, 1995).

15. Ibid., 236.

16. Michio Kaku, *Hyper Space* (Oxford: Oxford University Press, 1994).

17. John Horgan, *The End of Science: Facing the Limits of Knowledge in the Twilight of the Scientific Age* (Reading, Mass.: Addison-Wesley, 1996).

18. Louise L. Hay, *You Can Heal Your Life* (Santa Monica: The Hay House, 1984). Dozens of other books make this same point in various ways.

19. Robert C. Fuller, *Americans and the Unconscious* (New York: Oxford University Press, 1986).

20. Stuart Kauffman, *At Home in the Universe* (New York: Oxford University Press, 1995).

21. Steven C. Meyer, "The Origin of Life and the Death of Materialism," *Intercollegiate Review* 31, no. 2 (1996).

22. Rupert Sheldrake, *The Rebirth of Nature: The Greening of Science and God* (Rochester, Vt.: Park Street Press, 1994).

23. "The Private World of Bill Gates," *Time*, 13 January 1997.

24. Paul Davies and John Gribbin, *The Matter Myth* (New York: Simon and Schuster, 1992).

Selected Bibliography

Abegglen, James C. *The Japanese Factory: Aspects of Its Social Organization*. Glencoe, Ill.: The Free Press, 1958.

Albrow, Martin. *Bureaucracy*. London: Macmillan, 1970.

Allen, W. W. "Is Britain a Half-Time Country, Getting Half-Pay for Half-Work, under Half-Hearted Management?" *The Sunday Times* (London), 1 March, 1964.

Ardrey, Robert. *African Genesis*. New York: Atheneum, 1961.

———. *The Territorial Imperative*. London: Collins, 1970.

Bateson, Gregory. *Mind and Nature*. New York: Bantam Books, 1980.

Behe, Michael J. *Darwin's Black Box: The Biochemical Challenge to Evolution*. New York: The Free Press, 1996.

Bell, Daniel. *Work and Its Discontents*. New York: League for Industrial Democracy, 1970.

Bellah, R. N. *Tokugawa Religion: The Values of Pre-Industrial Japan*. Glencoe, Ill.: The Free Press, 1957.

Benedict, Ruth. *The Chrysanthemum and the Sword*. Boston: Houghton Mifflin, 1946.

Bennis, Warren, and Patricia Ward Biederman. *Genius: The Secrets of Creative Collaboration*. Reading, Mass.: Addison-Wesley, 1997.

Blinder, Alan. "Trading with Japan: Why the U.S. Loses Even on a Level Playing Field." *Business Economics*, January 1992, 86–92.

Bohm, David. *Wholeness and the Implicate Order*. London: Ark Paperbacks, 1980.

Branson, Noreen, and Margot Heinemann. *Britain in the 1930s*. London: Panther Press, 1963.

Briggs, John, and F. David Peat. *Turbulent Mirror: An Illustrated Guide to Chaos Theory and the Science of Wholeness*. New York: Harper & Row, 1989.

Burke, James, and Robert Ornstein. *The Axemaker's Gift: Technology's Capture and Control of Our Minds and Culture*. New York: G. P. Putnam's Sons, 1995.

Capra, Fritjof. *The Tao of Physics*. New York: Bantam Books, 1976.

———. *The Turning Point: Science and the Rising Culture*. New York: Bantam Books, 1983.

Chandler, A. D., Jr. *Strategy and Structure*. Cambridge: MIT Press, 1962.

Chia, Robert. *Organizational Analysis as Deconstructive Practice*. Berlin: Walter de Gruyter, 1996.

Chopra, Deepak. *Quantum Healing: Exploring the Frontiers of Mind and Body Science*. New York: Bantam Books, 1989.

Coon, C. S. *The Hunting Peoples*. Boston: Little, Brown, 1971.

Crozier, Michael. *The Bureaucratic Phenomenon*. Chicago: University of Chicago Press, 1964.

Darling, David. *Zen Physics*. New York: HarperCollins, 1996.

Darwin, Charles. *The Origin of the Species*. New York: W. W. Norton, 1975.

Davies, Paul C. *The Mind of God*. New York: Simon & Schuster, 1992.

———, and John Gribbin. *The Matter Myth*. New York: Simon & Schuster, 1992.

de Geus, Arie. *The Living Company: Habits for Survival in a Turbulent Business Environment*. Boston: Harvard Business School Press, 1997.

De Vore, Irvin, ed. *Primate Behavior*. New York: Holt, Rinehart, & Winston, 1965.

Drucker, Peter F. *The Age of Discontinuity*. New York: Harper & Row, 1968.

———. *The Concept of the Corporation*. New York: Mentor, 1983.

———. *The Practice of Management*. New York: Harper & Row, 1954.

Embree, John H. *The Japanese Nation, A Social Survey*. New York: Farrar & Rinehard, 1945.

Etzioni, Amitai. *Modern Organization*. Englewood Cliffs, N.J.: Prentice Hall, 1964.

Feignenbaum, A. V. *Total Quality Control*. New York: McGraw-Hill, 1983.

Ferris, Timothy. *Coming of Age in the Milky Way*. New York: Anchor Books, 1988.

Flannery, Thomas, David Hofrichter, and Paul Platten. *People, Pay, and Performance: Dynamic Compensation for Changing Organizations*. Philadelphia: The Hay Group, 1996.

Friedman, Milton, and Anna Schwartz. *A Monetary History of the United States, 1867–1960.* Princeton, N.J.: Princeton University Press, 1963.

Fujihara, G. *The Spirit of Japanese Industry.* Tokyo: Hokuseido Press, 1936.

Fukuyama, Francis. *The End of History and the Last Man.* New York: The Free Press, 1992.

Fuller, Robert. *Americans and the Unconscious.* New York: Oxford University Press, 1986.

Galbraith, John Kenneth. *The Affluent Society.* Boston: Houghton Mifflin, 1959.

———. *The New Industrial State.* Boston: Houghton Mifflin, 1967.

Gell-Mann, Murray. *The Quark and the Jaguar.* New York: W. H. Freeman, 1994.

Gerth, H. H., and C. Wright Mills, eds. and trans. *From Max Weber: Essays in Sociology.* New York: Oxford University Press, 1958.

Gleick, James. *Chaos: The Making of a New Science.* New York: Viking, 1987.

Goldratt, E., and Jeff Cox. *The Goal.* Rev. ed. Croton-on-Hudson, N.Y.: North River Press, 1992.

Goswami, Amit, Richard Reed, and Maggie Goswami. *The Self Aware Universe: How Consciousness Creates the Material World.* New York: G. P. Putnam's Sons, 1993.

Goulder, Alvin. *Patterns of Industrial Bureaucracy.* New York: The Free Press, 1964.

Gribbin, John. *In Search of Schroedinger's Cat: Quantum Physics and Reality.* New York: Bantam Books, 1984.

Halberstam, David. *The Powers That Be.* New York: Alfred A. Knopf, 1979.

———. *The Reckoning.* New York: Avon, 1986.

Hamel, Gary, and C. K. Prahalad. *Competing for the Future.* Cambridge: Harvard University Press, 1994.

Hammer, Michael, and James Champy. *Reengineering the Corporation.* New York: HarperCollins, 1993.

Handy, Charles. *Beyond Certainty: The Changing World of Organization.* London: Hutchinson, 1995.

Hay, Louise L. *You Can Heal Your Life.* Santa Monica: The Hay House, 1984.

Heilbroner, Robert L. *The Making of Economic Society.* 8th ed. Englewood Cliffs, N.J.: Prentice Hall, 1990.

Heisenberg, Werner. *Physics and Philosophy.* New York: Harper Torchbooks, 1956.

Herbert, Nick. *Quantum Reality: Beyond the New Physics.* New York: Anchor Doubleday, 1985.

Hobsbawm, E. J. *Laboring Men: Studies in the History of Labour.* Garden City, N.Y.: Doubleday, 1967.

Horgan, John. *The End of Science: Facing the Limits of Knowledge in the Twilight of the Scientific Age.* Reading, Mass.: Addison-Wesley, 1996.

Jantsch, Erich. *The Self Organizing Universe.* Oxford: Pergamon Press, 1980.

Jay, Anthony. *Corporation Man*. New York: Random House, 1971.

Jones, Daniel, James Womack, and Daniel Roos. *The Machine that Changed the World: The Story of Lean Production*. New York: Ransom Associates, 1990.

Kauffman, Stuart. *At Home in the Universe: The Search for the Laws of Self Organization and Complexity*. New York: Oxford University Press, 1995.

Keynes, John Maynard. *The General Theory of Employment, Interest, and Money*. New York: Harcourt Brace and World, 1965.

Kindleberger, Charles P. *The World in Depression, 1929–1939*. Berkeley and Los Angeles: University of California Press, 1973.

Kingdon, Jonathan. *Self Made Man: Human Evolution from Eden to Extinction?* New York: John Wiley & Sons, 1993.

Kuhn, Thomas. *The Structure of Scientific Revolutions*. Chicago: University of Chicago Press, 1962.

Kurten, Bjorn. *Not from the Apes*. New York: Pantheon Books, 1972.

Lederman, Leon. *The God Particle: If the Universe Is the Answer, What Is the Question?* Boston: Houghton Mifflin, 1993.

Lee, R. B., and Irvin DeVore. *Man the Hunter*. Chicago: Aldine, 1968.

Lindley, David. *The End of Physics: The Myth of a Unified Theory*. New York: Basic Books, 1993.

Lovelock, J. E. *Gaia*. New York: Oxford University Press, 1987.

Marshall, Ian, and Danah Zohar. *Who's Afraid of Schroedinger's Cat?: All the New Science Ideas You Need to Keep Up with the New Thinking*. New York: William Morrow, 1997.

Marx, Karl, and Friedrich Engels. *The Communist Manifesto*. London: Allen & Unwin, 1948.

Maturana, Humberto, and Francisco J. Varela. *Autopoiesis and Cognition: The Realization of the Living*. London: Reidl, 1980.

———. *The Tree of Knowledge: The Biological Roots of Human Understanding*. Boston: Shambala, 1992.

McGregor, Douglas. *The Human Side of Enterprise*. New York: McGraw-Hill, 1960.

McNamara, Robert S. *In Retrospect: The Tragedy and Lessons of Vietnam*. New York: Times Books, 1995.

Means, Gardiner C. *The Corporate Revolution in America*. New York: Collier Books, 1964.

Micklethwait, John, and Adrian Wooldridge. *The Witch Doctors*. New York: Times Business Books, 1996.

Mintzberg, Henry. *The Rise and Fall of Strategic Planning*. Hemel Hempstead: Prentice Hall, 1994.

Mitchell, Edgar. *The Way of the Explorer*. New York: G. P. Putnam's Sons, 1996.

Mitsubishi Co. *An Outline of Mitsubishi Enterprises*. Tokyo: Mitsubishi Co., 1930.

Mitsui Co. *A Record of Three Centuries*. Tokyo: Mitsui Co., 1923.

Morgan, Gareth. *Images of Organization*. 2d ed. London: Sage, 1997.

Morgan, Lewis H. *Houses and House Life of American Aborigines*. Chicago: University of Chicago Press, 1965.

Morton, Frederic. *Thunder at Twilight: Vienna, 1913–1914*. New York: Charles Scribner's Sons, 1989.

Nitobe, I. *Bushido*. Tokyo: Teibi Press, 1906.

Norman, E. H. *Japan's Emergence as a Modern State*. New York: Institute of Pacific Relations, 1940.

Okakura, Y. *The Japanese Spirit*. London: Constable, 1905.

Parkinson, C. Northcote. *Parkinson's Law*. Boston: Houghton Mifflin, 1957.

Penrose, Roger. *The Emperor's New Mind*. New York: Oxford University Press, 1989.

Peter, L. J., and Raymond Hull. *The Peter Principle*. New York: William Morrow, 1970.

Peters, Thomas J., and Robert Waterman. *In Search of Excellence*. New York: William Morrow, 1982.

Pfeiffer, John E. *The Emergence of Man*. New York: Harper & Row, 1969.

Porter, Michael. *Competitive Advantage*. New York: The Free Press, 1985.

Prigogine, Ilya, and Isabelle Stenger. *Order Out of Chaos: Man's New Dialogue with Nature*. New York: Bantam Books, 1984.

"The Private World of Bill Gates." *Time*, 13 January 1997.

"The Rising Sun in the Pacific." *Fortune Magazine*, September 1936.

Roberts, John. *Mitsui: A Record of Three Centuries*. New York: Weatherhill, 1976.

Rothlesberger, F. J., and W. J. Dixon. *Management and the Worker*. Cambridge: Harvard University Press, 1939.

Sansom, G. B. *The Western World and Japan*. New York: Alfred A. Knopf, 1950.

Senge, Peter. *The Fifth Discipline*. New York: Doubleday, 1990.

Sheldrake, Rupert. *The Rebirth of Nature: The Greening of Science and God*. New York: Bantam Books, 1991.

Skinner, B. F. *Beyond Freedom and Dignity*. New York: Alfred A. Knopf, 1971.

Sloan, Alfred P. *My Years with General Motors*. New York: McFadden, 1965.

Smith, E. Owen. *Productivity Bargaining: A Case Study in the Steel Industry*. London: Pan Books, 1971.

Stenger, Victor J. *The Unconscious Quantum: Metaphysics in Modern Physics and Cosmology*. Amherst, N.Y.: Prometheus Books, 1995.

Stewart, Thomas A. *Intellectual Capital: The New Wealth of Organizations*. New York: Doubleday, 1997.

Tawney, R. H. *Religion and the Rise of Capitalism*. New York: Mentor Books, 1955.

Tiger, Lionel, and Robin Fox. *The Imperial Animal*. New York: Holt, Rinehart, & Winston, 1971.

Wallace, William McDonald. "Cultural Values and Economic Development: A Case Study of Japan." Ph.D. diss. University of Washington, Seattle, 1963.

———. *How to Save Free Enterprise*. Homewood, Ill.: Dow-Jones Irwin, 1974.

———. "The Secret Weapon of Japanese Business." *Columbia Journal of World Business*, November–December 1972.

———. "Two Approaches to Human Labor." *Wall Street Journal*, 30 March 1972.

Weil, Andrew. *Spontaneous Healing*. New York: Fawcett Columbine, 1995.

Wesson, Robert. *Beyond Natural Selection*. Cambridge: MIT Press, 1994.

Wheatley, Margaret J. *Leadership and the New Science: Learning about Organization from an Orderly Universe*. San Francisco: Berrett-Koehler, 1992.

Wittfogel, Karl. *Oriental Despotism*. New Haven: Yale University Press, 1963.

Zohar, Danah. *The Quantum Self*. New York: William Morrow, 1990.

———, and Ian Marshall. *The Quantum Society*. New York: William Morrow, 1994.

Zukav, Gary. *The Dancing Wu Li Masters*. New York: Bantam Books, 1979.

Index